Conspiracy Theories

Conspiracy Theories

A Critical Introduction

Jovan Byford
Senior Lecturer in Psychology, The Open University, UK

First published 2011
First published in paperback 2015 by
PALGRAVE MACMILLAN

Palgrave Macmillan in the UK is an imprint of Macmillan Publishers Limited, registered in England, company number 785998, of Houndmills, Basingstoke, Hampshire RG21 6XS.

Palgrave Macmillan in the US is a division of St Martin's Press LLC, 175 Fifth Avenue, New York, NY 10010.

Palgrave Macmillan is the global academic imprint of the above companies and has companies and representatives throughout the world.

Palgrave® and Macmillan® are registered trademarks in the United States, the United Kingdom, Europe and other countries.

ISBN: 978–0–230–27279–8 hardback
ISBN: 978–1–137–52024–1 paperback

This book is printed on paper suitable for recycling and made from fully managed and sustained forest sources. Logging, pulping and manufacturing processes are expected to conform to the environmental regulations of the country of origin.

A catalogue record for this book is available from the British Library.

A catalog record for this book is available from the Library of Congress.

Contents

List of Figures

Acknowledgements

My thanks are due first of all to Michael Billig, who, as my PhD supervisor, introduced me, over a decade ago, to the fascinating, but also troubling topic of conspiracy theories. Michael Billig's classic work on the social psychological and ideological aspects of conspiracy theories is today surprisingly neglected in the literature on the subject, and I hope that the present book will go some way towards remedying this.

I am also grateful to Sabina Mihelj and two anonymous reviewers for their constructive comments on the manuscript. I thank Olivia Middleton and Melanie Blair of Palgrave Macmillan for their efficient handling of the publication process, and the team at Newgen Publishing and Data Services for copyediting and typesetting the manuscript with such care and attention.

Finally, I would like to thank my family, and especially my partner Sabina, for their consistent support and encouragement.

While acknowledging the contribution of others to this book, I should mention that the responsibility for any errors or omissions is, of course, solely my own.

1
Introduction

[...] even the most horrid deeds perpetrated during the French Revolution, every thing was foreseen and resolved on, was combined and premeditated: they were the offspring of deep-thought villany, since they had been prepared and were produced by men, who alone held the clue of those plots and conspiracies, lurking in the secret meetings where they had been conceived, and only watching the favourable moment of bursting forth.

—Augustin Barruel,
Memoirs, Illustrating the History of Jacobinism,
1799: xii

This movement among the Jews is not new. From the days of Spartacus-Weishaupt to those of Karl Marx, and down to Trotsky (Russia), Bela Kun (Hungary), Rosa Luxembourg (Germany), and Emma Goldman (United States), this world-wide conspiracy for the overthrow of civilization and for the reconstitution of society on the basis of arrested development, of envious malevolence, and impossible equality, has been steadily growing.

—Winston Churchill in *Illustrated Sunday Herald*,
8 February 1920: 5

How can we account for our present situation unless we believe that men high in this government are concerting to deliver us to disaster? This must be the product of a great conspiracy, a conspiracy on a scale so immense as to dwarf any previous such venture in the history of man. A conspiracy of infamy

1

so black that, when it is finally exposed, its principals shall be
forever deserving of the maledictions of all honest men.

—Senator Joseph McCarthy,
addressing the United States Congress, 14 June 1951,
cited in Hofstadter (1967: 7)

In September 2001, the World Trade Centre was attacked allegedly by terrorists. I am not sure now that Muslim terrorists carried out these attacks. There is strong evidence that the attacks
were staged. If they can make *Avatar*, they can make anything.

—Former Malaysian Prime Minister
Mahathir Mohammad, addressing the Conference
for the Support of Al-Quds (Jerusalem),
Kuala Lumpur, 20 January 2010

The above passages, written at different times over the past 250 years,
reflect the beliefs of four individuals of dissimilar social, cultural and
political backgrounds, citizens of different countries across three conti-
nents. The quoted observations have been made in response to diverse
historical and political events, ranging from the French Revolution to
the 11 September 2001 attacks on New York and Washington. And yet,
despite these and other differences, the remarks of a French Jesuit priest,
a British Conservative politician and future Prime Minister, an American
Republican Senator and the former head of the Malaysian government
share an important similarity. All contain within them the view that
a historical or political event (or a series of events) occurred as a consequence of a carefully worked out plan, plotted in secret by a small
group of powerful individuals. The passages invoke different conspiratorial bodies – the Illuminati, Jews, Communists or a shadowy elite within
the American establishment – but they are permeated by the same fundamental claim of the conspiracy theory: that there is 'an occult force
operating behind the seemingly real, outward forms of political life'
(Roberts, 1974: 29–30), and that visible reality is no more than an illusion, a smokescreen that conceals the sinister machinations of some
powerful, secretive and menacing cabal. Karl Popper referred to this
worldview as the 'conspiracy theory of society' according to which the
'explanation of a social phenomenon consists of a discovery of the men
[*sic*] or groups who are interested in the occurrence of this phenomenon
[...] and who have planned and conspired to bring it about' (1966: 95).

While the quoted passages suggest that conspiracy theories have been
around for at least two hundred years, it is often argued that we live

in an 'age of conspiracism' (Alter, 1997: 47). There is not a single significant event in the world today – an election result, economic crisis, death of a public figure, terrorist attack, natural disaster, plane crash, political assassination, military conflict, meteorological anomaly or flu pandemic – that does not generate at least a flutter of conspiracist speculation. Conspiracy theories are said to have migrated from the margins of society to the centre ground of politics and public life and have become a ubiquitous feature of contemporary political and popular culture – an 'everyday epistemological quick fix to often intractably complex problems' of the modern age, including secrecy in politics, increased surveillance and threat to privacy, the rise in influence of transnational corporate bodies and the sense of diminished personal agency (Knight, 2000: 8, see also Fenster, 2008, Goldberg, 2001). Throughout the world conspiracy theories have also become a popular means of articulating an opposition to the forces of international capitalism, globalisation, America's military and political supremacy, and the more general rise of a transnational political order.

Given their global proliferation and persistence, it is not surprising that, over the years, conspiracy theories have been the subject of numerous books and scholarly papers, not to mention hundreds of magazine and newspaper articles and, increasingly, blogs. Communities of historians, political scientists, psychologists, sociologists, anthropologists and philosophers as well as journalists, commentators and political pundits have sought to explain the enduring appeal of the conspiracy culture. They have looked for and found conspiracy theories in virtually every corner of the world, from Russia to Indonesia, from the United States to South Africa. They have delved into their past, present and future, scrutinising them from every possible angle, some with trepidation and contempt, and others with unconcealed fascination. They have sifted meticulously through thousands of pages of conspiracy materials, exposing even the smallest factual and logical flaws. They searched for the roots of conspiracy beliefs in every place imaginable, from the depth of the individual unconscious to something as impersonal as the 'postmodern condition'.

Despite this wealth of knowledge that has accumulated over the years, and the enduring public interest in and fascination with conspiracy theories, there has as yet been no attempt to offer a general introduction to this phenomenon and its historical, political and psychological dimensions. One reason for this is that writers on the subject tend to exhibit a certain reluctance to extend their enquiry beyond the bounds of their own discipline. For example, in the writing that belongs to the fields of anthropology, philosophy or cultural studies, one seldom finds references to psychological research, even though the appropriation of psychological vocabulary is common. Psychologists, on the other hand, often view conspiracy theories rather narrowly, as a matter of individual belief or attitude, without looking at them as a broader cultural phenomenon and historically bounded worldview. Writers focusing on the conspiracy culture in the United States often take little notice of developments overseas and tend to treat their subject matter as a uniquely American phenomenon, just as those focusing on conspiracy theories as a feature of contemporary mass culture have the tendency to neglect the continuities and discontinuities in conspiracist thought through history. What is more, in literature on conspiracy theories, consensus has been lacking even on some basic issues such as precisely what kind of explanation constitutes a conspiracy theory, or whether the enduring presence of conspiracy theories in society is a good or a bad thing.

In providing a critical introduction to conspiracy theories, the present volume does not offer a detailed overview of the different approaches to, and perspectives on the topic, nor does it seek to reconcile them. Also, it does not set out to examine in detail specific conspiracy theories, contemporary or historical, with the view of exposing their factual and logical flaws. Instead, drawing on literature from a variety of disciplines, the forthcoming chapters address a set of specific questions – six to be precise – which cut to the core of conspiracy theories as a global social, cultural and political phenomenon, and which offer a suitable starting point from which to begin to deconstruct their logic and rhetoric and analyse the broader social and psychological factors that contribute to their persistence in modern society.

The six questions, which will be introduced shortly, explore conspiracy theories as a *tradition of explanation*, characterised by a particular *rhetorical style*. Anyone who has had the opportunity to engage with conspiracy theories about 9/11, AIDS or the machinations of the Bilderberg group, the Illuminati or Jews will be struck by the fact that they often sound remarkably alike. Tales of conspiracy – whether expounded in Washington, London, Moscow, Damascus or Beijing and regardless of whether they purport to explain a political assassination, the cause of a disease or a financial crisis – are marked by a distinct thematic configuration, narrative structure and explanatory logic, as well as by the stubborn presence of a number of common motifs and tropes. American historian Richard Hofstadter (1967) referred to the common features of conspiracy theories as markers of a distinct explanatory or rhetorical 'style' which he chose to call 'paranoid'. He employed the term *style*, 'much as a historian of art might speak of the baroque or the mannerist style. It is, above all, a way of seeing the world and of expressing oneself' (ibid.: 4). For similar reasons, conspiracy theories are said to constitute a distinct culture – *conspiracism* – which encompasses a specific system of knowledge, beliefs, values, practices and rituals shared by communities of people around the world (Pipes, 1997, Barkun, 2006). The uniformity of the conspiratorial 'style' of rhetoric can be shown to persist over time. The worldview which defines contemporary conspiracy culture and the distinct manner of expression through which it is articulated bears a close resemblance to that found in the writings of nineteenth- and twentieth-century conspiracy theorists. Conspiracist interpretations of the 2008 financial crisis draw on the same armoury of arguments and tropes which were used to interpret the Great Depression of the 1930s. The 9/11 Truth movement draws extensively on the interpretative framework established in the 1940s, when the opponents of Franklin D. Roosevelt accused him of allowing Pearl Harbour to happen in order to create a pretext for taking America to war. Throughout post-communist Eastern Europe, criticism directed at the supposedly seditious and sinister activities of Western non-governmental organisations and human rights activists bears close resemblance to the late eighteenth- and nineteenth-century anti-Illuminati and anti-Masonic rhetoric. What is more, conspiracy theorists not only borrow their predecessors' arguments, but also acknowledge the enduring relevance of their work. The opening paragraph of this chapter includes a quote from Augustin Barruel's four-volume *Memoirs, Illustrating the History of Jacobinism*, one of the earliest elaborations of the Illuminati conspiracy theory, first published in London in 1797. For many conspiracy theorists today, the work of Barruel and his contemporaries is not just of historical significance. It is treated also as a body of knowledge which, if adequately interpreted, offers insight into the central problems of today. Other classics of the genre, including the writings of Nesta Webster, Henry Ford or Gary Allen, even the notorious *Protocols of the Elders of Zion*, are treated in the same way.

The thread of continuity that runs through the culture of conspiracy theory is sufficiently robust to make it possible to speak of conspiracism not just as an explanatory style, but also as a *tradition of explanation* (Billig 1978, 1987a). This tradition consists of a corpus of ideas, arguments, 'facts', 'revelations' and 'proofs' pertaining to the alleged world plot, which have accumulated over time, and which are referred to, cited, quoted and perpetuated by successive generations of conspiracy theorists. As we shall see later in the book, the conspiracy culture is defined (but also sustained) by the tendency among conspiracy writers to regurgitate, revamp and apply to new circumstances the body of knowledge, the explanatory logic and rhetorical tropes expounded in texts, books or pamphlets written and published by conspiracy theorists in the past.

The view of conspiracy theories as a tradition of explanation opens up a number of important questions which will be addressed in the forthcoming chapters. What are the defining characteristics of conspiracy theories and their rhetorical style? How does one differentiate conspiracy theories from legitimate inquiries into real conspiracies in politics? How long have conspiracy theories been around and to what extent are contemporary versions similar to those of yesteryear? Why do conspiracy theories sound alike and what ensures their persistence in modern society? Why do some people believe in conspiracy theories while others do not? Are conspiracy theories necessarily bad, or does the distrust in government and mainstream institutions which they invariably perpetuate harbour a progressive potential?

Before engaging with these questions and embarking on the exploration of the conspiracy tradition, it is necessary to survey the phenomenon under investigation, provide a brief tour of the contemporary conspiracy culture and examine why it is that conspiracy theories are worthy of critical examination.

Mapping contemporary conspiracy culture

The contention that at the dawn of the twenty-first century the world is undergoing a period of 'fashionable conspiracism' (Aaronovitch, 2008: 3) is not difficult to evidence. Opinion polls carried out around the world reveal that a substantial proportion of the population readily admits to believing in some form of conspiracy theory. In the United States, for example, polls have consistently shown that between 30 and 40 per cent of the population believes either that the official account of 9/11 is a cover-up or that the US establishment was involved in the attacks, either directly, by planting explosives that brought down the Twin Towers, or indirectly, through a deliberate failure to stop them from happening (Sales, 2006, Sunstein and Vermeule, 2009, Gillan, 2006). This view is shared by between a fifth and a third of the populations of Germany and Canada, and according to one survey at least, close to 40 per cent of Britons (Connolly, 2003, Sunstein and Vermeule, 2009, 'US base leads poll's top conspiracy theories', 2008, Knight, 2008). A poll carried out in five predominantly Muslim countries in

2004 found that more than three quarters of the sample did not believe that the 9/11 attacks were carried out by Al Qaida, alleging instead a conspiracy involving the US and Israeli governments (Gentzkow and Shapiro, 2004). In Egypt, the proportion of people who believe that Israel alone was behind 9/11 was found to be as high as 43 per cent (WorldPublicOpinion.org, 2008).

Other polls carried out in the United States, in Britain and elsewhere have also found that a high proportion of the population does not accept as true the official, non-conspiratorial explanations of a number of other dramatic events such as the 1963 assassination of John F. Kennedy, the 1996 explosion of the TWA 800 flight over the Atlantic, the death of Princess Diana or the Apollo moon landing (see Goertzel, 1994, Miller, 2002, Aaronovitch, 2009). What is more, recent surveys have found that between a half and two thirds of Americans agree with statements such as 'the US government know more about UFOs than they are telling us', which reveals not only that the majority of the American public believes in the existence of extra-terrestrial life, but also that such beliefs have become intertwined with the story of a vast government-sponsored cover-up (see Barkun, 2006, Goldberg, 2001).

The widespread popularity of conspiracy theories evidenced by the opinion poll data is reflected in (while at the same time being sustained by) what can be described as the veritable conspiracy theory industry, involving authors, publishers, the media, advertisers, event organisers, specialised tour operators and memorabilia vendors. In the past decade, conspiracy theory literature has featured on best-seller lists in the United States, Germany, France, Serbia, South Africa and China ('9/11 conspiracy theory books dominate debate at Frankfurt Book Fair', 2003, Connolly, 2003, Byford, 2006, Lewis and Kahn, 2005). In the 1980s, the number of books published in Japan on the topic of Jewish conspiracy was so great that some bookshops stocked them in a designated 'Jewish corner' (Kowner, 1997). 9/11 conspiracy theorists such as Thierry Meyssan or David Ray Griffin have become international celebrities after their work was published in dozens of languages worldwide.

Conspiracy literature features even in catalogues of major mainstream publishing houses. The commercial success of *Rule by Secrecy* (2000) and *The Rise of the Fourth Reich* (2008), two books by Jim Marrs, one of the doyens of contemporary American New World Order conspiracy theory, is undoubtedly linked to the fact that they were published and marketed by a reputable mainstream commercial publisher, HarperCollins. In China, *Currency Wars*, a bestseller by Song Hongbing, which alleges that a whole series of disparate events, from the battle of Waterloo, through the rise of Hitler, to the Japanese economic boom and climate change, are attributable to the machinations of the Rothschild family, was published by an imprint of the state-owned publishing house CITIC. Originally published in 2007, it is said to have sold more than 200,000 legal copies, and maybe twice as many pirated ones. Despite containing assertions such as that 'at present, 90 percent of the financial power on Wall Street is in the hands of Jews', the book received praise in state-controlled press in China (e.g. Jin, 2009) and attracted the attention of the higher echelons of the country's business and financial establishment (McGregor, 2007). In 2009, at the time when Song Hongbing was writing the sequel to *Currency Wars*, the website of *Bloomberg Business Week* included him on its list of 'China's most powerful people' (Bloomberg Business Week, 2009).

Recent years have also seen a proliferation of books such as *The Rough Guide to Conspiracy Theories* (McConachie and Tudge, 2008), *The Mammoth Book of Cover-ups* (Lewis, 2008), *Conspiracy Files* (Southwell and Twist, 2007) and others which offer an overview of the 'best known' or 'most bizarre' conspiracy theories of all time. Revised, updated or expanded editions of these compendia are printed every couple of years, ensuring a steady stream of new and old claims. A classic in this genre, Jonathan Vankin and John Whalen's *Fifty Greatest Conspiracies of All Time*, was updated four times between 1995 and 2004, eventually becoming *Eighty Greatest Conspiracies of all Time* (Harper, 2008). By 2010, the authors appear to have lost count, so the most recent edition is simply called *The World's Greatest Conspiracies* (Vankin and Whalen, 2010). These works, alongside a multitude of books devoted to conspiratorial explanations of single events such as the death of Princess Diana, 9/11, the origin of AIDS or the assassination of John F. Kennedy, reflect the recognition among publishers that there is a market for material of this kind.

Another branch of media industry involved in the dissemination of conspiracy theories is network television. Over the past decade, practically every major TV channel or network in the US and the UK has featured documentaries investigating one conspiracy theory or another. Meanwhile, cable networks specialising in historical documentaries, such as the History Channel or Discovery, have perfected the genre of 'speculative history'. This particular style of documentary is devoted to 'controversial' events which have been the topic of conspiracist speculation and which are set up in the programme as still awaiting a satisfactory and conclusive explanation. Although 'speculative history' documentaries tend not to endorse conspiratorial interpretations outright, they nevertheless fail to dismiss them as groundless. It is an inherent feature of the genre that conspiratorial and non-conspiratorial interpretations are presented as equally reasonable positions in a legitimate debate. Contributors to the programmes – be they scholars, engineers, forensic experts, trained historians, amateur enthusiasts, UFOlogists or conspiracy buffs – are typically accorded equal treatment as 'experts', and it is left to the viewer to weigh the arguments, consider the evidence and determine which of the rival interpretations is most plausible (Popp, 2006). The inevitable outcome of this approach, which shuns any firm conclusion or narrative closure in favour of doubt and ambiguity, is that the status of 'counterkonwledge' and conspiratorial pseudohistory is enhanced, at the expense of genuine scholarship (Thompson, 2008).

Conspiracism features in the mainstream electronic news media too. In 2008, at the time of the US presidential election campaign, CNN's Lou Dobs and several Fox News commentators and anchor men and women, publicised the agenda of the so-called Birther movement, which alleged that Barack Obama faked his birth certificate to conceal the fact that he was born in Kenya, which would have precluded him from standing for the US presidency. The Birthers, and their supporters within the mainstream media, were not simply pointing towards an individual act of fraud – the faking of a Hawaiian birth certificate – but hinted instead at a vast multi-million-dollar conspiracy to conceal the future president's real birthplace. This tale of conspiracy quickly became an important element in right-wing populist propaganda which used the 'doubts' and 'questions' about Obama's origins to emphasise the Democratic candidate's anti-Americanness, and the supposedly alien and 'un-patriotic' character of his 'socialist' policies (Pilkington, 2009a).

The rise of national 24-hour news channels has created new opportunities for the international dissemination of conspiracy theories. Russia Today, the English-language 24-hour news channel funded by the Russian state, which is available globally via cable or satellite, is a case in point. Established in 2005, the channel hoped to shake up the world of international news media by providing a fresh alternative to the likes of CNN or Sky News, which were seen, by RT's founders, as unquestioningly promoting the foreign policy agenda of Western powers. However, in the attempt to provide a novel 'critical' perspective on world affairs (the channel's motto is 'question more'), Russia Today opened its doors to conspiracy theorists from around the world, many of them from the US. The channel has provided the likes of Alex Jones, Webster Tarpley, David Ray Griffin and Jim Marrs with the opportunity to promote, to an international audience, their ideas about the New World Order, 9/11, the Bilderberg group or the climate change conspiracy, all while being treated with absolute deference by the channel's journalists. Embedded video clips of appearances on Russia Today have become a regular feature on the websites of American conspiracy theorists, where they are brandished as a sign of credibility and mainstream recognition.

Conspiracy explanations also feature in the press, and not just in tabloid publications such as the *National Enquirer* or *Weekly World News*, which have attained notoriety for their penchant for bizarre stories of conspiracy and cover-up. Over the past decade, a number of US periodicals, including *Discover*, a popular magazine devoted to issues related to 'science, technology and the future', as well as *Harper's Magazine*, *American Spectator* and *National Review*, have provided a platform for various conspiracy theories about the origins of AIDS (see Kalichman, 2009). In the United Kingdom too, since 1997, the Diana-related conspiracy theories have been the 'main marketing ploy' of the *Daily Express*, which frequently sought to boost circulation by adorning its front page with a photograph of the glamorous Princess of Wales, accompanied by a claim casting doubt on the official version of her death (Aaronovitch, 2009: 152).

A particularly regrettable instance of conspiracism in the mainstream British press was the front cover of the 14 January 2002 issue of the left-wing news magazine the *New Statesman*, which featured an image of the Union Jack pierced by a glittering, golden Star of David, accompanied by the caption 'A kosher conspiracy?'. The contemptible conspiratorial motif reminiscent of the Nazi propaganda of the 1930s, which portrays Jews as using the power of gold and money to work against the interest of the nation, was clearly signified on the cover, announcing the issue's headline story – an exploration of the workings of Britain's 'pro-Israel lobby'. Although the outrage that followed the magazine's publication led to a swift apology from the editor-in-chief, the fact that it was ever published reminded the British (and international) public that antisemitic motifs and conspiracy theories are not the prerogatives of the Right, but an increasingly common trope in the rhetoric of some left-wing critics of Israel and its policies (see Hirsh, 2007 and Harrison, 2006).

The principal medium for the transmission of conspiracy theories today, however, is neither the press nor television, but the internet. The kind of conspiracy theorising that a generation ago was disseminated in photocopied newsletters and pamphlets, in books sold in specialist bookshops or through mail order catalogues, or in amateur videos that were costly to produce and distribute can now reach, via the world wide web, a large proportion of the (developed) world instantly and at minimal cost. Over the past 15 years, conspiracy theories have spread like wildfire through the internet, to the point where, in September 2010, the search-term 'conspiracy' yielded close to 30 million results on Google. A more recent development in the online dissemination of conspiracy theories, which has enabled them to reach a new generation of consumers, has been the emergence of video-sharing websites such as YouTube or Google Videos. Amateur documentaries are today an indispensable tool of conspiracy theorists, alongside websites, internet chartrooms and forums. One of the most successful postings on YouTube to date has been the 9/11 conspiracy film *Loose Change*, created by a group of 20-something year-olds on a laptop, using unauthorised footage from news channels and some basic graphic design and animation software. Within a month of being posted on the internet in April 2005, *Loose Change* was viewed by 10 million people, rising to number one on the Google video chart (Sales, 2006). The success of this film inspired a whole generation of amateur documentary makers, who have posted, over the past five years, thousands of conspiracy-related videos on YouTube and other similar websites. Crucially, YouTube, and the internet more generally, are used by conspiracy theorists in conjunction with traditional media, including books and radio (Fenster, 2008). The popular syndicated daily radio show produced and presented by Alex Jones, one of America's best known conspiracy theorists, is today part of a sophisticated and lucrative multimedia franchise which includes books, DVDs, a website (infowars.com), a web-based television channel (prisonplanet.tv), a YouTube channel, daily podcasts and merchandising.

Conspiracy-related themes have also become an unavoidable feature of fictional genres. The global success, in the 1990s, of *The X-Files* is an obvious and much written about example of the popularisation of conspiracy theories through fictional narratives (see Kellner, 2003, Fenster, 2008). Conspiracy motifs have also featured in Hollywood blockbusters such as *JFK* or *Conspiracy Theory* and (in a somewhat watered-down form) in a number of successful recent American TV productions such as *24*, *Prison Break* and *Lost*. Tales of occult knowledge, plots and cover-ups have featured also in a number of bestselling novels published in the past decade. Dan Brown's *The Da Vinci Code* (2003), *Angels and Demons* (2000) and *The Lost Symbol* (2009) are obvious examples. The plot of *The Da Vinci Code* was influenced by the central claim of Michael Baigent, Richard Leigh and Henry Lincoln's 1982 bestseller *The Holy*

Figure 1.1   Loose Change 9/11: An American Coup (2009) DVD sleeve (with permission from Microcinema International)

Blood and the Holy Grail, a book which by the time Brown's novel hit the best-sellers list had already attained cult following among conspiracy theorists worldwide (see Barkun, 2006, Aaronovitch, 2009). *Angels and Demons* focuses on the epitome of secret societies, the Illuminati, while in Brown's most recent work, *The Lost Symbol*, attention is turned to the Freemasons and the idea that Washington D.C. was built in accordance with Masonic teachings, a claim that has featured in anti-Masonic conspiracy theories for decades (Barkun, 2006). Arguably, the popularity of Brown's novels is not unrelated to their underlining conspiratorial theme. Writing in the *Guardian*, journalist and literary critic Mark Lawson attributed the success of the *The Da Vinci Code* to the fact that 'this story of a conspiracy lasting two millennia [...] chimed with a time of paranoid suspicion about official institutions and religions' ('What we were reading', 2009: 2). What Brown's novels did was to take a number of motifs out of the world of conspiracy theory, 'sanitise' them by incorporating them into a fictional genre, while at the same time obscuring, deliberately and cleverly, the boundaries between fact and fiction, between conspiracy theory and genuine history. This blurring of boundaries continues in a variety of spin-offs in the form of books and documentaries purporting to 'unlock' the mysterious Da Vinci code or 'decode' the lost symbols of the Freemasons.

The 'paranoid suspicion about official institutions' which Lawson identified as a factor fuelling the proliferation of conspiracy theories is apparent not only in the stance towards religious institutions, but also towards the mainstream of science. Scepticism about the authority of science permeates contemporary conspiracy culture. For many conspiracy theorists, the whole of science is in the service of greedy pharmaceutical companies, pressure groups, international organisations and other sinister bodies set on manipulating and exploiting the public. Evidence of global warming is often dismissed, even in the mainstream press, as a manipulation, a scare tactic, and an instrument of an international plot orchestrated by those benefitting from 'climate change industry', including the UN Intergovernmental Panel on Climate Change, the World Wildlife Fund and multinational insurance companies (Booker, 2010, North 2010). Conspiracy theories have been embraced also by exponents of creationism and intelligent design. *Expelled: No Intelligence Allowed*, the 2008 documentary by the filmmaker Ben Stein, which banked up to 10 million dollars and became the thirteenth highest grossing documentary in US history, alleged that Darwin's theory of evolution owes its popularity to centuries of systematic suppression of disconfirming evidence by exponents of secular and materialist philosophies who dominate the scientific establishment.

The most dramatic example of the conspiracist suspicion of science, which illustrates poignantly also the lethal potential of conspiracy theories, are the claims about HIV and AIDS. For the past 30 years, what has become known as the denialist movement has questioned the well established link between HIV and AIDS, attributing the public concern about the spread of HIV to a vast conspiracy by the pharmaceutical industry and (Western) government agencies. Denialists claim that antiretroviral drugs administered to HIV patients are more harmful than the virus itself, and that their use is motivated either by greed or by the more sinister aim of genocide. Over the years, the AIDS denialist movement has become sufficiently influential to affect public policy. The reliance of the former South African president Thabo Mbeki on the 'expertise' of some of the world's most prominent AIDS denialists (including Peter Duesberg and David Rasnick) and the opposition, from within his administration, to the use of antiretroviral drugs caused important delays to the treatment of millions of those affected by HIV in South Africa (Kalichman, 2009). According to some estimates, the delay contributed to the death of as many as 330,000 HIV patients between 2000 and 2005 (Chigwedere et al., 2008, Nattrass, 2008).

Another, somewhat different set of AIDS-related conspiracy theories have been shown to be especially common among the African American community in the United States (Bird and Bogart, 2005, Simmons and Parsons, 2005). Bird and Bogart (2005) found that 70 per cent of respondents from an African American sample reported believing that 'a lot of information about AIDS is being withheld from the public', half reported believing that a cure from AIDS exists but is being withheld from the poor, while 40 per cent agreed that recipients of antiretroviral drugs are guinea pigs for the US government (for data from earlier opinion polls see Thomas and Quinn, 1991, 1993). The high percentage of African Americans who reportedly believe in conspiracy theories is not limited to AIDS-related claims. In the 1990s, 60 per cent agreed with the statement that 'the government deliberately makes sure that drugs are easily available in poor black neighbourhoods in order to harm black people' (Crocker et al., 1999, Goertzel, 1994). Also, as many as 50 per cent of African Americans surveyed endorsed the claim that the government is taking measures to keep the numbers of black people down, with between 20 per cent and 30 per cent believing that birth control is being used for this purpose (Bird and Bogart, 2005). Although the impact of these beliefs has not been as dramatic as in South Africa, their prevalence has become an important obstacle to the success of public health campaigns in the United States.

The example of AIDS-related conspiracy theories clearly illustrates how dangerous it would be to dismiss conspiracism as a mere curiosity or a harmless feature of contemporary mass culture. In addition, a number of dramatic events over the past 20 years have provided unwelcome reminders of the link between conspiracy culture and mass violence.

Timothy McVeigh's 1996 terrorist attack on the federal building in Oklahoma, for instance, turned out to have been inspired by *The Turner Diaries*, a dystopian account of American society caught in the grip of a dictatorship by Jews and Blacks, which was popular in the 1990s among far-right conspiracy theorists and supporters of supremacist movements. Members of the pseudo-Buddhist Aum Shinrikyo sect who, in 1995, released sarin gas on a Tokyo subway killing 16 and injuring 5,000 commuters were also motivated by the desire to strike a blow to the sinister plot by Jews and Freemasons (Goodman, 2005). To the present day, conspiracy theories remain the staple ingredient of the propaganda not just of far-right militias or totalitarian sects but also of terrorist movements around the world. The charter of the Palestinian terrorist organisation Hamas cites the notorious *Protocols of the Elders of Zion* as evidence that 'Zionists' are striving for world domination and uses the antisemitic hoax to legitimise its attacks on Israeli military and civilian targets. It has been suggested that even in the case of 9/11, Al Qaida's choice of target reflected the preoccupation, within the radical Islamist movements, with Wall Street and the whole of New York's financial district as the centre of Jewish power in the US (Küntzel, 2007).

Also, because conspiracy theories are so often stories of *global* power and influence, they tend to fall on fertile ground among political cultures, societies and movements which feel in some way marginalised, threatened or victimised by the global political order. Critics of Western military, economic and diplomatic supremacy, and those eager to challenge the authority of the liberal-democratic political agenda and values, often project their fears and discontents into a general thesis of conspiracy. Leaders of authoritarian regimes in particular readily reach out for conspiracy theories as a means of reinforcing their grip on power and as a source of convenient excuses for economic failures, and their respective countries' marginal status in world politics. In Serbia in the 1990s, under the regime of Slobodan Milošević, conspiracy theories were the dominant paradigm for interpreting the country's conflict with the international community (Byford, 2002, 2006, Byford and

Billig, 2001). In 2009, the Libyan president Muammar Qaddafi delivered an hour-and-a-half-long speech before the General Assembly of the United Nations in which he claimed that the swine flu virus was manufactured in a laboratory, that Kennedy was assassinated because he 'wanted to investigate the nuclear reactor of the Israeli demon' and that the assassination of Martin Luther King was the result of a government-sponsored plot (Pilkington, 2009b). In recent years, the Iranian regime has not only offered patronage to Holocaust deniers and 9/11 conspiracy theorists from around the world, but even pinned the 2010 Haitian earthquake and the harsh winter that struck Europe that year on a conspiracy orchestrated by 'the US-Zionist regime' (IRIB, 2010). Dramatisations of the *Protocols of the Elders of Zion* showing Jews plotting world domination have been broadcast on state-sponsored television channels in Egypt, Lebanon and Syria.

On the opposite side of the world, in Chavez's Venezuela conspiracy theories have also become an intrinsic part of the regime's missionary politics, used to justify the suppression of political dissent and cement the president's grip on power (Pérez Hernáiz, 2009). The pro-regime

Figure 1.2 Screen shot from the TV series *Ash-Shatat* (The Diaspora) broadcast in 2003 on Hezbollah's TV station Al-Manar in Beirut (courtesy of The Middle East Media Research Institute, www.memri.org)

press routinely links Chavez's political opponents not just to the US or the CIA but also to Israel and Jews, blaming economic problems on 'Semitic bankers' or 'Israeli-Zionist associations', which are said to have the Venezuelan ruler's opponents in their grip (Pantin, 2008, Lomnitz and Sánchez, 2009). Chavez, like his political hero Fidel Castro, has also promoted conspiracy theories about 9/11 as well as about the US military's supposed use of secret tectonic or meteorological weapons against nations in Asia and South America (Tran, 2007, Wood, 2007). The fact that stories of plot and subversion have made their way into the rhetoric of a whole host of regimes from around the world, right wing as well as left wing, religious as well as secular, Christian as well as Muslim, exposes not just the popularity and geographical spread of conspiracy theories, but also their disregard for ideological barriers and their remarkable ability to 'bend the political spectrum and fuse its extremes into an endless circle of paranoia' (Olmsted, 2009: 174).

Chapter outline

This brief survey of the contemporary conspiracy culture illustrates the extent to which conspiracy theories have become a global phenomenon, one that pervades contemporary societies, from the wider margins inhabited by extremists of various persuasions, to the mainstream of politics, media and entertainment industry. Of course, among the plethora of conspiracy theories in circulation at any one time, some will be of passing relevance and local consequence and will remain confined to a small proportion of the world's population. Others, such as those about 9/11, about the assassination of Kennedy, or about the Jews ruling the world's finances and the media have, by contrast, become part of a more 'robust belief system' which, as well as being widespread and persistent, acquired symbolic significance and the capacity to mobilise sections of the public (Heins, 2007: 791). The forthcoming chapters focus primarily on the latter, as these form the core of the conspiracy theory as a tradition of explanation.

As already mentioned, the approach taken in this book is to offer a critical introduction to conspiracy theories through six specific questions. The first question concerns the definition of the term 'conspiracy theory'. Defining conspiracy theories is not as straightforward as it seems. In everyday conversation, 'conspiracy theory' is not a neutral term. To refer to an explanation as a 'conspiracy theory' or its exponent as a 'conspiracy theorist' implies criticism and alludes to a tendency towards faulty reasoning, irrationality or political bias. At the same time, plots, collusion and cover-ups are a regular feature of contemporary politics, which means that a theory about a conspiracy might be a perfectly reasonable view to hold. Chapter 2 sets the scene for the subsequent discussion by looking at *how legitimate analyses of secrecy and collusion in politics might be differentiated from conspiracy theories.* It also looks at why it is important (although not always easy) to maintain the distinction between the two types of explanation.

Chapter 3 focuses on the origins and the history of conspiracy theories as a tradition of explanation and considers *how long conspiracy theories have been around and where they have come from.* The chapter starts off by tracing the roots of the conspiracy tradition to the immediate aftermath of the French Revolution and examines the social, political and cultural factors that contributed to its emergence. It then provides an overview of the vicissitudes of conspiracism over the subsequent two centuries, highlighting a number of landmark events. Among them are the incorporation, in the nineteenth century, of the European conspiracy theories into the American political culture and the emergence of antisemitic motifs; the shift, in the early twentieth century, from a preoccupation with external threat to the fear of the 'enemy within'; and changes in the conspiracy culture after 1945. In tracing the origins of the conspiracy tradition and identifying the continuities and discontinuities in its development, Chapter 3 also provides a kind of *dramatis personae* of the conspiracy culture and introduces some of its main exponents, whose work is considered in later chapters.

As was already pointed out, one of the distinguishing features of conspiracy theories worldwide is that they are often remarkably similar. Ruminations about the historical role of mysterious clandestine forces tend to share a distinct narrative structure, an internal logic and a set of recurring motifs. Chapter 4 looks in more detail at the anatomy of conspiracy theories, and asks *what are the principal features of the explanatory or rhetorical 'style' of the conspiracy theory?* The chapter focuses in particular on three central elements of any conspiracy narrative, namely the identity and the character of the conspirators, their nefarious plan and the means of mass manipulation through which they keep their endeavours secret.

Chapter 5 turns the attention to antisemitism, a phenomenon that has an intrinsic connection with conspiracy theories. Contemporary antisemitism has a distinct, even unique, conspiratorial nature: Jews are the only ethnic or religious group that consistently gets accused of being wealthy and powerful and of masterminding world domination. Also, as the chapter shows, even conspiracy theories that do not explicitly target Jews often include subtle allusions to Jewish involvement in the plot. The chapter carefully examines the link between antisemitism and conspiracy theory and considers *why it so often seems unavoidable.*

Chapter 6 turns to the psychological dimension of conspiracism. In the literature on conspiracy theories, there is an overwhelming tendency to talk of them as a manifestation of individual or collective fears, fantasies, projected aggression or – most commonly – paranoia. The chapter looks at whether the comparisons between conspiracy beliefs and paranoia stand up to scrutiny and then considers *what psychological factors distinguish believers in conspiracy theories from the sceptics, and what psychological benefits the belief in a conspiracy theory brings to those who subscribe to it?*

The concluding chapter, Chapter 7, casts a critical eye on some of the recent literature on conspiracy theories which adopts a more sympathetic view of their role in modern society. A number of scholars of contemporary conspiracy culture, especially in the United States, have suggested that since the 1960s conspiracy theories have developed a somewhat playful character and that rather than being an inherent feature of political extremism, they are a response to genuine anxieties and grievances of the turn-of-the-millennium reality. Chapter 7 engages in a dialogue with this literature and asks *whether conspiracy theories can indeed be seen as a worldview with a playful, ironic side, or are they something to be feared – a relic of a populist, rightwing, political tradition, which refuses to go away?* To address this question, the chapter revisits the arguments presented throughout the book and calls for the distinction to be preserved between, on the one hand, conspiracy theories as a tradition of explanation and, on the other hand, the more general discourses of suspicion, cynicism and irony which permeate modern society. It argues that the failure to preserve such a distinction not only leads to conceptual confusion, but also implies that conspiracy thinking might be acceptable or inevitable, thereby instilling it with legitimacy. Given the historical legacy of the conspiracy theory, which is examined throughout the book, and the fact that, in the words of Richard Hofstadter (1967: 5), it 'has a greater affinity for bad causes than good', this, it will be suggested, is something that is best avoided.

2
Towards a Definition of Conspiracy Theories

> We must speak the truth about terror. Let us never tolerate
> outrageous conspiracy theories concerning the attacks on
> September 11, malicious lies that attempt to shift blame away
> from terrorists themselves, away from the guilty.
>
> —US President George W. Bush,
> speaking at the United Nations, 10 November 2001

> People can reach different conclusions, but for heaven's sake
> let's do away with all these conspiracy theories that it was about
> oil, it was about George Bush telling Tony Blair what to do ...
>
> —Alistair Campbell,
> Tony Blair's Director of Communications
> between 1997 and 2003, speaking before the
> War Crimes Inquiry, 12 January 2010

Before conspiracy theories can be meaningfully examined within their
appropriate social, historical and ideological context, it is necessary to
spend a bit more time furnishing a working definition of the phenomenon, and in doing so set the basic parameters for the forthcoming
discussion. At first sight, the meaning of the term 'conspiracy theory'
might seem obvious. The word 'conspiracy' is well established in the
English language. Derived from the Latin *conspirare*, meaning 'to breath
together', it signifies the joining together of two or more individuals and
their acting in collusion to achieve a desired outcome. Phrases such as
'conspiracy to commit murder', 'conspiracy to defraud' and 'conspiracy
to commit genocide' are enshrined in legal systems around the world
and refer to offences involving an arrangement or a joint endeavour to
perpetrate a crime. In the broadest sense, therefore, a conspiracy *theory*

would be an explanation, either speculative or evidence-based, which attributes the causes of an event to a conspiracy or a plot (Keeley, 1999, Basham, 2003).

Although any explanation that suggests collusion between individuals is, in a *literal sense*, a 'conspiracy theory', in everyday language the term is used to signify a much narrower class of phenomena. Regardless of the level of intentionality or personal agency that it entails, a causal account will rarely be labelled a 'conspiracy theory' if its subject matter is a petty and obvious plot, or one with straightforward or benevolent objectives. The epithet 'conspiracy theory' tends to be reserved for conspiracy-based explanations which deal with large scale, dramatic social and political events (such as the AIDS epidemic, the assassination of John F. Kennedy or 9/11); for explanations that do not just describe or explain an alleged conspiracy, but also *uncover* it and in doing so expose some remarkable and hitherto unknown 'truth' about the world (such as that the Illuminati orchestrated the French Revolution or that the Bush administration had a hand in 9/11); and for accounts that allege the existence of a plot with nefarious and threatening aims (to destroy Christianity, establish the New World Order, take a country to war or eliminate a racial group).

More importantly, a causal account is unlikely to be labelled a 'conspiracy theory' if it is believed to be true. In colloquial language, 'conspiracy theory' is not a neutral label used merely to describe a certain type of explanation. It is an *evaluative* term with significant pejorative connotations. To allude to an account as a 'conspiracy theory' is to make a judgment about its epistemic status; it is a way of branding an explanation untrue or insinuating that it is based on insufficient evidence, superstition or prejudice (Coady, 2006). The quotations at the start of the chapter illustrate this point. Both George W. Bush's rejection of 9/11 conspiracy theories and Alistair Campbell's call for challenges to the official explanation of Britain's involvement in the Iraq War to be 'done away with' used the tag 'conspiracy theory' to signpost the false and unsubstantiated nature of the rival explanation and to exclude its exponents from 'the imagined community of reasonable interlocutors' (Husting and Orr, 2007: 127).

These examples also point to the inherently dialogic nature of the label 'conspiracy theory'. Positioning an explanation as a 'conspiracy theory' serves to legitimise the competing one as rational, reasonable and evidence-based. It maintains the boundary between what are deemed the beliefs of competent actors and those of 'paranoid' conspiracy theorists (Husting and Orr, 2007: 141). Yet, what is noteworthy about the quotations from George W. Bush and Alistair Campbell is that, in each case, an explanation was dismissed as a 'conspiracy theory' without acknowledgment that the alternative, officially sanctioned account – the one that is set up as rational and 'non-conspiratorial' – also contains an allegation of an organised plot. According to the official version of 9/11, the attacks on the World Trade Centre and the Pentagon were the outcome of a well-coordinated conspiracy – a sinister Al Qaida plot orchestrated in secret from the caves of Afghanistan. The justification for the invasion of Iraq presented to the British public in 2003 alleged a conspiracy within the Iraqi regime to manufacture weapons of mass destruction with the purpose of using them against targets in the West. And yet, neither President Bush nor Alistair Campbell called upon the public to reject one 'conspiracy theory' in favour or another. The phrase was reserved for those explanations whose epistemic status the speakers wanted to question and which they sought to present as unwarranted or unworthy of the consideration. In fact, Catherine Olmsted (2009) has shown that in the United States, many of twentieth century's most widely disseminated conspiracy theories emerged in response to official explanations that also alleged the existence of a plot, usually one that required more power to be given to the state. Yet, in each case the epistemologically damaging label 'conspiracy theory' was applied only to those explanations which were deemed to be bogus and which were judged to lie beyond the boundaries of legitimate opinion.

The effectiveness of the label 'conspiracy theory' as a 'strategy of exclusion' (Husting and Orr, 2007) and the means of 'cutting out' (Smith, 1978) rival interpretations rests on the existence of the widespread 'intellectual presumption' against, or even 'hostility' towards, conspiracy theories (Pidgen, 1995, Clarke, 2002: 132). As Jeffrey Bale put it, 'very few notions nowadays generate as much intellectual resistance, hostility and derision within academic circles as a belief in the historical importance or efficacy of political conspiracies' (2007: 47). In the world of academia, characterising someone as a 'conspiracy theorist' is a form of character assassination. Noam Chomsky referred to this label as 'the intellectual equivalent of four letter words and tantrums' or a 'curse word' which is used to dismiss or marginalise dissident views, including his own (Chomsky, 2004). Swami and Coles (2010) have recently argued that the reluctance among psychologists to engage with conspiracy theories might be attributed to 'fear of being branded as conspiracy theorists themselves', presumably if their analysis should lead to a conclusion that falls short of outright condemnation and censure. Conspiracy-based explanations are also regularly parodied and ridiculed in the elite press, where their exponents are portrayed as suffering from some kind of psychological deficit (Harper, 2008, Husting and Orr, 2007). The term's negative connotations are even more apparent in the German language where the word for conspiracy theory is *Verchwörungsmythos* – the conspiracy *myth* – therefore something that is assumed to be imaginary or false. Furthermore, conspiracy theorising is perceived not just as crazy, paranoid or absurd but also as *politically* suspect and antithetical to 'proper' democratic politics (Fenster, 2008, Bratich, 2008). It is believed to be the sanctuary for kooks and extremists and therefore beyond the limits of respectable enquiry and legitimate political dissent.

Conspiracy theory operates as a resource for delegitimation not only at an individual level, as a means of undermining the credibility of an individual author, academic, politician or activist but also on a collective level. Whole societies, communities or religions can be presented as 'paranoid' or as subscribing to absurd or politically discredited beliefs. As we will see in Chapter 6, the demonstrable popularity of conspiracy theories in the Muslim world has led some to present Middle Eastern cultures as a hotbed of anachronistic, backward irrationality, superstition and prejudice.

Conspiracy theories are, however, not the only example of what Michael Barkun (2006: 26) calls 'stigmatised knowledge', a set of beliefs and assumptions about the world that is marginalised by 'institutions that conventionally distinguish between knowledge and error – universities, communities of scientific researchers, and the like'. The epistemic status of other forms of knowledge – paranormal beliefs, astrology, claims about the existence of extraterrestrial life or religious mythologies – is similar to that of conspiracy theories. All of them are commonly held by the population at large, but are nevertheless seen as unwarranted by the more authoritative regimes of knowledge and truth. Also, just like conspiracy theories, they can be and are used to marginalise rival explanations, belittle them and eliminate them from the realm of rational discourse. It is, in fact, not uncommon for conspiracy theories to be ridiculed by being compared with these other forms of stigmatised knowledge.

However, an important difference exists between conspiracy theories and other forms of stigmatised knowledge. Believing in the existence of conspiracies is, in and of itself, neither objectionable, nor irrational or misguided. Conspiracies (unlike alien visitations, religious miracles or telekinesis) happen all the time. Even the greatest sceptics, such as Karl Popper (1966, 1972), Richard Hofstadter (1967), or Seymour Lipset and Earl Raab (1978), when it comes to the explanatory value of conspiracy theories acknowledge that conspiracies occur regularly and are even a 'typical social phenomenon' (Popper, 1966: 95). Political assassinations, dramatic transfers of power, political scandals and cover-ups, terrorist attacks, as well as much of everyday politics and governance – from the negotiations of coalition agreements to the setting of interest rates – involve the collaboration of multiple agents who collude in the attempt to bring about a desired outcome. So, whatever the epistemic status of conspiracy theories, claims about conspiracies are the staple diet of perfectly legitimate forms of enquiry, including investigative journalism, political punditry and even mainstream historiography (Pidgen, 1995). In fact, revelations about the Watergate scandal, the Iran Contra affair, or the Enron fraud suggest that excessive disinclination to believe in conspiracies could be as much an 'intellectual vice' as the tendency to uncritically embrace conspiracy-based explanations (Coady, 2003: 197).

The regularity with which conspiracies occur in everyday life and the negative connotations associated with the label 'conspiracy theory' warrant further examination. If conspiracy theories are to be made into an object of inquiry and critical analysis, it is important to be able to differentiate 'rational hypotheses about actual conspiracies' from the kind of speculation which warrants criticism and dismissal (Heins, 2007: 788). Much of contemporary literature on the subject assumes that it is necessary to make an analytical distinction between what Jeffrey Bale (2007: 45) calls *genuine conspiratorial politics* – 'a regular if not omnipresent feature of national and international politics', and *bogus conspiracy theories* – 'elaborate fantasies that purport to show that various sinister, powerful groups with evil intentions, operating behind the scenes, are secretly controlling the course of world events'. Similar distinctions have been made between dysfunctional 'clinical' or 'pathological paranoia' and the more acceptable 'healthy' or 'critical paranoia' (Harper, 2008; Kellner, 2003) or between explorations of 'the natural threat of global conspiracy' – posed by the secretive and hierarchically organised international political and economic order – and the 'sort of mindless McCarthyian witch-hunts' that are to be discarded (Basham, 2003: 101–102). Underpinning all of these distinctions is the same question: How do we tease apart claims of conspiracy that are based in reality from those that are spurious?

Negotiating the boundaries of the term 'conspiracy theory'

Any attempt to differentiate between the two types of knowledge claims and to derive a clear and unambiguous definition of 'conspiracy theory' will be hampered by the effectiveness of the label as a strategy of exclusion. While there may be agreement about the necessity of maintaining a distinction between real and bogus conspiracies, there is no consensus in sight when it comes to deciding precisely where this boundary lies. Instead, what counts as a 'conspiracy theory' (vis-à-vis legitimate exploration of real conspiracies) is a topic of continuous debate and disagreement. The meaning of these categories and their conceptual limits are constantly reconstructed and renegotiated, as those debating the issue, including scholars, journalists, commentators and conspiracy theorists, use language flexibly not just to describe the world around them and derive explanations of social events, but also to accomplish rhetorical goals: to manufacture accusations, refute criticism, apportion blame and legitimise or contest particular versions or descriptions of reality (Potter and Wetherell, 1987, Billig, 1987b, Edwards, 1997).

Several examples can be cited to illustrate this point. In his 1997 book *Conspiracy: How the Paranoid Style Flourishes and Where It Comes From*, Daniel Pipes discriminates between 'conspiracies, which are real' and 'conspiracy theories, which exist only in the imagination' and which are no more than a manifestation of an irrational 'fear of non-existent conspiracies' (1997: 20–21). Throughout the book, the distinction between 'real' and 'imagined' conspiracies is treated as largely self-evident and unproblematic, although Pipes does acknowledge the potential fuzziness of the boundaries when he suggests that some left-wing writers have been allowed to get away with promoting bogus conspiracy theories, in large part due to an anti-right-wing bias among critics of conspiracism.

Among this elusive brand of sophisticated left-wing conspiracy theories Pipes includes the work of Noam Chomsky, the American linguist and long-standing critic of the US establishment and its foreign policy. For Pipes (1997: 160), Chomsky 'forwards a conspiracy theory that blames the US government for virtually every ill around the world, including environmental pollution, militarism, economic poverty, spiritual alienation and the drug scourge'. Chomsky is portrayed as a purveyor of 'harebrained ideas' and a prominent exponent of 'anti-secret society' mythology. On the pages of *Conspiracy*, his name is mentioned in the same breath as the John Birch Society and various right-wing anti-Masonic sites on the internet.

Pipes's critique of Chomsky is not new. Since the 1980s critics of Chomsky's political activism have drawn parallels between his institutional analysis and conspiracy theory, although most have been more generous than Pipes. Holsti and Rosenau (1984: 174), for example, suggest that Chomsky's propaganda model of the media articulated in the book *Manufacturing Consent* (Herman and Chomsky, 1988) is 'almost conspiratorial'. The notion that in contemporary Western democracies 'consent' is somehow 'manufactured' has been criticised as implying a kind of intentionality often associated with conspiracy theory (Klaehn, 2002, see Rai, 1995 for a defence of Chomsky).

The debate about whether Chomsky is a conspiracy theorist, 'almost' a conspiracy theorist or whether his writing is distinguishable from contemporary conspiracy culture is not solely about Chomsky and the relative merits of his intellectual engagement. It is also about the conceptual limits of 'conspiracy theory' and where legitimate analysis of secrecy in politics ends and conspiracy theory begins. When Chomsky responded to criticism, he did so by challenging the applicability of the damaging label to his perspective (Chomsky, 2004). He too made a distinction between legitimate analysis of current affairs, such as his own, which is based on evidence drawn from 'historical' or 'documentary record' and the far-fetched and speculative 'conspiracy theories' from which he wanted to be dissociated. Among the latter Chomsky includes 9/11 or Kennedy assassination conspiracy theories which he has dismissed on several occasions as baseless and as diverting attention and energy form the more intellectually sound exploration of real abuses of power in the United States (e.g. Chomsky, 2006, see also Hari, 2009). Therefore, in responding to criticism, Chomsky sought to reconstitute the meaning of the word 'conspiracy theory' and renegotiate its boundaries in a way that would exclude his kind of enquiry and limit the damaging label to a narrower set of (rejected) explanations.

This however was not the end of the debate. Chomsky's distancing from the Kennedy conspiracy thesis provoked a reaction from a number of its exponents who retorted by proffering their own interpretation of where the boundaries of 'conspiracy theory' lie. Michael Parenti (1996: 172), for example, contended that the conspiracy to assassinate the former president of the United States belongs to the same realm of real conspiracies as Watergate or the Iran-Contra affair and is therefore distinguishable from 'kooky fantasies or unimportant aberrations' and 'wacko conspiracy theories'. What is noteworthy is that Parenti responded to Chomsky's critique with an argument identical to that which Chomsky utilised to answer his own critics. Parenti argued that Chomsky uses 'conspiracy theory' as a dismissive label to silence political opponents, and that he deliberately sets up for disparagement the perfectly legitimate investigations into the plot to assassinate Kennedy by linking them to motifs which have come to symbolise the irrationality of conspiracy theories.

The second example comes from the work of Robin Ramsay, the British writer and journalist who over the past two decades has published extensively on the topic of 'parapolitics' and conspiracy theories (Ramsay, 2000, 2008). Much of Ramsay's writing is devoted to delineating, on the one hand, the kind of analysis he advocates, namely the exploration of 'the activities of covert groups, intelligence agencies, secret societies and agendas' (Ramsay, 2008: 15) and on the other hand the countless 'wacky' and eccentric explanations which attribute causes of events to 'Jews (and Jewish bankers), the Freemasons, the Catholics, the Communists, the Illuminati, or the Devil' and which 'strike the orthodox rational Western mind as absurd' (Ramsay, 2000: 9). At first sight, Ramsay's argument echoes the aforementioned efforts to differentiate between the legitimate analysis of secrecy in politics and 'bogus' conspiracy theories. However, the key issue is *where* Ramsay places the boundary between the two. In addition to Watergate, the Iran-Contra affair or the well-publicised secret medical experiments on American citizens carried out by US government agencies in the 1950s and 1960s, Ramsay includes, among real 'political conspiracies', also the assassinations of John F. Kennedy, Martin Luther King, Malcolm X and the attempted assassination, in 1972, of the former Governor of Alabama George Wallace. In each of these events (which have been the topic of much conspiracist speculation over the years and where no plot has ever been proven) he suspects the involvement of the US government or rogue elements within the state apparatus and security services. Therefore, just like Parenti (1996), Ramsay frames 'conspiracy theories' in a way that places a number of accounts that are commonly associated with 'wacky' conspiracy explanations within the domain of legitimate analysis acceptable to the 'orthodox rational Western mind'. Crucially however, this categorisation of conspiracy theories did not go unchallenged: in *Voodoo Histories* David Aaronovitch (2009) refers to Robin Ramsay as the 'doyen of British [conspiracy] theory', a qualification which again is not just a judgment on Ramsay personally but also, implicitly at least, a way of (re-)setting the boundary between 'conspiracy theory' and the more respectable and plausible explanations of political events.

The negotiation of the meaning of 'conspiracy theory' is apparent also in the frequent use of disclaimers which accompany views that might be recognised as conspiratorial. 'I am not a conspiracy theorist, but...' has become a regular tool for forestalling and neutralising potential criticism and avoiding being affiliated with an epistemologically damaging label. For example, in the foreword to Edward S. Herman and Noam Chomsky's (1988) aforementioned book *Manufacturing Consent*, the authors accurately anticipated the criticisms that followed by stating that 'institutional critiques such as we present in this book are commonly dismissed by establishment commentators as "conspiracy theories", but this is just an evasion. We do not use any kind of "conspiracy" hypothesis to explain mass-media performance' (Herman and Chomsky, 1988: xii). Just like the debates which followed the book's publication, this disclaimer reflected the assumption that a distinction can and should be made between legitimate analysis and 'conspiracy theories', and that only the latter are intellectually suspect.

The use of disclaimers is not limited to analyses of, or commentary on, international politics. Since the 1960s, there has been a tradition in American feminist writing to employ the idea of a conspiracy as a metaphor so as to give shape to the complex issues of blame, responsibility and agency, in other words, give 'a name to a faceless "problem"' of female subjugation (Knight, 1997: 55). Betty Friedan's classic work *Feminine Mystique* (1992/1963), for example, presents women as victims of a coordinated attempt by welfare, educational, medical and media institutions to manipulate them into accepting a life of domesticity (Knight, 1997). Women are said to be the target of 'brainwashing' that leaves them acting 'like a puppet with someone else pulling the strings' (Friedan, 1992/1963: 246). Just like in traditional conspiracy theory, ordinary people, in this case women, are presented as helpless victims of mass manipulation.

The motif of 'conspiracy of male domination' (Palmer, 1989: 69) is accompanied in feminist writing by a clear recognition that there are gains to be made from *not* being seen as a conspiracy theorist. Attempts at distancing are particularly apparent in *Feminine Mystique* which is unsurprising given that the book was first published in the post-McCarthy era, when conspiracy theories were seen, particularly on the left, as 'a mark of an unacceptable political demonology' (Knight, 1997: 45–46). Thus Friedan is keen to point out that claims about the economic subjugation of women are not an allegation of an 'economic conspiracy', or that the contribution of psychoanalysis to the brainwashing of women does not infer 'a psychoanalytic conspiracy' (Friedan, 1992/1963: 181, 109).

However, it is among the critics of American foreign policy that it is easiest to find the more problematic examples of disclaimers. The writing of the veteran British journalist and author Robert Fisk is a relevant example. Fisk is no stranger to controversy or to accusations that he is delving in conspiracy theorising. His writing on the supposed power of the Zionist/Israel/Jewish lobby in America and the 'stranglehold' that it supposedly has over the political, financial, academic and media institutions in the US frequently crosses the line of good taste and comes dangerously close to the rhetoric characteristic of antisemitic agitators (see Chapter 5). In an article in the *Independent* in 2007, however, Fisk turned his attention to a different topic, namely the events that took place on 11 September 2001. The aim of the piece was to express doubts about the veracity of the official version of 9/11, according to which the attacks were perpetrated by a group of airline hijackers belonging to Al Qaida. Crucially, before outlining his argument, Fisk voiced a disclaimer: he emphasised that he is 'not a conspiracy theorist' (Fisk, 2007). He drew a line between 'real plots' of the kind that, as an experienced journalist, he witnessed and reported on from 'Lebanon, Iraq, Syria, Iran, the Gulf' and the various 'imaginary [plots] in Manhattan' espoused by the likes of David Icke (whom he dismisses as 'crazed') and other 'ravers'. However, having established the distinction between 'real' and 'imagined plots' and dissociated himself from conspiracy theories and conspiracy theorists, Fisk goes on to pose the very same questions about 9/11 (e.g. why no debris from the Boeing 757 had been found at the site of the Pentagon crash) which continue to fuel the imagination of those same traders in 'imaginary [plots] in Manhattan' whom he supposedly dismisses (e.g. Meyssan, 2002, Griffin, 2008). In fact, given that most of these questions have been addressed by experts (see Dunbar and Reagan, 2006), 9/11 conspiracy theorists are the only people who still consider them to be relevant. Through the use of disclaimers, therefore, Fisk distanced himself from 'conspiracy theories' as a category of explanation, while at the same time elevating conspiracist suspicions about the 'real' causes of 9/11 into the domain of legitimate political analysis.

Setting the epistemic threshold between real and bogus conspiracies

The inherently contested nature of the term 'conspiracy theory' illustrated through the earlier examples presents a problem for anyone engaging with the topic. The ubiquity of plots and cover-ups in modern society, coupled with the 'intellectual presumption' against conspiracy theories, means that debates will always be had about what exactly *is* a 'conspiracy theory' and about what burden of proof is required to demonstrate that a conspiracy is 'real', just as the nature and validity of that evidence will also be disputed (Keeley, 1999). The controversy surrounding the Watergate scandal – a paradigmatic 'real conspiracy' – provides an additional example of the conundrum in question. At the time of the affair, as the scale of conspiracy within the US government was coming to light, there were concerns, even among the *Washington Post*'s editorial team, that the newspaper's investigation was crossing the line between journalism and 'fantasy'. There was, in other words, an awareness that the boundary between investigative journalism and conspiracy theory (one that a reputable newspaper should never be seen to cross) is not always clear to see. On the other hand, when Bob Woodward and Carl Bernstein published one of their reports on the illegal tapping at the Watergate Hotel, the White House sought to discredit the *Washington Post* by claiming that the newspaper was propagating 'conspiracy theories' as a means of discrediting political opponents. Nixon's aides went as far as to accuse the *Post* of 'McCarthyism' (Goodnight and Poulakos, 1981: 308). Thus, within the editorial offices of the *Washington Post*, just as in the conflict between the newspaper and the Nixon administration, the meaning of the term 'conspiracy theory' was intrinsically tied up with the argumentative contexts within which it performed its rhetorical functions and the complex 'machinery of interaction' within which it was constituted and disputed (Husting and Orr, 2007: 128).

If the meaning of the term conspiracy theory is, as has been suggested, flexible, negotiated and contested, how does one go about setting the epistemic threshold that distinguishes 'real' from 'bogus' conspiracy theories? The fact that some explanations are referred to as 'conspiracy theories' more often than others has led some to emphasise the importance of *power* in the labelling process. Sociologists of deviance have long argued that those in positions of authority have the wherewithal to determine what a 'reasonable' person is expected to believe and what constitutes a normal and rational as opposed to a deviant and irrational view of the world (e.g. Douglas and Waksler, 1982). It could be argued therefore that which explanation will attract a pejorative label like 'conspiracy theory' depends mainly on whether it has been endorsed and sanctioned as an 'official' and 'authoritative' account of an event. Equally, this means that those in powerful social positions can make claims about plots, without fear of being called 'paranoid' or a 'conspiracy theorist' (Harper, 1996, Knight, 2008).

And yet, as the examples cited in the previous sections suggest, those in power clearly do not have a monopoly over the interpretation of reality. They are unable to create a consensus about what a conspiracy theory is or impose on the public their preferred definition of the term. After all, people are not passive recipients of ideological constructs and interpretations, who accept communication from relevant power structures without challenging or disputing ideological claims. What counts as a 'conspiracy theory' as opposed to a rational and legitimate explanation is continually recast in the course of the struggle between multiple and competing interpretative communities and regimes of knowledge and truth, each with its own basis for 'knowing about reality and for assessing whether a belief is true' and each seeking to defend, legitimise and enforce their own assumptions about the workings of society, history and politics (Heise, 1988: 263). After all, conspiracy theorists have a strategy of exclusion of their own. Just as the reputation, character and reasoning ability of conspiracy theorists is continuously challenged by the more conventional regimes of truth, so, in the company of conspiracy theorists, it is the sceptics who will be confronted for their supposed naïveté and gullibility and subjected to scorn and ridicule.

For those faced with the difficult task of setting the threshold between real and bogus conspiracies, a tempting solution might be to steer clear of this problem and resort simply to common sense and – instinct. A precedent for this approach has been set by the US Supreme Court Justice Potter Stuart who, in 1964, in response to the challenge of having to define pornography – a concept which, not unlike 'conspiracy theory,' lacks well-defined parameters and whose boundaries are vague, abstract and, most importantly, disputed – simply stated, 'I know it when I see it' (see Bratich, 2008). One could apply the same principle to conspiracy theories. The philosopher Brian Keeley (1999: 111) made this point when he alluded to the 'strong, common intuition' that makes it possible to mark out a set of explanations that belong to the domain of 'unwarranted conspiracy theories' and distinguish them analytically from 'those theories which deserve our assent'.

Arguably however, one can do better than resort to 'intuition' or 'common sense' especially as the latter is, as we have seen, rarely as common, or as 'intuitive' as it is assumed to be. This is especially so given that the broad range of claims about conspiracies, which circulate at any point in time, is not a seamless continuum of assertions, ranging from the likely to the impossible, on which people arbitrarily place a boundary marker, in line with their rhetorical needs, ideological inclinations or intuition. There is, instead, a particular, *qualitatively distinct class of personalised explanations* which stands out from the rest. At its core is not only an allegation of conspiracy, the assumption about the importance of human agency and the suspicion of government and official explanations, but also much more than that. As hinted in the previous chapter, this class of explanations is identifiable by a distinct narrative structure, thematic configuration and explanatory logic, as well as by the fact that it is embedded within a particular tradition of explanation. Its precise boundaries may not always be possible to demarcate, for reasons that I will return to later in the book, but it is nevertheless distinguishable. It is this class of explanation that in this book is referred to as *the conspiracy theory*.

How do explanations that belong to the conspiratorial tradition of explanation differ from legitimate and rational explorations of secrecy and collusion in politics? The conspiracy tradition and the rhetorical style through which it is articulated is explored in more detail in subsequent chapters, so the discussion here is limited to three characteristics which relate specifically to its explanatory logic and underlying assumptions. These include the view of conspiracy as the motive force in history, the approach to evidence (or the absence of it) and the conspiracy theory's essential irrefutability.

The explanatory logic of the conspiracy theory

As already noted, there is nothing a priori wrong with the assumption that conspiracies happen. Over the past 60 years, for example, a number of plots have been uncovered in the United States. In the 1950s and 1960s, the CIA and other agencies of the state carried out a series of covert and illegal medical experiments on unassuming US citizens. Around the same time, the FBI engaged in illegal surveillance and intimidation of civil rights activists. The CIA plotted to kill Fidel Castro. Richard Nixon condoned illegal surveillance and wiretapping of the Democratic National Committee at the Watergate Hotel. In the aftermath of 9/11, as part of the War on Terror the CIA ran secret prisons and participated in 'extraordinary rendition' missions which involved extra-judicial transfers of terrorist suspects to countries where they could be tortured. And so on.

An important feature of the more mainstream and sound inquiry into these and other similar events, which differentiates it from explanations belonging to the conspiratorial tradition of explanation, is the recognition that they involved different groups of conspirators, with disparate aims, working independently of each other. Social and political life might be replete with plots and cover-ups, but these need to be recognised as *multiple*, and in most instances unrelated events which cannot be reduced to a single, common denominator.

The assumption about the existence of a variety of unrelated plots is vital because it reduces the temptation to allocate to the notion of conspiracy a central place in the interpretation of politics. Real conspiracies rarely work out according to plan, and one reason why this is so is precisely because there are so many different conspiracies going on at the same time (Cubitt, 1993, Keeley, 1999). Between any one instance of intent, collusion or design and the wished-for outcome is not just 'a more or less resilient or brittle framework of institutions and traditions' with all their unforeseen and unforeseeable elements, but also other individuals and organisations (journalists, fraud investigators, researchers, political rivals, prosecutors and others) with their own (often concealed) goals and intentions (Popper, 1966: 95). The latter are a source of interference or 'conscious counteraction' to any conspiracy, standing in the way of its successful conclusion (ibid.).

Also, it is sufficient to look at Watergate or the arms-for-hostages deals in the 1980s to see how hard it is, in real life, for plotters to keep their clandestine endeavours under wraps. This is not just because people make mistakes, or because institutions are typically flawed information processors prone to errors, delays and loss of information, which makes secrecy less likely to be maintained, but also because contemporary society awards incentives for telling the truth and rewards acts of dissidence (Harrison and Thomas, 1997, Heins, 2007). This is important because it suggests that both the size and complexity of a conspiracy and its level of nefariousness will be inversely proportional to its chance of success: the greater the number of people involved in a plot, and the more evil it's character, the more likely it is that someone will make a mistake or that a whistleblower will come forward (Keeley, 1999). It is considerations such as these that led Karl Popper (1972: 123–124) to argue that in history, *'nothing ever comes off exactly as intended'* and that the relevant question is not 'who wanted something to happen?' but 'why things *did not* happen exactly in the way that somebody wanted?'

Through the prism of the conspiracy theory, however, the world looks very different. Conspiracy theorists are generally not interested in the multitude of conflicting conspiracies, but in a smaller number of them, which are often reduced to a single overarching plot which supposedly explains everything. The essential tenet of the 'conspiracy theory of society' is not that conspiracies happen, but that they are the motive force in history. This assumption gives conspiracy theories an exceedingly *comprehensive* and *all-encompassing* character (Popper, 1966, Lipset and Raab, 1978). As the British fascist writer A.K. Chesterton put it in the book *The New Unhappy Lords*, history is nothing more than 'a series of conspiracies that involve power groups which may often differ about methods but which direct their thoughts and acts to the attainment of the same broad objective' (1975: 211). Also, the chronic disregard for the impact of unintended consequences of human actions, or forces above and beyond human intent, sustains the assumption that the *greater the alleged conspiracy, the more likely it is to succeed.* Those believed to be powerful enough to influence the course of history will also be seen as having the skill, the power and the resources to keep their actions, intentions and even their existence hidden from view.

Let us consider, for example, the 9/11 conspiracy theories. It is often argued that what makes these explanations so implausible is the level of organisation and collusion which is assumed to have existed on that fateful day in 2001. The planning and co-ordination needed to bring down the World Trade Centre (in a way that makes it look as if Al Qaida did it), and the assumption that thousands of complicit individuals (secret service agents, military personnel, engineers, pyrotechnics experts and others) conspired to keep the truth about the attacks from coming out makes these explanations seem far-fetched, even absurd. But for conspiracy theorists, the sheer scale and complexity of the required plot is precisely the point. The fact that there have been no whistleblowers and the absence of any other kind of definitive proof in favour of the conspiracy thesis simply demonstrates the conspirators' ability to cover up their tracks and illustrates the power at their disposal. Therefore, the very same thing that critics argue makes conspiracy theories unbelievable is, for conspiracy theorists, the strongest evidence in favour of their claims.

The second difference between conspiracy theory and legitimate analysis of secrecy and collusion in politics lies in the topics of their respective investigations. None of the aforementioned post-Second World War, real life plots has been exposed by conspiracy theorists. Most came to light as a result of state-sponsored inquiries, initiated, more often than not, by administrations that conspiracy theorists believed were in the hands of the shadowy elite of the sinister, anti-American, creators of the New World Order. The CIA's domestic spying programme that targeted dissidents within the US was first revealed, in 1974, by the *New York Times* – a publication despised by conspiracy theorists of all political persuasions (Hersh, 1974). The source of the revelation was, it is worth noting, a whistleblower from within the security services. The subsequent special commission which investigated the illegal activities of executive agencies (including CIA's experiments with 'behaviour influencing drugs') was headed by none other than Nelson Rockefeller, who was at the time the favourite target of conspiracist speculation, and someone whom many conspiracy theorists believed was a key figure among the cabal which pulls the strings of world politics (e.g. Allen, 1972). Subsequent reviews of various abuses of power by the intelligence agencies and other government bodies were also headed by people at the heart of the US establishment (Olmsted, 2009, Miller, 2002). Most importantly, since the 1970s, the driving force behind many revelations about real conspiracies within the US government has been the Freedom of Information Act – a key institution of political transparency.

Conspiracy theorists generally have an ambivalent stance towards documented and verifiable instances of collusion and cover-up. For them, the proven abuses of power are not worthy of attention in their own right, in part because the manner in which they were uncovered leads them to suspect that these revelations were themselves a cover-up for something a lot more sinister. Watergate is a clear example. In the 1985 update of Gary Allen's classic conspiracy theory pamphlet *None Dare Call It Conspiracy* (1972), Larry Abraham argues that the Watergate affair is not what it seems and that Nixon was in fact set up by Henry Kissinger, Nelson Rockefeller and a suite of other members of the Council on Foreign Relations intent on subverting the presidency (Abraham, 1985). At the same time, conspiracy theorists will occasionally allude to real conspiracies, but as mere starting points, as a kernel of truth upon which implausible stories about the activities of the would-be rulers of the world can be constructed. Thus, the revelations about the CIA plot to assassinate Fidel Castro are, in the context of the conspiracy theory, transformed into 'proof' that assassinations (successful or otherwise) of John F. Kennedy, Martin Luther King Jr, John Lennon or Ronald Reagan must have been the work of the US intelligence agencies. The CIA's experiments with mind manipulation are interesting to conspiracy theorists only in so far that they 'prove' that the government is up to no good and therefore that events such as the cult suicides committed by Jim Jones's followers in Guyana in 1978, or Timothy McVeigh's bombing of the Federal Building in Oklahoma are linked to CIA's 'brainwashing experiments'. Similarly, the revelations about the government-sponsored, secret medical experiments have served as a catalyst for claims that every imaginable disease, from AIDS, through Ebola to avian and swine flu is the product of some clandestine complot, the aim of which is genocide or population control. The real-world conspiracies are therefore the springboard for what Hofstadter (1967: 37) identified as the 'big leap from the undeniable to the unbelievable' that lies at the core of the conspiracy narrative.

This brings us to what is probably the most important feature of conspiracy theories: they are by their very nature irrefutable. Logical contradictions, disconfirming evidence, even the complete absence of proof have no bearing on the conspiratorial explanation because they can always be accounted for in terms of the conspiracy: the lack of proof about a plot, or any positive proof against its existence, is turned around and taken as evidence of the craftiness of the secret cabal behind the conspiracy and as confirmation of its ability to conceal its machinations. Conspiracy theories thus become 'the only theories for which evidence against them is actually construed as evidence in favour of them' (Keeley, 1999: 120).

It is important to mention, however, that unfalsifiability is not something that *a priori* disqualifies conspiracy theories. In the natural sciences, where falsifiability – the logical possibility that a claim could be proven to be false – is indeed the principal requirement for a good theory, the object of knowledge (the natural world) is devoid of agency with respect to the scientific investigation. Nature does not wilfully react to the scientist's enquiry, nor does it set out to deliberately hamper its progress. By contrast, when dealing with investigations into political cover-ups, scandals and conspiracies (including those that are real), a researcher is dealing with evidence and data which someone is deliberately trying to conceal or destroy. In those instances falsified evidence, or the lack of it, is what the theory *expects* to find. In some ways, a conspiracy theory, by its very definition, *has* to be unfalsifiable because it predicts that evidence will be hampered with, concealed or destroyed by the forces eager to cover up their tracks (see Basham, 2003).

The problem with conspiracy theory is that it takes this position to the extreme. The existence of a plot is not treated as a testable hypothesis, but as a fundamental, unshakeable principle. The possibility that the conspiracy theory may be wrong, or that its basic assumption could be, at least in theory, disconfirmed by new evidence, is not even entertained. And this is the key point. In the face of the possibility of a conspiracy, the approach to evidence adopted by investigative journalists, historians, prosecutors or judges would demand the sources to be checked and the claims to be verified, all while resisting the temptation to interpret the presence of disconfirming evidence or the absence of proof as confirmation that there has been a cover-up. The conspiracy theorist is in an entirely different game. For him or her, the latter is not a temptation to be avoided, but the starting point and a raison d'être.

The 'leap of imagination', and the irrefutable explanatory logic that it helps to establish, enables conspiracy theory not only to 'tie together the untidiness of the social world into a tale of deception and conspiracy' but also to weave a tale of secret collusion that has no temporal or geographical limits (Billig, 1988: 203). By denying the existence or relevance of mistakes, failures and ambiguities, conspiratorial narrative gradually slides towards a view of society and history as coherent and predictable, but at the same time deceptive. It establishes connections between diverse historical events and assumes that conspirators are ubiquitous and omnipresent, active in every part of the world and unaffected by logistical constraints. It becomes not just a personalised explanation, but a belief in a 'vast and sinister conspiracy, a gigantic and yet subtle machinery of influence set in motion to undermine and destroy a way of life' (Hofstadter, 1967: 9).

Crucially, the assumption that outward forms of political life are just a front for an evil, global plot gives conspiracy theories a distinct 'self-sealing' quality (Zarefsky, 1984: 72). It transforms them into a 'monological belief system', one that, while looking outwards and seeking to convert the outside world, is, in fact, engaged in dialogue only with itself (Goertzel, 1994). As we shall see in later chapters, this closed, self-isolating quality plays a key role in sustaining the ideological tradition of the conspiracy theory and ensures its continuity through time.

3
Conspiracy Theories and Their Vicissitudes

As already noted in Chapter 1, contemporary debates about conspiracy theories, particularly in the media, are often underpinned by the implicit assumption that there is something distinctly modern (or postmodern) about their presence in society. The findings that a particular conspiracy theory is believed by a high proportion of the population, or the realisation that yet another conspiracy theory book made it onto the bestsellers list, tend to be accompanied by concerns that paranoia, suspicion and mistrust are sweeping the planet and that the present, more than any other period in history, deserves the label 'the age of conspiracism'.

The view of conspiracy theory as a response to unique challenges of today is in part the consequence of the fact that it is only in the past 30 years that conspiracism attracted media attention as a phenomenon in its own right (Bratich, 2008). Before the 1980s, the term 'conspiracy theory' was, for example, virtually absent from the columns of the *New York Times*. Between the middle of that decade and the end of the 1990s, however, the frequency of its use almost quadrupled, with a substantial further rise between 2000 and 2004 (Husting and Orr, 2007, Bratich, 2008). Similarly, it is only in the last quarter of a century that opinion polls exposing the prevalence of conspiracy beliefs are routinely carried out, published and pondered over by the media and by scholars. The fact that there is little historical data with which to compare these results, inevitably contributes to the belief that before the onset of globalisation or the arrival of the internet, conspiracy thinking was not as widespread as it is today. The relatively recent origin of the preoccupation with conspiracy theory is reflected also in the fact that it was only in the 1990s that the term got sufficiently firmly established in the English language to warrant a separate entry in the *Oxford English Dictionary*.

There is, however, ample evidence that suggests that the manifest popularity of conspiracy theories is not all that new. For example, contemporary conspiracy culture is saturated with claims that the interests of the 'military industrial complex' is driving the foreign and defence policy agendas of Western powers and that decisions about whether or not to go to war are made in smoked-filled rooms, by a shadowy cabal of politicians, arms manufacturers, profiteers, speculators and oil merchants. Such claims are at the core of much of the 9/11 conspiracy theories which, according to a number of opinion polls, as we have seen, are believed by between a third and half of the population of the United States. If we go back 70 years to 1939, and look at the result of an opinion poll carried out at the time, we find that one-third of Americans believed that their country should have stayed out of the 1914–1918 war, for reasons very similar to those cited today: because the war was thought to be driven exclusively by the interests of big business. This stance towards America's involvement in the First World War reflected the thinking of conspiracy theorists who for years had promoted the idea that 'London gold' (i.e. a group of pro-British bankers led by the American industrialist J.P. Morgan) conspired to take America to war in order to protect their long-term financial interests (see Olmsted, 2009). American soldiers battling in Europe were portrayed as 'high-class muscle men for Big Business, for Wall Street and for the Bankers' and 'gangsters for capitalism' (cited in Aaronovitch, 2009: 86). The similarity in the rhetoric aside, the comparison of the poll data from 1939 and today suggests not only that, even before the onset of the internet, conspiracy theorists had the means of influencing public opinion, but also that contemporary conspiratorial accounts of the US government's foreign policy are not entirely explicable in terms of the post-Watergate decline in public trust or anxieties brought on by globalisation. Similarly, if we could retrospectively measure the proportion of the population of Europe or the United States who in the 1920s believed that Jews were behind the 1917 Bolshevik Revolution, the results would probably dwarf anything yielded by contemporary opinion polls. Even as late as in 1944, at a time when news of the Holocaust had already reached the United States, a survey found that as many as 24 per cent of Americans regarded Jews as a 'menace' to their country while between 30 and 50 per cent stated that they would have supported a (hypothetical) antisemitic campaign (*Encyclopaedia Judaica*, 2007: 391). Evidently, the 'age of conspiracism' encompasses a longer historical period than is usually acknowledged.

The aim of the present chapter is to look at the history of conspiracy theories and consider their origins and trajectory over time. This is an important task if we are to provide an adequate explanation of conspiracism as an evolved *tradition of explanation*. If conspiracy theory is conceptualised as a set of arguments, narrative themes and rhetorical tropes which are passed on from one generation of conspiracy theorists to the next, and which link accounts from the earlier periods to those in circulation today, then an awareness of the historical development and evolution of conspiracy theories is a necessary prerequisite for any further inquiry into their nature and continuing appeal. Providing a comprehensive historical analysis within the confines of a single chapter is, of course, impossible, so the focus will be on identifying the key events and junctures. The first question to be addressed, however, concerns the origins of conspiracy theories. How old are they and where have they come from?

The origins of a tradition of explanation

The roots of the modern conspiracy culture are often traced to a variant of the mythology of secret societies which developed at the end of the eighteenth century, in the immediate aftermath of the French Revolution (Hofstadter, 1967, Lipset and Raab, 1978, Billig, 1978, Cohn, 1967, Roberts, 1974). Specifically, two works on the causes of the Revolution, which were published almost simultaneously in 1797, are cited as the first examples of the modern political conspiracy theory. One is the four-volume *Memoirs pour servir a l'histoire du Jacobinsme* by Augustin Barruel, a French Jesuit priest exiled in England. The other is *Proofs of conspiracy against all religions and governments of Europe, carried on in the secret meetings of Free Masons, Illuminati and the Reading Societies* written by a Scotsman, John Robison, Professor of Science at the University of Edinburgh.

Both Barruel and Robison saw the French Revolution as the work of a nexus of clandestine organisations, including the Freemasons, the Philosophes, the Jacobins and most importantly the Bavarian Illuminati, a secret society which was said to have played a central role in the revolutionary plot. The Illuminati were, in reality, a relatively obscure Bavarian secret society founded in 1776 by Adam Weishaupt, a professor of law at the University of Ingolstadt. Just like the Freemasons, the Illuminati pursued a progressive social agenda: they advocated the Enlightenment values of rationalism and anti-clericalism, championed causes such as the abolition of torture and of witchcraft trials and campaigned for the improvement of education (Roberts, 1974). Contrary to the claims made by Barruel and Robison, there is no evidence that the Illuminati, which had no more than a thousand members, ever 'controlled' the Freemasons or anyone else, or that they wielded any significant political influence. They were not even 'secret' in the way in which the term is understood today. In the eighteenth century, the term 'secret society' denoted 'voluntary association of like minded people' which was unaffiliated and unaccountable to the state, the church or any mainstream institution (von Bieberstein, 1977: 1). More importantly, the Illuminati were dissolved in 1786, which means that they were no longer active when the Revolution began. This however only made them more attractive to the likes of Barruel and Robison who interpreted such timely 'disappearance' as incontrovertible proof of culpability. Thus, by the end of the eighteenth century, Weishaupt's Illuminati, a small and ultimately unsuccessful organisation that functioned for less than a decade, took centre stage in the conspiracy theory as the most iniquitous and the most powerful of all secret societies.

The claim that Barruel's and Robison's work on the causes of the French Revolution represent foundational texts of the conspiracist tradition of explanation warrants further examination. It would be naïve to assume that the conspiracy theory has a fixed point of origin that could be unequivocally traced to a particular book or to the thinking of a specific individual or individuals. After all, Barruel and Robison were not the first to focus on the sinister activities of the Illuminati, nor was it by chance that they honed in on the same organisation. By the time Barruel and Robison embarked on their literary projects, Illuminati had already been accused of subversion and treachery by opponents of their progressive agenda (Roberts, 1974, Wood, 1982, Hofman 1988). A number of pamphlets published in Germany in the 1780s went as far as to suggest that the order was in league with Satan (von Bieberstein, 1977). The anti-Illuminati literature soon reached France and Britain. Rev. E. Erskine, a reviewer of Robison's book, commented in 1800, that 'some of the most shocking facts' in Robison's work 'I knew before its publication' (cited in Payson, 1802: 14). Clearly, Barruel's *Memoirs* and Robison's *Proofs* were building on a set of explanations which had developed in decades preceding their publication.

Also, Barruel and Robison were certainly not the first to allege that a political event is explicable by reference to someone's volition and design. Questions such as 'Cui bono?' (Who benefits?) or 'Cui prodest?' (To whose advantage?), which are invoked even today to justify intentionalist interpretations of political events, date back to antiquity. In

G. V. *Mansinger pinx.*

Figure 3.1   Portrait of Adam Weishaupt by C. K. Mansinger (ca 1799) (reproduced from Webster, 1924)

Ancient Athens, speeches and writings of public figures, philosophers and politicians contained a 'rich lexicon of conspiracy' which was used to denote different kinds of plots, intrigues or secret collusion (Roisman, 2006: 6, see also Glass, 1988). Orations were 'full of alleged plots to kill, to deceive, to subvert the government, to betray friends and nation, even to start a war' (ibid.). The level of anxiety apparent in Athenian political discourse led Eli Sagan (1991) to postulate that paranoia constituted a key element of the collective Athenian psyche.

Allegations of conspiracy were also ubiquitous in ancient Rome: the assassination of Julius Caesar in 44 BC endures in popular imagination as the epitome of political betrayal and conspiratorial collusion - the paradigmatic 'inside job'. Tales of conspiracy also marked the political culture in subsequent centuries, up to the Middle Ages and beyond. In Early Modernity in particular, conspiracies and speculation about them were so common that many commentators drew parallels between the politics of the day and that in ancient Rome, in terms of the regularity of clandestine political manoeuvring (see Swann and Coward, 2004).

With all this in mind, what is it about the late eighteenth-century writing on the French Revolution that signalled a turning point in the history of conspiracy theories and what is it that makes Barruel and Robison such key figures in their development? According to Geoffrey Cubitt (1989), post-revolutionary conspiracy theories differed from those which existed before 1789 in a number of important ways. First, the older versions of conspiracy theory tended to deal with fairly specific intrigues, plots and collusion among powerful figures and persons of authority who were said to be conspiring for the purpose of financial or political benefit. These were, in other words, accounts of multiple, often interacting conspiracies with different agents and somewhat prosaic, worldly aims. By contrast, the conspiracy theory about the French Revolution did not focus on the machinations of influential public figures of the day. The hub of the alleged plot was located among mysterious secret societies whose composition, political character and modus operandi were shrouded in mystery. Second, while in the past conspirators were said to be motivated by personal gain, in the writing of Barruel and Robison conspirators were working for a less-tangible reward, namely the implementation of an evil, secret and subversive plan. The plot was no longer limited either temporally by the length of the conspirators' term of office, political career or life or spatially by their finite sphere of influence. The conspiracy that Barruel and Robison imagined was timeless, and it had the destruction of Christianity and the social order as its ultimate aim. This also meant that every event, past, present or future could be explained (retrospectively or otherwise) by the overarching conspiratorial explanation. It is at this juncture in history, therefore, that tales of conspiracy acquired the comprehensive and all-encompassing character which was cited in Chapter 2 as the key characteristic of the conspiracist tradition of explanation. What is it that brought about this transformation, and why did the conspiracy theory emerge in the aftermath of the French Revolution, rather than at any other point in history? According to J.M. Roberts (1974: 212–213), a key factor was the unprecedented nature of the Revolution, which shook the foundations of society like no other event before it:

> What the Revolution had brought about in men's minds was the conviction that there was almost no institution, no traditional value, no social landmark which was not threatened in some way, and a ready audience was available to someone who could link together in an ordered scheme the various plot theories which were lying about and provide with their aid a rationale for the colossal psychological and political changes which men [*sic*] felt they were undergoing.

For the frustrated advocates of the old aristocratic order, in France as well as abroad, routine canons of explanations, which typically appealed to the inertia of history, providence or petty conspiracies among the ruling elite, could not adequately account for the dramatic and sweeping societal transformation. This is especially so given that the Revolution was 'ideologically founded on the attribution of sovereign authority to an abstract entity', namely the people or the nation, rather than to something more familiar like God or King (Cubitt, 1993: 305). The claim about a large scale, universal and comprehensive plot gave a concrete form to the new entity's elusive will.

Also, during the eighteenth century, mechanistic causality – the assumption of a link between cause and effect – which had become the dominant principle in the natural sciences had begun to affect the way in which people viewed and interpreted causal relations in society. It was assumed that every event has an identifiable cause, one that has little to do with chance or providence. In conjunction with the principle of free will that was rooted in Christian morality, it led to the tendency to explain events in terms of human intentionality: things happen because people want them to happen (Wood, 1982, Roberts, 1974). This was not a difficult assumption for people to accept, given that eighteenth-century politics was marked by a 'cloak and dagger' culture of scheming and backstabbing among a small number of members of the aristocracy who wielded all the power. In the face of turmoil brought about by the Revolution, the Illuminati conspiracy theory was accepted as yet another political plot, but one whose unprecedented size and scope was commensurate with its perceived consequences.

Finally, in Barruel's case in particular, the assumed anti-Christian and anti-Catholic nature of the conspiracy, suggests that the tale of the Illuminati plot drew also on the existing discourse of heresy which in eighteenth-century France was directed mainly at Protestantism. The anti-Protestant rhetoric included allegations that 'men of letters' and members of the nobility were using their influence in court to promote Protestanism, and that immoral, impious and even Satanic rituals were being performed so as to sabotage the existing moral and religious orders. In the post-revolutionary writing, the Illuminati took over from the Protestants as the definitive heretics and archenemies of true faith (Hofman, 1988). The reliance on the discourse of heresy gave the conspiracy theory its inherent Manichaeism, which is explored in more detail in the next chapter.

From the perspective of the conspiracy tradition, therefore, the significance of Barruel and Robison is not that they were the first to target the Illuminati, or that they invented the idea of a conspiracy. It is, rather, that they responded to the needs of a turbulent time, and drawing on the pool of discourses available to them, created a simple and comforting explanation for why bad things were happening to good people (Groh, 1987).

Equally important is the fact that Barruel and Robison provided an endless source of inspiration for subsequent generations of conspiracy theorists. Roberts (1974: 204) describes Barruel's work as 'the bible of the secret society mythology' which has been cited, quoted and recommended in conspiracy literature ever since, often alongside Robison's *Proofs*. The fact that no work published before 1797 occupies the same status suggests that Barruel and Robison are rightfully accorded the accolade (if it can be called that) of the founding fathers of the conspiracy tradition.

Barruel and Robison were also the conspiracy theory's first international celebrities. Multiple editions of their work were published in Germany, France, England, Russia and, most importantly, in the United States where they were met by a particularly sympathetic audience. Among Barruel's and Robison's earliest American followers was the Boston Congregationalist minister Jedidiah Morse, whose sermons in the late 1790s warned the Americans about the threat posed by Illuminism. In 1802 Seth Payson, a pastor from New Hampshire, published *Proofs of the Real Existence and Dangerous Tendency of Illuminism*, a single volume 'abstract of the most interesting parts of what Dr Robison and the Abbé Barruel have published on the subject'. Payson, who was actively encouraged in his endeavour by Morse, sought to 'preserve my country from that vortex of anarchy, which has ingulphed the liberties, civil and religious, and the peace, property, and the lives of millions' (Payson, 1802: iv).

The reason behind America's receptiveness to the emerging conspiracy culture lies in the fact that since before the American Revolution, the political elite in the New World perceived itself under threat from conspiracy by colonial powers, especially Britain (Bailyn, 1975). Already in the 1770s, Thomas Jefferson – a leading figure of America's fight for independence – argued that the British were engaged in 'a deliberate, systematical plan of reducing us to slavery' (cited in Wood, 1982: 421). This kind of thinking permeated revolutionary discourse and in the words of David Brion Davis (1972: 23) 'conditioned Americans to think of resistance to a dark, subversive force as the essential ingredient of their national identity.' In the aftermath of the War of Independence, the likes of George Washington and John Adams turned their attention to France and warned of an imminent French-led conspiracy aimed at subverting the fledgling republic (Lipset and Raab, 1978). The literature on the Illuminati arriving from the Old Continent helped not only to articulate but also to reinforce such fears.

However, in America, as well as in Europe, the interest in the Illuminati subsided relatively quickly. As Lipset and Raab (1978: 221) point out, the appeal of a conspiracy theory lies not just in the assumption that there is 'a mysterious cabal' engaged in subversion, but also in the existence of 'some less mysterious, more visible target group associated with the cabal' which makes the perceived threat more tangible. By the early 1800s, the Illuminati, of whom there had been no trace since 1786, had become too abstract, so the focus of conspiratorial fantasy shifted to more visible targets. In the United States, the role of the Illuminati was taken on by the Freemasons and the Catholics, in Europe by Freemasons and increasingly by Jews. By the second half of the nineteenth century, the Jews will have replaced the Illuminati and the Freemasons as the masterminds behind the alleged world conspiracy, relegating the secret societies to the position of foot soldiers and pawns in the hands of the international Jewish elite.

The myth of the Jewish conspiracy

In 1806, almost ten years after the publications of *Memoirs*, Augustin Barruel received a letter from a Florentine army officer by the name of Jean Baptist Simonini. The letter sought to draw the attention of a recognised expert on secret societies, to the activities of a financially powerful 'Judaic sect', whose members supposedly founded and controlled the Illuminati and the Freemasons. The aim of this sect was to 'turn Christians into slaves' and set up a world government (Cohn, 1967, von Bieberstein, 1977, Benz, 2007).

The 'revelations' made in 'Simonini's letter' (which was undoubtedly a hoax) were not themselves particularly original. The link between the Illuminati, the Freemasons and Jews had featured in German anti-Illuminati literature for years. Since the 1770s, secret societies had been referred to as 'puppets manipulated by Jews' and a 'veritable haven and a highly desirable base' for the machinations of 'Christ-hating Jewry' (cited in von Bieberstein, 1977). Barruel himself speculated on Jewish involvement in the Illuminati conspiracy before he received the letter from the Italian officer. The German translation of *Memoirs* published in 1800 includes an author's footnote alleging a link between Freemasonry and Jews. And yet, the allegations made in 'Simonini's letter', as well as its precise timing, are revealing. First, the document offers a poignant example of a pattern of reasoning which is fundamental to the conspiratorial explanatory style. It reveals the tendency to infer causality from an event's consequence. The granting of full citizenship rights to French Jews in 1791 meant that Jews were seen to have benefited (and indeed did benefit) from the Revolution. This was enough for some to conclude that Jews must have had a hand in the event itself, that they planned it or at least exercised control over those who did, that is, the Freemasons and the Illuminati (Cohn, 1967). In subsequent decades, in other parts of Europe, the granting of full citizenship and property right to Jews provoked comparable allegations about the Jewish origins of liberal reform (see Wistrich, 1991, Poliakov, 1974 Vol.3). More importantly, the publication of 'Simonini's letter' in 1806 coincided with Napoleon's decision to assemble the leading Jews of France at a meeting which he regrettably called the 'Great Sanhedrin' after the ancient Jewish court. This gave the meeting unnecessary political connotations and fuelled rumours about the Emperor's 'collusion' with Jews. The publication and distribution of 'Simonini's letter' was without a doubt a response to these rumours and an attempt to assimilate the emerging antisemitic sentiment within the Illuminati conspiracy theory.

The idea of a Jewish plot 'revealed' in 'Simonini's letter' was not instantly picked up by the wider conspiracist community. In France, the Jewish conspiracy theory took off only in the 1860s with the publication of Henri Roger Gougenot des Mousseaux's notorious *Le juif: le judaïsme et la judaïsation des peuples chrétiens* (1869), an elaborate account of a satanic plot supposedly orchestrated by 'kaballistic Jews'. A distinguishing feature of des Mousseaux's treatise is its pronounced mystical dimension, and the fact that it explicitly draws on the longer tradition of medieval antisemitic demonology which perceived Jews as 'killers of Christ', sorcerers, poisoners of wells and murderers of children (Trachtenberg, 1983). Des Mousseaux modernised the traditional Christian antisemitic motifs and brought them in line with contemporary reality, ensuring their persistence in the modern age of secular politics, Enlightenment values and Reason. In the nineteenth century, 'the Jew' was thus no longer perceived as, in a *literal* sense, the 'spawn of Satan' and 'a diabolic beast fighting the forces of truth and salvation with Satan's weapon' (which was a common view in the Middle Ages) but rather as a *political force* using money, influence and arcane knowledge 'to conquer the world, to refashion it in its own craven image, enslave it to his own alien ends' (Trachtenberg, 1983: 18, 3). Together with a number of other antisemitic authors like Arthur de Gobineau and Edouard Drumont, Des Mousseaux helped transform nineteenth-century French society into 'a kind of laboratory of antisemitic concepts, ideas and slogans' (Wistrich, 1991: 126).

The proliferation of antisemitic conspiracy theories was also helped by the publication, in 1844, of the novel *Coningsby; or, The New Generation* by the British politician and future Prime Minister Benjamin Disraeli. In the book, a Jewish character by the name of Sidonia informs the novel's hero, Henry Coningsby, that 'the world is governed by very different personages from what is imagined by those who are not behind the scenes' (Disraeli, 1844, vol. 2: 204). This sentence follows the claim that finance ministers in major European countries are Jews. Ever since the book was first published, conspiracy theorists interpreted this passage from *Coningsby* as an important admission, straight from the pen of a famous and influential Jew, that the Jewish financial elite is 'the hidden hand' behind European politics. The fact that this was a work of fiction and that none of the finance ministers of countries mentioned in the book was Jewish did not seem to matter.

The impact which *Coningsby* had on the conspiracy culture is noteworthy for two reasons. First, it illustrates the *fact-fiction reversal* commonly found in conspiracy literature. The conspiracy theorist believes not only that 'what the world at large regards as fact is actually fiction', but sometimes also that the reverse, namely that 'what seems to be fiction is actually fact' (Barkun, 2006: 29). More importantly, the quote from Disraeli appears as an epigraph in numerous conspiracy texts from des Mousseaux's 1869 work *Le juif: le judaïsme et la judaïsation des peuples chrétiens*, to Jim Marrs's bestseller *Rule by Secrecy* (2000) published 140 years later. It has been cited as evidence of the 'hidden hand' in world history by scores of other conspiracy theorists, from Nesta Webster (1924: 382) in the 1920s, through the ideologues of the John Birch society in the 1960s and 1970s (see Lipset and Raab, 1978: 250), to contemporary conspiracy theory websites. This is a clear example of continuity within the conspiracy tradition which is explored in more detail in Chapter 5.

The wave of Jewish emancipation in Europe in the 1860s and 1870s, which contributed to the proliferation of antisemitic conspiracy theories, influenced also the events in Russia, the country with the largest number of Jews among its population. In the 1880s, in the face of inevitable pressure to offer equal rights to Jews on its territory, Russian authorities embarked on a campaign to reduce the size of the Jewish community through a mixture of restrictive administrative measures and violent pogroms. The result was a wave of Jewish emigration, primarily to the United States. The expulsion of Jews was accompanied by virulently antisemitic propaganda, which made Russia especially receptive to antisemitic literature and ideological motifs that were emerging in other parts of Europe. In particular, under the influence of German antisemitic literature which appeared after the revolution of 1848, Jews were seen as the force behind the revolutionary, terrorist movements that emerged in Russia at the time. Such rhetoric planted the seed for the myth about the Jewish nature of Bolshevism, which, as we shall see, blossomed in the first decades of the twentieth century. Crucially, in Russia, unlike elsewhere in Europe, the idea of a Jewish conspiracy was propagated not just by nationalist writers and publishers, or by traditionally conservative clerical authorities, but also by the all-powerful state apparatus, raising antisemitism to the status of an official doctrine.

Protocols of the Elders of Zion

Developments in nineteenth-century Russia are of particular importance to the history of conspiracy theory given that it was there that the most infamous antisemitic document of all time – *Protocols of the Elders of Zion* – was created. The *Protocols*, a pamphlet of no more than a hundred pages, divided into 24 chapters (or 'protocols'), lays out the plan for world domination supposedly drawn up by a group of Jewish elders. Written partly in first person – it was promoted as a detailed record of an actual meeting by a group of conspiring Jews – the *Protocols* reveal the aims of the ongoing Jewish plot, outline the means by which world domination is to be achieved and offer an insight into what life would look like under the future Jewish world government.

The *Protocols* were first published in book form in 1905, when they appeared as an appendix to the second edition of *The Great in the Small*, a collection of mystical writings by a shady character by the name of Sergei Nilus. Nilus's biography has been the source of much confusion: in some of the literature on the *Protocols* he is referred to as a monk, an Orthodox theologian or a Rasputin-like figure with good connections within the Russian imperial family (Hagemeister, 2008). In reality, he was little more than an antisemitic agitator and an Orthodox Christian mystic of little consequence. Crucially, Nilus was not the author of the *Protocols*. He merely published a copy of one of several versions of the pamphlet which was being passed around among Russian antisemites in the late 1890s (Cohn, 1967). Nilus was, nevertheless, instrumental in bringing *Protocols* to a wider audience, which is why his name has become intrinsically tied with this work.

The precise origins of the *Protocols* have been the subject of much speculation. The most popular account (although one that is usually accompanied by caveats and qualifications) is that they were created by the Russian secret police, the Okhrana (specifically by Piotr Rachkovskii, head of Okhrana's Paris-based foreign branch), with the purpose of inciting and legitimising pogroms against Russian Jews. However, much more important than the precise authorship of the document is the fact that this was an unsophisticated and obvious forgery. One source for the *Protocols* is the novel *Biarritz* (1868) by the second-rate German author and notorious antisemite Hermann Goedsche, who published under the pseudonym John Retcliffe. *Biarritz* contains a chapter entitled 'In the Jewish cemetery in Prague', which depicts a fictional meeting by the representatives of the 12 Tribes of Israel who gather in the night to discuss global conquest. The fact that such a motif appeared in a fictional novel is itself indicative of the emerging preoccupation, in Goedsche's native Germany, with the idea of Jewish conspiracy (see Cohn, 1967). Shortly after the publication of *Biarritz*, the chapter depicting the event at the Prague cemetery was taken out of its fictional context and publicised separately, as an account of a real event. First in Russia, and then in France and Germany, the chapter was printed as an 'authentic' document exposing a secret plan by Jews to take over the world. 'The Rabbi's speech', as it came to be known, was attributed to different 'reliable' sources, such as an 'English diplomat' (who had allegedly been killed for divulging the secrets of the Jewish conspiracy) or one of several different Jewish rabbis.

By the turn of the century, the chapter from Goedsche's novel was combined with extracts from another work of fiction – *Dialogues en Enfer entre Montesquieu et Machiavelli*, by the Swiss writer Maurice Joly – to produce the *Protocols of the Elders of Zion*. *Dialogues* was a thinly veiled critique of the reign of Napoleon III which used the format of an imagined dialogue between two philosophers, Montesquieu and Machiavelli, to pit the values of liberalism (represented by Montesquieu) against those of Napoleonic despotism (symbolised by Machiavelli). The authors of the *Protocols*, without making too much effort to conceal their plagiarism, lifted whole paragraphs from this little known work. Specifically, Machiavelli's defence of despotism was blended with the chapter from Goedsche's book, to produce the definitive 'proof', supposedly from the horse's mouth, that there is a Jewish world government which controls everything, including world finances, politics, public opinion and cultural life.

The *Protocols* proved popular in Russia. Several reprints of Nilus's work and other editions of the hoax were published between 1905 and 1915 and received praise even from Tsar Nicholai II (Bronner, 2000). The esteem in which the *Protocols* were held needs to be seen in the context of the anxieties about the impending Bolshevik Revolution. The *Protocols* provided a simple, albeit terrifying, framework that, drawing on the deeply engrained antisemitic stereotypes, could accommodate popular anxieties about the impending upheaval. With the onset of the First World War, the antisemitic motifs were blended with anti-German prejudice, as the press in Russia began to promote the idea that the revolutionaries were being bankrolled by a syndicate of American-based Jewish bankers of German descent, led by Max Warburg.

Around the time of the Russian Revolution, the claim about the Jewish-German-Bolshevik connection reached the Western audience. In Britain, Robert Wilton, the Russia correspondent of the *Times* and Victor Marsden of the *Morning Post* led the way with regular reports from Russia alleging the Jewish origins of the revolution. Later, the claim acquired some endorsement from British state authorities, who, driven mainly by opportunism, incorporated it into the more general anti-Soviet and anti-German propaganda. The situation was similar in the US. In 1917 and 1918, Edgar Sisson, an American diplomat based in St Petersburg procured, from a Russian journalist, a series of documents 'proving' the link between a group of Jewish bankers and the Revolution. The documents, which just like the *Protocols* were an antisemitic hoax (see Poliakov, 1987), fooled even the American government, which published them in 1918 in the form of a pamphlet entitled *The German Bolshevik Conspiracy*. In its earliest incarnation in the West, this conspiracy theory emphasised the *German* rather than the Jewish nature of the alleged plot (the network responsible was referred to as 'Rheine-Westphalian syndicate'), although the protagonists were clearly identified as *Jews* of German descent (Aaronovitch, 2009). In subsequent years, the notoriously antisemitic White Russian émigré organisations active in the US and Europe worked hard to embellish the conspiratorial claims with further 'proofs' and 'eyewitness reports' and fed them to the surprisingly receptive local politicians and journalists.

The idea of collusion between Jews and Communists caught the imagination of populist ideologues in the US. Ever since the 1870s, North American agrarian and producerist movements had resented wealthy bankers and financiers from the East Coast of the US who were often referred to as the 'corporate Jew class' and portrayed as enemies of the (white and protestant) American worker (Lipset and Raab, 1978). By 1920, the East Side of New York was perceived by many reactionaries as a 'cradle of Bolshevism' with Warburg, Kuhn, Loeb, Schiff and the inescapable Rothschilds cast in the role of the puppeteers in control of Russia's new rulers (Poliakov, 1974: 36).

It is in this context that the *Protocols of the Elders of Zion* made an entrance in the Western world and acquired international fame. In Britain, the United States, Germany, France and elsewhere, the key role in their dissemination was played, once again, by opportunistic individuals and activists of various right-wing White Russian émigré organisations who were intent on turning the world against the Bolshevik government. When the Russian officer by the name of Piotr Shabelskii-Bork escaped the revolution and fled to Berlin, he brought with him a copy of the 1911 edition of Sergei Nilus's *The Great in the Small*. The first German translation of the *Protocols* appeared in 1919 and became an instant bestseller. More than 30 German editions were printed prior to 1933 (Kellogg, 2005).

Soon after they first appeared in Germany, the *Protocols* were published in Britain. At the time, the Conservative Party and sections of the media sympathetic to it embarked on a campaign to subvert Prime Minister Lloyd George's initiative to re-open trade negotiations with Communist Russia. The idea of a sinister, Jewish, Moscow-based international conspiracy aimed at world domination, presented itself as a convenient means of opposing the rapprochement with the Bolshevik government. A series of articles in *The Times* on 'Jews and Bolshevism' was followed by the official endorsement, by the same newspaper, of the *Protocols of the Elders of Zion*. Soon after, the *Protocols* were published in London under the title *The Jewish Peril* (1921). Arguments similar to those found in *The Times* were espoused by the *Morning Post* which devoted hundreds of column inches to interpreting the *Protocols* for its readers (Gwynne, 1920). This unprecedented publicity in the mainstream press, in conjunction with the fact that *The Jewish Peril* was published by a respectable publisher with links to the government, gave the forgery the impetus it needed, effectively launching its international career (Poliakov, 1974).

The arrival of the *Protocols* in Britain coincided with the rise to prominence of another significant figure in the history of the conspiracy theory, the British socialite and writer Nesta Webster. In the years leading to the Bolshevik Revolution, Webster wrote a number of successful books on the French Revolution, which, among other things, sought to revive the ideas of the late eighteenth-century French counterrevolutionary tradition, especially the work of Augustin Barruel. In the early 1920s, at a time when the *Protocols of the Elders of Zion* were receiving significant publicity, many, including the editors of the *Morning Post* saw 'Mrs. Webster's' work as providing valuable context for Sergei Nilus's sensational discovery. In 1921, Webster published *World Revolution: The Plot against Civilisation* which was followed three years later by *Secret Societies and Subversive Movements* (Webster, 1921, 1924). The main thesis of these books was that there is a thread of continuity which links the French Revolution and the events in Russia in 1917. Both, according to Webster, were orchestrated by a network of secret societies whose activities can be traced back to the machinations of Weishaupt's Illuminati in the 1780s. More importantly, Webster saw Jews as playing a central role in the history of conspiracy, and as a dominant force behind the Illuminati, both in the past and in the present.

Although Webster's ideas were rejected by most mainstream historians of that era, making her something of a laughing stock in academic circles, her work was not confined to the margins. Winston Churchill's claim, quoted in the opening paragraphs of this book, that Jews played a longstanding role in the 'world-wide conspiracy for the overthrow of civilisation' was based on the work of 'a modern writer, Mrs. Webster' who has 'so ably shown' the role of Jews in the 'tragedy of the French Revolution' (Churchill, 1920: 5).

Nesta Webster's lasting contribution to the conspiracy culture is that she managed to integrate the whole of the nineteenth-century and early twentieth-century conspiracy tradition into a coherent and chronologically ordered narrative that explains all events between 1789 and 1917. She also revived the interest in the Illuminati and made the nineteenth-century obsession with this secret society relevant to the audience in twentieth-century Britain and the United States (Barkun, 2006). Also, Webster's scholarly credentials, her academic writing style and detailed knowledge of arcane nineteenth-century sources made the claims appear far more reputable than those made by shady White Russian émigrés for whom antisemitism was as much a commodity as a conviction. Through her writing in the *Morning Post* in particular, Webster helped sanitise the principal message of the *Protocols* enabling it to survive the revelations about the book's origins (see below). Finally, in reviving the work of nineteenth-century writers like Des Mousseaux, she re-introduced occult themes into the mainstream conspiracy culture and made them appear respectable. According to Thurlow (1978: 12), Webster represents 'the root source of practically all occult knowledge in reactionary right and neo-fascist movements' not just in her native United Kingdom, but also in the United States, and not just in the 1920s but also in subsequent decades (see also Ruotsila, 2004).

The *Protocols* reached the US around the same time as Britain, through the writing of another Russian, Boris Brasol who published a detailed commentary of the alleged blueprint for world domination under the title *Protocols and World Revolution*. This was one of several books published by Brasol, which he hoped would 'do the Jews more harm than ten pogroms' (cited in Poliakov, 1974, Vol. 4: 236). However, it was the American industrialist Henry Ford who was instrumental in bringing the *Protocols* to the American public. Between May 1920 and January 1922, the *Dearborn Independent*, a newspaper of which Ford was proprietor, published a series of articles on the Jewish conspiracy. These articles were based on the *Protocols* and other similar literature which Brasol fed to Ford's personal secretary (Aaronovitch, 2009). The articles were later published in four volumes entitled *The International Jew: The World's Foremost Problem*. Half a million copies of this work were distributed in the United States alone.

In subsequent years, *Protocols* were translated into Polish, French and later also into Italian, Japanese, Spanish, Arabic and most other languages of the world. Millions of copies were sold throughout Europe, Asia, the Middle East and South America. In the period between 1920, when it acquired international fame, and the defeat of Nazism in 1945, the *Protocols* were outsold only by the Bible (Cohn, 1967). Crucially, in the 1930s, the *Protocols of the Elders of Zion* became the cornerstone of Nazi propaganda. They were disseminated and popularised throughout the world by the Third Reich's propaganda machinery and were instituted as compulsory literature in Germany's schools (Wegner, 2002, Herf, 2006). This antisemitic hoax, which arrived into the world on a wave of antisemitic pogroms in Russia, became as Norman Cohn aptly called it, 'a warrant for genocide' against six million European Jews.

A particularly intriguing feature of the history of the *Protocols* is that shortly after they were published in Germany, Britain and the United States, they were exposed as a forgery. In August 1921, *The Times* in London revealed the *Protocols* as a hoax, exposing the similarities with Joly's *Dialogues en Enfer*. In New York, the same evidence was presented in Herman Bernstein's book *The History of a Lie* (1921). Following the publication of the *Protocols* in Switzerland in the 1930s, a highly publicised trial was held in Berne which definitively proved the work's provenance, and its status as a forgery. Crucially however, this did not seem to undermine the book's cult status among millions of readers around the world who fell under its spell. Many of the book's admirers simply dismissed the evidence against it as a campaign by Jews to undermine the 'leaked' document which exposes so clearly their sinister secret. On the other hand, there were those, among them the Nazi ideologue Alfred Rosenberg, who were aware from the outset that the *Protocols* are not genuine, but for whom this simply did not matter. This is primarily because what made the *Protocols* such an object of fascination was not so much their provenance, but as Nesta Webster (1924: 409) put it, their 'prophetic nature'. In part because they are written in vague terms without reference to specific historical events or dates, but also because they outline a slowly unfolding plan, the *Protocols* function like the antisemitic divination, offering perpetual affirmation of what the antisemitic conspiracy theorist already believes to be true: that there is a vast Jewish conspiracy aimed at world domination (Bennett, 2007). The *Protocols* are therefore treated as a 'secret/sacred conspiratorial text' (Boym, 1999: 99), one that contains the 'key that unlocks all the perplexing mysteries of the modern world' (Levy, 1996: 7). Henry Ford captured the essence of this view when he stated, in 1921, that the only thing that matters about the *Protocols* is that they 'fit in with what is going on. They are sixteen years old and they have fitted the world situation up to this time. They fit it now' (cited in Kosmala, 1978: 20). In *Mein Kampf*, Hitler similarly states that it is enough to look at the 'historical development of the last hundred years' to recognise the intrinsic worth of the

Figure 3.2   Jewish Peril: The front cover of the French edition of the *Protocols of the Elders of Zion* (ca 1934) (United States Holocaust Memorial Museum)

Protocols (Hitler, 1992/1926: 297). In other words, for the antisemitic conspiracy theorist the *Protocols* function like the Bible: they are an ahistorical document that 'invites incantation, not critical interpretation' (Boym, 1999: 99).

Conspiracy at the heart of the US government

In the early twentieth century, the conspiracy culture in the United States underwent another significant development whose consequences are still apparent today. For much of the nineteenth century, the main preoccupation of conspiracy theorists in the US was the protection of American democracy, values and way of life from the imminent threat posed by the Freemasons, the Illuminati, Catholics or Jews. In the twentieth century, this began to change. After decades of anxieties about whether America might be taken over by alien forces, conspiracy theorists began to entertain the possibility that such a takeover had taken place, that the people were already dispossessed, and that the conspiracy is, in fact, acting through the government (Hofstadter, 1967, Bell, 1962). The driving force behind this change was the rise of the modern, powerful federal state, manifested in the foundation of the Federal Bureau of Investigation (1908), the establishment of the Federal Reserve (1913), and the introduction of legislation which allowed the government to initiate a draft and compel young men to go into war beyond America's borders (1917). These developments were seen by detractors as symptoms of the kind of potent, totalitarian order that conspiracy theorists of yesteryear feared might be brought to America (Olmsted, 2009). During the First World War in particular, there was widespread belief that America's foreign policy was no longer in the interest of its citizens, but was under the control of a small group of pro-British presidential advisers, international capitalists and arms manufacturers. Politicians and the media were seen as mere puppets in the hands of what late nineteenth-century populists had already identified as the 'secret cabals of international gold ring' (cited in Hofstadter, 1967: 8). Later events, such as the suspension of the gold standard and the introduction of the New Deal (1933) only helped to reinforce such anxieties. President Franklin D. Roosevelt in particular, was placed at the heart of the alleged plot and presented as a totalitarian leader intent on turning Americans into slaves.

In the 1920s and 1930s, this new breed of conspiracy theory became infused with the antisemitic variant epitomised by the *Protocols* and Ford's *The International Jew* (Olmsted, 2009). By the time of the introduction of the New Deal and Roosevelt's re-election in 1936, claims about the president's collusion with Jewish capital were rife. Charles Coughlin, the Canadian born Catholic priest, who was among the first to use the radio for the transmission of conspiracy theories, attacked the president's 'Jew Deal' and publicised the various 'revelations' about the 'Jewish capital's' communist connections. In subsequent years, conspiracy theories influenced the interpretation of all major events, including the Japanese attack on Pearl Harbour on 7 December 1941. The raid instantly revived the anti-interventionist discourse of 1914–1918, leading to the ludicrous claim that Roosevelt had foreknowledge of the raid but allowed it to happen as part of a conspiracy to lead the country into war. Remnants of this theory are clearly apparent today in the rhetoric of the 9/11 conspiracy theory, where the attacks on the World Trade Centre are referred to as the 'new Pearl Harbour' (Griffin, 2008).

The most dramatic and long-lasting effect of the early twentieth-century developments in conspiracism is that it acquired a significant and enduring subversive character. Since then, the goal of successive generations of conspiracy theorists, including the modern-day militia movements and far-right groups, has been to reclaim what was lost, uncover the secret behind the American establishment, and expose it for what it is: a façade for the machinations of 'Communists', 'New World Order', the 'Zionist Occupational Government' or the transnational financial and political oligarchy. An obsession with the former dominated conspiracy theories in the aftermath of the Second World War.

Senator McCarthy vs the communist conspiracy

After the victory over Germany and Japan, the key item on the political agenda in the United States was the rising threat of communism. For many, but especially those under the influence of the pre-1941 conspiracy culture, the perceived danger from communism extended above and beyond America's rivalry with the Soviet Union. Communist movements world wide, while undoubtedly helped financially and logistically by the USSR, consisted mostly of local movements of national grassroots communist party organisations. This led to fears that communist organisations might be operating clandestinely in and against the United States. Moreover, President Harry Truman's apparent failure to prevent the expansion of communist influence around the world was seen by many as evidence that communist subversion is already at work in Washington's corridors of power (Lipset and Raab, 1978).

Such anxieties paved the way for the arrival of McCarthyism. In 1950, Joseph McCarthy, the Republican senator from Wisconsin, initiated a campaign against the communist 'fifth column' within the American establishment. Using as a convenient tool the Senate's Permanent Subcommittee on Investigations of which he was Chair, McCarthy set out to expose communist stooges in all spheres of public life, including the arts, the academia and the media. Thousands of people were stigmatised as 'communist sympathisers', employers were issued with 'black lists' and libraries were under pressure to remove potentially suspect publications from their catalogues.

The conspiracy theory propagated by McCarthy differed from those which focused on the Illuminati or Jews in the sense that there was no identifiable conspiratorial body to speak of but merely a principle, or an ideology – 'the atheistic communist world'. The hub of the conspiracy was of course in Moscow, but the target of Senator McCarthy's endeavour was its agents on American soil. Nevertheless, McCarthyism exhibited all the signs of the warped explanatory logic of the conspiracy theory, including its inherent unfalsifiability. For example, when Owen Lattimore, a scholar and East Asia expert at Johns Hopkins University in Baltimore was accused of holding Maoist views, it was pointed out,

Figure 3.3 Senator Joseph R. McCarthy speaking (Wisconsin Historical Society, Image #8006)

in his defence, that he had been attacked on several occasions in the Communist Party newspaper, the *Daily Worker*. In the classic style of the conspiracy theory, this disconfirming evidence was interpreted by McCarthy as supporting the conspiracy thesis. The attacks in the *Daily Worker* were attributed to a deliberate ploy by the communists to protect their stooges from 'exposure' by having them criticised in party publications (Aaronovitch, 2009).

The witch-hunts initiated by McCarthy lasted several years. By the mid-1950s, however, McCarthy had become, in the words of one biographer, 'America's most hated senator' (Herman, 1999). His approach to combating the threat of Soviet espionage, which left thousands of lives and careers in ruin, appalled even some of the staunchest anticommunists in America. His support base was soon reduced to the narrow circle of seasoned conspiracy theorists, many of whom saw McCarthy's fall from grace as a sign of America's further decline before the threat of communist takeover of the world. They retreated from the spotlight into a smaller network of right-wing organisations, the most influential of which was the John Birch Society. 'The Birchers' are in many ways the epitome of the American conspiracy culture in the 1960s and 1970s.

The new mythology of secret societies

For inspiration, organisations such as the John Birch Society returned to the classic, pre-war right-wing conspiracy culture but endeavoured to give it a more 'respectable' image. The populist politics within which this movement was embedded was tainted by the legacy of pre-war antisemitism. After the Holocaust, it had become impossible to champion the idea of a Jewish conspiracy with the same degree of openness as before the war (Poliakov, 1974, Billig 1978). In the face of the new reality, Robert Welch, the founder of the John Birch Society, went to great lengths to distance himself and his organisation from allegations of antisemitism. In 1963, he denounced *Protocols* as a 'communist forgery' and in subsequent years expelled several members of the Society who expressed anti-Jewish prejudice in public (Lipset and Raab, 1978). The 'medieval scarecrow of antisemitism' was even weaved into the conspiracy theory and portrayed as 'a ploy to distract public attention from the real problem and the real causes' and most importantly, the 'real operators' behind the conspiracy (Sutton, 1974: 189).

Whether or not this sanitation operation was successful will be explored in more detail in Chapter 5. For now it suffices to say that in the attempt to deal with the antisemitic legacy of the conspiracy theory, the ideologues of the John Birch Society and similar institutions revived the older tradition of secret society mythology which characterised the works of Barruel and Robison. In the first instance, the 'real operators' were sought among the inner circles of transnational institutions, such as the International Monetary Fund and the United Nations, which were identified as precursors to a future (communist) world government. Eventually more 'mysterious' and exclusive bodies took centre stage (Thurlow, 1978, Berlet, 1994, Billig, 1978). Among them were the London-based Royal Institute of International Affairs, also known as Chatham House (founded in 1920), the Council on Foreign Relations (founded in 1921), the Bilderberg group (founded in 1954) and the Trilateral Commission (founded in 1973). The secrecy with which these talking shops for the international elite appeared to be obsessed enabled conspiracy theorists to project onto them the different elements of the conspiratorial fantasy and imagine them as 'tentacles' of a single, sinister, conspiratorial beast (Abraham, 1985). Also, as the loyalty of these institutions was said to lie above any single country or nation, they could be linked with the kind of internationalism that had been associated in the past with the Illuminati or communism. From the 1960s onwards (and especially after the publication, in 1964, of Phyllis Schlafly's pamphlet *A Choice, Not an Echo*) the Bilderberg group became a particular favourite, in part because it was the most 'mysterious', but also because, unlike the Council on Foreign Relations or Chatham House, it was explicitly transnational. Through the Bilderberg group, conspiracy theorists could finally plausibly place representatives of governments, financial institutions and royal families from around the world in the same room (Berlet, 1994, Ronson, 2000).

In the 1960s and 1970s, conspiracy theories focusing on the machinations of the new generation of 'secret societies' became a successful cultural export. The far-right in the English speaking world, including Britain, became heavily reliant on literature by American authors (Thurlow, 1978, Billig, 1978). The idea of the Bilderberg conspiracy also managed to cross the cold war divide and was endorsed by Soviet propaganda (Pipes, 1998). Even today, throughout the world, from post-communist Eastern Europe, to the Middle East and beyond, one frequently encounters references to works which epitomise this strand of conspiracy theory, such as Garry Allen's *None Dare Call It Conspiracy* (1972), Pat Robertson's *The New World Order* (1991) or John Coleman's *The Conspirators Hierarchy: The Committee of 300* (1992). The fact that the Bilderberg group was founded in Europe, by a member of the Dutch royal family, made this organisation appealing also to European conspiracy theorists who, drawing extensively on the work of American authors, projected onto the Bilderbergers their anxieties about European integration or transatlantic military cooperation.

An important implication of the global influence of American right-wing conspiracy literature in the 1960s and 1970s is that from this period onwards, the United States came to occupy a central place in the conspiratorial tale, either as the arch-villain or as the puppet through which the 'real' rulers of the world exercise their influence. This is the case even in parts of the world, such as Zimbabwe for example, where, historically, American influence has been negligible. There, AIDS-related conspiracy theories routinely invoke 'American scientists' or 'American government' as the force behind the alleged genocidal plot against Africa's black population (Rödlach, 2006). Also, as already noted in Chapter 1, in many parts of the world, conspiracy theories featuring the US have become the staple ingredient of anti-imperialist, anti-American, anti-capitalist, or anti-Western political arguments.

When examining the cross-cultural influences within the conspiracy culture after the Second World War, it is important to bear in mind that the influence did not go in one direction. In the aftermath of the assassination of John F. Kennedy, the first elaborate theories about the complicity of the US administration in the murder came from Europe (Hofstadter, 1967). Similarly, book-length elaborations on the alleged 9/11 conspiracy penned by European authors Thierry Meyssan or Andreas von Bülow, predated those of American conspiracy theorists by more than a year (Knight, 2008). The claim that AIDS was created by the US government for purposes of racial genocide – which is today widespread within the African American community and parts of sub-Saharan Africa – was first put forward, in 1986, by the East German biologist Jakob Segal (Kalichman, 2009). Also, as Daniel Pipes (1996: 318) points out, there always existed a 'ping pong of mutual influence' between the West and the Muslim world. Most antisemitic and anti-Western conspiracy motifs arrived in the Middle East from Europe and the US, and, as we shall see shortly, also from the Soviet Union. These were then elaborated upon and applied to a specific set of local political concerns (first and foremost the Israel-Palestine conflict) before being returned for consumption by the Western conspiracist community, only to eventually find their way back to the Middle East.

Old wine in a new bottle

In the aftermath of the Second World War, conspiracy theories continued to flourish east of the Iron Curtain too, particularly in the

Soviet Union. Just as McCarthy was embarking on his infamous crusade against the communist 'fifth column' within the American establishment, the Kremlin began its own campaign of counter-subversion, against the agents of Western imperialism – the 'Zionists'.

In the final years of his life, Josef Stalin (who was both a notorious antisemite and a clinical paranoiac) used the absolute power at his disposal to pursue a personal vendetta against Jews whom he believed were conspiring both against him personally and against the Soviet Union. He eradicated Jews from his immediate surrounding, from politics and public life. Jewish cultural institutions were closed down, leading figures arrested, tried for treason and subversion, and in many instances executed. It was only Stalin's death in 1953 that put a stop to the planned finale of the antisemitic campaign, namely the mass deportation of Soviet Jews to Siberia (see Laqueur, 2006, Wistrich, 1991).

Because in a communist society, which professed an ideological commitment to equality between peoples and nations, Jews could not be openly persecuted as Jews, the old antisemitic conspiracy theory was given a 'Marxist-Leninist' makeover: the ethnic category of 'the Jew' was replaced with a political one 'Zionist'. The purges of the early 1950s accused the Zionists/Jews of being 'rootless cosmopolitans' whose loyalty lay not with the Communist Soviet Union, but with the Jewish bourgeoisie in capitalist countries, especially in the US and Israel. Jews were targeted as disloyal, hypocritical, treacherous, power hungry agents of 'world Zionism', exponents of a dangerous and inherently anticommunist ideology in the service of Western imperialism (Hirszowicz, 1979, Wistrich, 1991).

The Soviet anti-Zionist campaigns continued even after Stalin's death, reaching their pinnacle in the aftermath of Israel's victory in the 1967 Six-Day War. The defeat of Moscow's allies in the Middle East sparked an anti-Zionist frenzy both in the Soviet media and on the international stage. Zionism was portrayed as an intrinsically chauvinistic and expansionist ideology, and Israel was cast in the role of the epitome of Evil, on a par with Nazi Germany. Through the works of a number of official Soviet 'Zionologists', including Yuri Ivanov, author of *Beware: Zionism!* (1970) and Vladimir Begun, who penned the particularly controversial book *The Encroaching Counter-Revolution* (1975), the disparaging claims about Israel and Zionism were placed in an elaborate (and familiar) conspiratorial narrative. The same cabal that was once accused of masterminding communism (including the familiar names of Kuhn, Loeb, the Rothschilds) was now portrayed as its worst enemy and an extended arm of capitalism and Western imperialism. The sinister force of international Jewry, which in an earlier era was said to have financed the Bolshevik Revolution, was, in its Zionist incarnation, accused of bankrolling and colluding with – the Nazis. Zionists were even held responsible for the Holocaust. Most importantly, Zionism came to be imagined as an independent and wealthy international movement, 'the great invisible power whose influence extends into every sphere of politics, finance, religion and the communications media in capitalist countries' (Wistrich, 1979: 288).

Clearly discernible behind the seemingly novel image of the 'Zionist' was that of 'the old mythical Jew, the faceless enemy, the cunning foe' (Lendvai, 1972: 6). This is unsurprising given that official 'Zionologists' drew inspiration directly from Nazi literature. Vladimir Begun, for example, was later shown to have plagiarised Hitler's *Mein Kampf* (see Spier, 1988), while the numerous anti-Zionist cartoons published in the Soviet press were clearly and unashamedly replicating the pre-Second World War antisemitic imagery (Hirszowicz, 1979, Vogt, 1975, Cooper, 1984).

Anti-Zionist campaigns similar to those organised in the Soviet Union took place in other countries of the Eastern Bloc (Laqueur, 2006, Lendvai, 1972, Wistrich 1979). What is more, the Soviet regime transformed anti-Zionism into a 'valuable export commodity' (Hirszowicz, 1979: 65). According to William Korey (1984: 157), in the 1960s and 1970s, the Soviet Union became 'the world's largest exporter of anti-Jewish hate materials'. The anti-Zionist campaign beyond the borders of the USSR helped to introduce antisemitic stereotypes, and the

Figure 3.4 'Change of horses', Nazi magazine *Der Stürmer* (1941) and 'The Cart of Zionism', Soviet magazine *Trud* (1972) (reproduced from Cooper, 1984)

conspiracy tradition, to societies where they were hitherto absent. Soviet anti-Zionism also helped shape the anti-Israeli rhetoric in the Muslim countries of the Middle East, where Soviet propaganda was particularly intensive and where it fell on fertile soil. Comparisons drawn between Israel and the Apartheid regime in South Africa, or the portrayal of Zionism as imperialism *par excellence* were carefully chosen so as to make anti-Zionist rhetoric appealing also throughout Africa and Asia, all with the aim of securing the international isolation of Israel (Hirszowicz, 1979). Crucially, it also influenced the far-left in Europe. Throughout the 1970s and the 1980s, the far-left in Britain and on the continent viewed Middle Eastern politics almost exclusively through the prism of Soviet anti-Zionism (see Billig, 1987a, Cesarani, 2004).

The language of Soviet anti-Zionism did not disappear with the fall of the Berlin Wall and the dissolution of the Soviet Union. Vladimir Begun, for example, continued to peddle his ideas as an ideologue of the Russian ultra-nationalist organisation Pamyat (Memory) whose activities in the late 1980s and early 1990s helped shape the ideas of the contemporary Russian far-right (Spier, 1988). The notion of a Zionist/Jewish conspiracy became an important tenet of what Oushakine (2009) labelled 'patriotism of despair': a sense of collective vulnerability, identity loss, dispossession and alienation caused by the dissolution of the Soviet empire and the tribulations of post-communist transition. The motifs of Soviet anti-Zionism, especially the parallel between Zionism and Nazism, persist also in the anti-Israeli propaganda in the Middle East and in the discourse of a segment of the contemporary liberal and leftist intelligentsia, where, albeit in a somewhat watered down, sanitised form, it continues to colour attitudes towards Israel (see Chapter 5).

The Kennedy assassination and its aftermath

The assassination of President John F. Kennedy, on 22 November 1963, is often seen as a landmark event in the post-war history of conspiracy theories. According to Knight (2000: 76), the Kennedy assassination 'inspired more conspiracy thinking in America than any other event in the twentieth century.' More importantly, it brought into the open a new breed of conspiracy theorists and a new way of doing conspiracy theory.

Within weeks of the Kennedy assassination, in order to restore public faith in government institutions and put a lid on widespread rumours about who was to blame for the president's death, the newly inaugurated president Lyndon B. Johnson set up a congressional inquiry into the event, lead by Chief Justice Earl Warren. After a ten month-long investigation, the Warren Commission concluded that there was no conspiracy to kill the president: Lee Harvey Oswald, a communist sympathiser arrested after the assassination, was identified as the 'lone gunman' whose actions on the Dealey Plaza in Dallas, Texas were unconnected to the CIA, the Mafia, the Cuban government or any other force named in conspiracy theories at the time.

Soon after they were published, the findings of the Warren Commission came under sustained criticism from a loose network of activists, investigators and campaigners, most of them amateurs, who were convinced that the Commission's findings were a cover-up. They believed that the assassination was the outcome of a conspiracy at the heart of the American establishment, masterminded by the network of individuals and groups which was later to acquire the collective name the 'military industrial complex'. These early conspiracy theories set the tone for much of subsequent speculation about the assassination of John F. Kennedy, which is still ongoing. What is particularly interesting about the motley crew of amateur detectives who pioneered the John F. Kennedy conspiracy theory is that many of them, including Harold Weisberg, the author of *Whitewash* (1965) – an early work condemning the Warren Report – had been victims of Joseph McCarthy's anticommunist crusade in the 1950s (Olmsted, 2009). This was not a coincidence. Many of those who lost their reputations, jobs and livelihoods during McCarthyism, saw themselves as victims of a government-led conspiracy to silence and discredit progressive public opinion. In the outcome of the Warren Comission, these individuals saw another government lie, one that concealed the FBI's or the CIA's complicity in the death of the country's most liberal and progressive president in a generation. All that was missing was proof.

The 26 volumes of the Warren Commission's findings became an obsession for this new generation of conspiracy theorists, who analysed the report's every word in the quest for inconsistencies or contradictions which might prove the cover-up. Much has been written about the Warren Report and more generally the assassination of John F. Kennedy, but for the present purposes, it suffices to say that the report did have substantial flaws which had to be put right by subsequent investigations, but this does not mean that conspiracy theorists were ever onto something (see Posner, 1993). Also, it later emerged that the left-leaning investigators into the secrets behind the assassination (including Jim Garrison, the District Attorney from Louisiana who is the central character of Oliver Stone's 1991 film *JFK*) had not only traded information and 'revelations' with conspiracy theorists on the right, but they made themselves vulnerable also to Soviet propaganda which promoted the idea of US government's involvement in the Kennedy assassination, in the hope that conspiracy theories would undermine its international reputation (see Holland, 2001).

In terms of the history of the conspiracy culture, the fallout from the John F. Kennedy assassination is important because it marked a point in time when the distinction between the producers and the consumers of conspiracy theories became obscured. At the core of the DIY investigations carried out by the critics of the Warren Report was the belief that the 'the truth is out there', that official experts – from doctors and scientists to lawyers and government officials – are trying to conceal it, and that it is up to the ordinary man or woman to go and seek it out, against all odds. Rather than being aimed at passive consumers who were supposed to lap up the interpretations served to them by others, conspiracy theory became a call to mobilisation, inspiring readers to gather 'evidence', share it with others and become part of a community.

This *participatory approach* to conspiracism inaugurated in the 1960s realised its full potential only 30 years later, in the 1990s, with the arrival of the internet. Shane Miller (2002: 45) cites the explosion of TWA 800 flight over the Atlantic in 1996 as the 'first major conspiracy of the internet age'. Theories about the causes of the explosion spread like wildfire from individual postings on internet message boards to the mainstream electronic media and the press. Conspiracy theorising in the age of the internet is underpinned by the conviction that anyone with the time and patience to sift through thousands of often highly technical and jargon-filled documents posted online (which are obtained, more often than not, through freedom of information requests from the very government which is being accused of conspiracy) might stumble upon some key piece of evidence that will cause the 'truth' to unfold. This methodology, pioneered in the 1960s by Kennedy assassination conspiracy theorists has since become the trademark of conspiracy theories about 9/11, AIDS, the death of Princess Diana, and other similar events.

The mistrust not just of the government, but also of science, medicine and expertise, which fuelled the JFK conspiracy theories, persisted in subsequent decades. It intensified further in the aftermath of the Watergate scandal and revelations about the CIAs covert activities at home and abroad (see previous chapter). Evidence that the state conspired not just against political opponents but also against its own citizens blew wind in the sails of conspiracism. This is why the 1970s are often identified as the point where conspiracy theories moved from the ideological extremes to the mainstream of politics (Goodnight and Poulakos, 1981). The revelations about the government's involvement in illegal (or at least ethically unacceptable) medical and scientific experiments also proved damaging. The disclosure of the details of the Tuskegee syphilis study carried out by the US Public Health Service between 1932 and 1972 is especially important in the light of the effect it had on race relations. The study involved 600 African American men being denied treatment for syphilis over four decades, as part of government-funded research on the natural course of the disease (Jones, 1981). In conjunction with the experience of decades of discrimination by the health care system, the revelations helped to create a pervasive climate of suspicion about the government and public health provision (Bird and Bogart, 2005, Simmons and Parsons, 2005). With the spread of HIV and AIDS in the late 1980s and 1990s, the distrust came to be expressed in the form of a conspiracy theory. What is important, however, is that the African American conspiracy culture did not develop independently of that which in previous decades and centuries had been the prerogative of white men and women. Accounts of the anti-Black plot draw extensively on the ideological tradition of the conspiracy theory, adopting its key motifs, rhetorical style and explanatory logic. They even became tainted with antisemitism. Nation of Islam, the African American religious organisation founded in the 1930s, which has been under the leadership of Louis Farrakhan since the 1970s, has become notorious for promoting old antisemitic canards about Jews being behind communism and capitalism or about their control over the world's finances and Hollywood. These motifs, some of which, paradoxically, have been adopted from literature of white supremacist movements (see Berlet and Lyons, 2000, Goldberg, 2001) are often promoted as the context within which the causes of AIDS, poverty and the alleged 'racial genocide' being perpetrated against the African American community are to be understood.

Conclusion

This whistle-stop tour of the history of the conspiracy theory, which began with the examination of late eighteenth-century accounts of the French Revolution, brings us all the way to the present and the contemporary conspiracy culture that was surveyed in Chapter 1.

Several broader conclusions emerge from this overview. First, although it is only in the last 30 or so years that conspiracy theories have become the topic of public interest and concern (if not 'panic', see Bratich, 2008), they have been a stable feature of social life and political discourse for more than two centuries. Over that time, their prominence ebbed and flowed, depending on the circumstances, but what usually brought them to the fore were dramatic social events such as wars, revolutions and financial or political crises. Although the current popularity of conspiracy theories is often attributed to the rise of the internet, the history of conspiracism appears to suggest that that digital media and computer technology merely accelerated a process that has been in place for centuries. Today, conspiracy theories about an event can circumnavigate the globe within days, if not hours, of it happening. In the early twentieth century, it may have taken *Protocols of the Elders of Zion* several years to do so, but they nevertheless managed to take root in virtually every corner of the planet. In fact, the international success of Barruel's and Robison's work a century earlier shows that from its inception, the conspiracy tradition had a 'global' appeal, at least in an eighteenth century sense of that term. Thus, while there may be more conspiracy theories today, and while they may appear more diverse, this is less to do with conspiracy theories themselves and more with the greater accessibility of information generally, and the fact that a greater number of people are involved in the creation of the public sphere.

Second, although a thread of continuity can be observed through conspiracy theory's history (in that conspiracy theories of every era clearly built on the assumptions and claims of previous ones), there is also clear evidence of evolution and fluidity. As we will see in Chapter 5, the ability to change and adapt ensured the conspiracy theory's survival, although at the same time (as one might expect from a tradition of explanation) each new incarnation or mutation retained ideological links with previous forms. This is especially so given that, as conspiracy theories underwent various changes, remnants of the older versions survived. Conspiratorial discourse today consists of numerous variants, ranging from the seemingly outdated and 'old fashioned' to the contemporary and topical. These different forms exist side by side and, more importantly, feed off each other. As we shall see later on, the fact that the different types of conspiratorial explanation share a common ideological heritage means that the boundaries between them are fuzzy and clear distinctions often difficult to draw.

Finally, regardless of the transformations which they have undergone over the years and the various developments which affected their dissemination, the most striking feature of conspiracy theories is their common and distinctive manner of expression. The explanatory style of conspiracy theory, with its characteristic narrative structure, rhetorical organisation and underlying assumption about politics, power and history links together the leather-bound volumes by Augustin Barruel, the *Protocols of the Elders of Zion* and Alex Jones's syndicated radio show broadcast daily across the United States. It is to the features of this style that we turn next.

4

The Anatomy of the Conspiracy Theory

At the core of every conspiracy theory is the assumption about the decisive role of human agency, intentionality and collusion in social and historical causality (Popper, 1966). However, there is much more to conspiracy theories than the supposition that events in the world can be attributed to someone's volition and design; they are also intricate and often enthralling *stories*. Since their inception in the eighteenth century, conspiratorial explanations have taken the form of complex tales of secret identities, covert plans and arcane knowledge weaved into the classic morality tale about the battle between Good and Evil. In addition, conspiracy theories are rhetorically organised to be seen as *fact*. Hence, they are replete with elaborate arguments, evidence and 'proof' which purport to validate the conspiratorial perspective on history and politics. The narrative configuration and rhetorical organisation of the conspiracy theory combine to create the distinct and enduring conspiracist explanatory style and manner of expression (Hofstadter, 1967). This style, in conjunction with the irrefutable logic considered in Chapter 2, is the defining feature of the conspiracist tradition of explanation.

The investigation into the anatomy of the conspiracy theory begins with a look at a triad of narrative elements without which no conspiracy theory can be complete: the *conspirators*, the *plan* and the *endeavour to maintain secrecy*.

The conspiratorial group

In every conspiracy theory, significant attention is devoted to the identity and the character of the cabal behind the alleged plot. The preoccupation with the conspirators is such that, in the words of Daniel Bell (1962: 16), conspiracy theorists often seem to be 'mesmerised by the enemies they have studied so assiduously and with such horrified fascination.'

When identifying and describing the conspiratorial clique, writers of conspiracy theory face a dilemma. As the ultimate causal agent in history, the conspirators have to be clearly identifiable. And yet, as the conspiracy is by definition secret, the conspirators must also be, to some extent at least, obscured from public view. In the early days of the conspiracy theory, the mysterious secret societies fitted the bill perfectly: they were real and yet at the same time also mysterious and secret. After the Second World War, the Bilderberg group and the Council on Foreign Relations caught the attention of conspiracy theorists for the same reasons. For writers not focusing on secret societies, an alternative solution to the dilemma has been to refer to the conspirators in vague terms, for example, by means of symbolic geographical locations such as 'New York', 'Wall Street', the 'East Coast', 'Vatican', or 'Kremlin'. That way a specific (although vaguely defined) body of people – bankers, Catholics, Communists or Jews – is given a 'secret, arcane centre' (Lipset and Raab, 1978: 16), enhancing the mystery surrounding the conspiracy without compromising the conspirators' concrete identity. The same principle underpins the use, in the post-Kennedy assassination era, of the term 'military industrial complex' to refer to the warmongering arms manufacturers, rogue elements within the intelligence establishment and corrupt politicians intent on subverting democracy (Olmsted, 2009). Or indeed the tendency among AIDS conspiracy theorists to talk of the 'Big Pharma' as an overarching entity encompassing pharmaceutical companies, government agencies, AIDS charities, the UN and the World Health Organisation (Kalichman, 2009). Crucially, no matter how broad or vague a category is used to describe the conspirators, the assumption of plotting and decision making usually invokes *personal* attribution. The conspiracy theorist treats collective, symbolic entities as having 'a kind of group-personality' and regards them as 'conspiring agents, just as if they were individual men' (Popper, 1972: 125, see also Billig, 1978).

The use of broader categories such as 'international bankers', 'military industrial complex' or 'Big Pharma' has the additional advantage of being sufficiently broad to include potentially anyone. An important task for any writer of conspiracy material is to populate the narrative with names of those who are supposedly involved in the plot and situate them within the broader conspiratorial network. This obsession with lists gives conspiracy theory a distinct 'odour of card index' (Cubitt, 1989: 20). Lists of conspirators produced in the appendices of

conspiracy theory literature or on websites are, however, never definitive: they are in constant need of updating as new names are added
and fresh connections are exposed. More importantly, the conspiracy
theorist's endeavour is continuously frustrated by the inevitability that,
because of the cunning of the secret cabal, the *real* masterminds, the
top of the conspiratorial hierarchy, will forever remain elusive and
shrouded in mystery.

In populating the conspiracy theories, writers often exhibit the tendency towards what is known as the *associational shift*, whereby someone who is believed to be involved in the conspiracy is given attributes
associated with the conspiratorial body (Cubitt, 1989, Byford, 2006).
Thus, in an antisemitic conspiracy theory, not only will the presence
of Jews in public life be accentuated, but powerful public figures who
are *not* Jewish, but are deemed to be part of the conspiracy, will be
'Judaised'. For example, Edouard Drumont's antisemitic book *La France
Juive* (1885), which sought to blend the French counter-revolutionary
literature with antisemitic conspiracy theory, alleged that Adam
Weishaupt, the founder of the Bavarian Illuminati, was himself Jewish
(von Bieberstein, 1977).

The conspiratorial body is usually represented not just as a list of
names, but also graphically, in the form of complex diagrams and sche-
mas illustrating the ties between different individuals and organisations. Although writers will sometimes focus on a single entity, the plot
is usually conceived as a complex hierarchy of secret or not so secret
organisations which are occasionally referred to in terms of 'hyphen-
ated or composite entities' (Cubitt, 1989: 12), such as 'Judeo-Masonry' or
'the Illuminati-Jacobin conspiracy.' Intricate drawings are used to show
the infinite number of connections that link the different branches of
the conspiracy. Individuals and organisations are placed side by side or
indeed as concealed within one another. Secret societies in particular are
assumed to be organised 'on the conspiratorial pattern of circle within
circles' (Allen, 1972: 80), or as Pat Robertson, the televangelist, onetime
presidential candidate and the author of the 1991 conspiratorial classic
The New World Order explains, 'there is a tiny secret core ring, a larger
and slightly less secret middle ring, then a much broader and more public group' (Robertson, 1991: 72). Therefore, while linear diagrams are
used to convey the hierarchical structure of the conspiracy, the idea of
concentric circles, with a 'secret core ring' enables the conspiracy theorist to account for the fact that the Council on Foreign Relations or the
Freemasons can, at the same time, have a seemingly innocuous public
presence and be involved in sinister conspiratorial activity.

A particularly notorious example of a visual representation of the Jewish conspiracy, one which is paradigmatic of the way in which conspiratorial networks are imagined, was published in December 1941 in the Nazi propaganda ministry publication *Parole der Woche* (see Figure 4.1). The diagram, embedded in an article on 'Jewish wire pullers', presented Churchill, Roosevelt and Stalin as linked by a sinister Jewish influence, epitomised by the names 'Baruch' (reference to the American financier and presidential adviser to F.D. Roosevelt, Bernard Baruch) and 'Mosessohn' (reference to Lazar Kaganovich, Stalin's henchman of Jewish descent whose father's name was Moses) and by a caricature of the Jew that symbolises international Jewry generally (Herf, 2006). All three leaders are, therefore, imagined as no more than tools of a secretive and mysterious force, conspiring against Germany and the rest of the world.

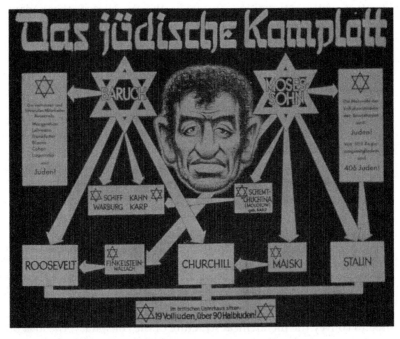

Figure 4.1   Detail from the Nazi propaganda poster 'Das judische Komplott' [The Jewish Conspiracy] published in *Parole der Woche* in 1941 (United States Holocaust Memorial Museum)

In the conspiratorial imagination, organisations and individuals are linked by the plot in a way that defies conventional logic, as traditional enemies are conceived as standing shoulder to shoulder. This is only to be expected. After all, the main tenet of the conspiracy theory is that nothing is as it seems, so the *appearance* of opposition between different forces is obviously revealed to be precisely what the conspirators want everyone to believe. This is why the apparent opposition between communism and capitalism, or the Catholic Church and Freemasonry, is routinely presented, by conspiracy theorists, as little more than 'another dastardly trick to confuse the unsuspecting public' (Billig, 1989: 156, see also Figure 4.2).

The character of the conspirator

Apart from naming the individuals involved in the conspiracy and exploring the network of organisations, secret societies and interests behind the alleged plot, conspiracy theory also attaches considerable importance to the conspirator's personality and disposition. The conspirator is typically construed as 'the perfect model of malice, a kind of amoral superman: sinister, ubiquitous, powerful, cruel, sensual, luxury-loving' (Hofstadter, 1967: 31–32). Adam Weishaupt, the founder of the Illuminati, has been compared by different authors to 'Satan' (Barruel, 1799, Vol. 4: 68), a 'monster' (Allen, 1972: 80) or even the antichrist (see Barkun, 2006). The use of religious imagery to capture the essential iniquity of the conspirators is common even in the overtly secular conspiracy theories. David Ray Griffin, one of the founders of the 9/11 'Truth' movement, which for the most part builds its legitimacy on 'scientific' or intellectual credentials of its exponents, spoke of America being 'entranced by demonic power, so focused on lust for wealth and control that almost anything becomes possible' (cited in Powell, 2006).

Descriptions of the pathological characteristics of the conspirators often include references to illicit sexual behaviour, debauchery and hedonism (Davis, 1972; Billig, 1978, 1989). Nesta Webster, for instance, perceived the evil 'Jewish caballa' to be not just 'magical' but also 'perverted' (Webster, 1921: 166). Gougenot des Mousseaux also dwelled in his most infamous work on the sexual orgies allegedly practiced by the secret plotters whose symbol is the serpent and the phallus (see Cohn, 1967). The obsession with sexual impropriety of the secret rulers of the world persists to the present day. Alex Jones, David Icke and other writers concerned with the annual gathering of the world's elite at a site called the Bohemian Grove claim that the 'ancient Canaanite, Luciferian, Babylon mystery religion ceremony' performed there involves orgies, depravity and child sacrifices (*Dark Secrets: Inside Bohemian Grove*, 2000, Ronson, 2000). It is difficult not to see in the imagery evoked by Jones, Icke and many others, an ideological link not just with the socially conservative political agenda within which the conspiracy theory is rooted, and which accounts for much of its preoccupation with puritan values, but also with the medieval antisemitic demonology in which motifs of ritualistic child abuse were all-pervading.

In the context of the alleged immorality of the conspirators, one also finds regular accusations of homosexual practices. Senator McCarthy's crusade against the communist conspiracy in the United States alluded to the existence of a 'homosexual international' set on undermining traditional Christian morality. Jim Garrison, the District Attorney from Louisiana who promoted conspiracy theories about the Kennedy assassination also speculated about the involvement, in the assassination, of a homosexual cabal envious of the president's virility (see Olmsted, 2009). The homophobic element of the conspiracy tradition is of course not limited to the United States: throughout the world, conspiracy theorists often claim that Hollywood, and the Western entertainment industry more generally are in the grip of a powerful 'gay lobby' whose aims are identical to those alleged by McCarthy in the 1950s.

The most important and ubiquitous characteristic of the conspirators, however, is their elite status: the villains of any conspiracy theory are typically found in universities or within the higher echelons of business and politics. The position of privilege is believed to give them control over education, the press and technology while also providing endless financial resources, which in turn enables them to control the masses and keep everyone in ignorance about their sinister aims. Also, the anti-elitism contributes to the conspiracy theory's populist appeal: just like the conspirators' assumed immorality, their elitism drives a wedge between the conspiratorial minority and the moral majority of ordinary men and women whom the conspiracy theorist explicitly or implicitly addresses. Therefore, the conspiratorial elite is presented above all as 'secret and alien' (Lipset and Raab, 1978: 16).

The conspiratorial plan

The emphasis on specific individuals involved in the conspiracy and the concern with their identity, character, activities and sources of influence is central to the conspiratorial narrative, but it is only part of the story. Individuals, no matter how powerful or sinister, come and go, but the conspiracy persists through time. As Gary North put it, if someone had blown up J.D. Rockefeller, Andrew Carnegie and other industrialists in early twentieth century, the conspiracy still would have happened. It is because 'it is the script, not the players, who are central' (North, 1985: 260). For that reason the account of the conspiracy must always go beyond individual power-holders and consider the grander scheme of things, a network of power that determines the course of history. The conspirators are, after all, just a personification of something less tangible, but more sinister – the 'demonic power' mentioned by David Ray Griffin. As Nesta Webster (1921: viii) put it, a conspiracy theorist is dealing with 'an occult force, terrible, unchanging, relentless, and destructive which constitutes the greatest menace that has ever confronted the human race.'

The 'occult force' that Webster refers to is most frequently conceived as a plan. In fact, at the heart of the conspiracy theory is the pairing of a conspiratorial body and a plan (Cubitt, 1989). Antisemitic conspiracy theories, for example, are as much about specific Jews controlling the world of finance and politics, as they are about a more general scheme for global domination explicated in the *Protocols of the Elders of Zion* and similar material.

In contemporary conspiracy culture, the most commonly encountered 'plan' behind the conspiracy is the creation of a 'New World Order'. Although this term featured in conspiracy literature since the 1960s (e.g. Allen, 1987), it was a speech by President George Bush Sr. before the US Congress in March 1991 – in which he referred to a 'new world coming into view, a world in which there is the very real prospect of a new world order' – that propelled the concept into the centre of the conspiracy culture. The New World Order filled the void left by the demise of 'international communism' which preoccupied conspiracy theorists in the West until the late 1980s. Bush's speech signalled a new and equally dark post-communist reality, in which the prospect of a sinister world government looms over humanity. The fact that Bush's speech coincided with the publication of Pat Robertson's bestselling conspiracy theory treatise *The New World Order* (1991) helped to reinforce the formulation's new status within the conspiracy culture (Goldberg, 2001).

According to Michael Barkun what makes the idea of the New World Order so appealing to conspiracy theorists is not just that it explicitly alludes to global domination as the ultimate aim, but also its inherently *abstract* nature: 'the New World Order is invisible, always cloaked in garb that disguises its true nature, whether it takes the form of the UN, philanthropic foundations, or academic organisations' (Barkun, 2006: 65). The vagueness surrounding its structure and membership means that there is always something new to discover about it. Also, the New World Order created scope for a truly 'ecumenical' conspiracy theory – the concept is sufficiently broad to allow conspiracy theorists from the left and from the right, from religious and secular organisations to project onto it their disparate ideas and concerns regarding world domination. This, however, is not a unique feature of the New World Order. The plan for Jewish domination 'revealed' in the *Protocols of the Elders of Zion* is similarly vague, which has made the hoax 'all things to all men' (Cohn, 1967: 174). In the 1920s, German (and to some extent American) antisemites saw in it proof of a Jewish conspiracy originating in London, while British antisemites located the heart of the plot in Germany. To Germans the *Protocols* explained the defeat in the First World War and the ensuing economic crisis, to Russians the advent of communism bankrolled by American industrialists, and to Americans the decline of puritan morality, and so on. Since the 1960s, in the Muslim countries of the Middle East it has been used to explain the existence of Israel, while in the late 1990s, Serbian conspiracy theorists claimed that the *Protocols* contain the blueprint for the 1999 NATO bombing of Serbia (Byford, 2006).

The conspiratorial plan is often believed to be revealed in some secret document. The *Protocols of the Elders of Zion* is, of course, the best known example, although it is neither the first nor the only one (see Cohn, 1967). For example, even before the publication of the hoax in 1905, a number of antisemitic conspiracy theorists in Germany, Austria, France and Russia exhibited a comparable fascination with Judaism's sacred text, the Talmud. In medieval times, the Talmud was seen across Christian Europe as containing the secrets of Jewish magic, sorcery and devil-worship (see Trachtenberg, 1983). In the nineteenth century, with the emergence of the conspiracy tradition, it came to be seen as a secret blueprint for Jewish world domination. Authors such as August Rohling, Gougenot de Mousseaux, Justinas Pranaitis and others, systematically mistranslated, de-contextualised and deliberately twisted the meaning of selected extracts from this religious text and presented Jews as a community intent on subjugating the non-Jews and ruling the world. This writing left an enduring mark on the conspiracy tradition: the nineteenth-century attacks on the Talmud, echoed in Nesta Webster's work, continue to be regurgitated even today on websites around the globe, from the United States to the Far East (see Anti-Defamation League, 2003).

Such treatment of religious texts is however not limited to Judaism. Right-wing political movements which espouse Islamophobic rhetoric in the West have latched onto this tradition and started to treat the Koran in a way not dissimilar to how the Talmud was treated by conspiracy theorists in the nineteenth century. The claim that a vast Muslim plot is under way, the aim of which is the Islamisation of Western societies, is today often accompanied by the assumption that Islam's holy text, when decoded appropriately, reveals itself to be the 'handbook for conquering people's countries' (Wood and Finlay, 2008: 715).

Manipulation of many by the few

The third key preoccupation of conspiracy theorists is the *effort at secrecy*, that is, the means by which the plot, its aims and the masterminds behind it are kept hidden from view (Cubitt, 1989). The effort at secrecy is essential to a conspiracy theory because it underpins the idea that there is more to social and political reality than meets the eye and, therefore, that there is something for the conspiracy theory to explain and reveal (Hofstadter, 1967, Billig, 1978). As J.M. Roberts (1974: 365) observed, at the core of the conspiracy mythology is a 'community unaware of its true nature. Apparently self-conscious and self-regulating, it is unknown to itself, in fact directed by concealed hands'. Also, it is the apparent secrecy of the plan that sets in motion the irrefutable logic of the conspiracy theory: it is because conspirators are so good at hiding evidence and manipulating reality that the absence of proof about the conspiracy can be taken as incontrovertible evidence of its existence. Finally, mass manipulation accounts for why most people do not believe the conspiracy theorist: 'the failure of the people to see the truth could only be explained by the political establishment evolving techniques to hide the facts from the public' (Thurlow, 1978: 23).

The methods that the conspirators are said to have at their disposal range from the plausible to the preposterous and include anything from news management, propaganda and 'information warfare' to the transmission of subliminal messages, microchip implants, brainwave manipulation or holograms. Generally, the greater the mainstream pretentions of a conspiracy theorist, the more likely it is that they will allude to the more plausible methods and techniques, primarily media manipulation. The emphasis on the media is, however, not new: in Gougenot des Mousseaux's *Le Juif: le judaïsme et la judaïsation des peuples chrétiens*, money and the control of the press feature prominently among the list of tools at the disposal of 'cabalistic Jews', although these means of mass manipulation stand side by side with various occult practices, sorcery and magic (Cohn, 1967). The control of the media became ubiquitous in conspiracy narratives with the advent of radio and the rise of Hollywood. In the 1930s, opponents of US President Franklin D. Roosevelt blamed his popularity on the manipulation of the public by the Jewish controlled press, by Hollywood (to which they attributed increasing influence on the hearts and minds of the American public) and radio which Roosevelt had used to mobilise Americans at the time of the New Deal. Charles Lindbergh, the first man to fly over the Atlantic and one of the leading opponents of US involvement in the war against Hitler identified Jewish 'ownership and influence in our motion pictures, our press, our radio and our Government' as the greatest danger to America (cited in Olmsted, 2009: 53).

In the case of conspiracy theories that claim to be about science or expertise, such as those promoted by AIDS denialists or the 9/11 Truth movement, censorship features as the dominant instrument of mass manipulation. The fact that AIDS denialists have been ostracised from mainstream scientific institutions or have difficulties obtaining funding is attributed to the actions of the 'Big Pharma' eager to conceal its sinister motivations, stifle dissenting voices and maintain the so-called AIDS industry, the 'global, multibillion-dollar juggernaut of diagnostics, drugs, and activist organizations' (Farber, 2006). The whole of biomedical science and public health enterprise is perceived as nothing less than the product of a vast conspiracy involving scientists, researchers, medical doctors and public health officials (Kalichman, 2009). In 9/11 conspiracy theories, the same arguments are used to dismiss aeronautical, mechanical and structural engineers, forensic experts, government officials and others who support the official version of the events of 9/11.

In addition to the *materialist* thread in conspiracy theories, which focuses on money and corruptions as the main source of the conspirators' power and influence, we also find an *occultist* thread which focuses on the conspirators' possession of arcane powers and their ability 'to monopolise and use knowledge which is not readily available to others' (Thurlow, 1978: 7). It is among the latter that we encounter references to the more bizarre and less plausible means of manipulation. John Robison, for instance, referred to a type of tea that causes abortion, or a stench bomb that would fill 'a bedchamber with pestilential vapours' (Robison, 1797: 137). Nesta Webster referred to hypnotism as the means by which the 'modern Illuminati' manipulate the unsuspecting public (see Thurlow, 1978). As we have seen in the opening paragraphs of the book, the former Malaysian Prime Minister Mahathir Mohammad reflected on the possibility that the whole of 9/11 as we know it was no more than a Hollywood style special effect.

In conspiracy theories with overtly Christian overtones, manipulation is often formulated in terms of hidden satanic symbolism which affects the public subliminally. The antichrist features in the narrative not simply as an epitome of evil, but also as 'part of a system of control' through which the public is manipulated (Barkun 2006: 44). Honouring of Lucifer, audible when pop records are played backwards, the apparent omnipresence of the number 666 in everything from McDonald's food to barcodes to Microsoft software, or the existence of hidden messages in political speeches, newspapers and on TV, are only some of the 'favourites'. Also, the assumption that conspirators have at their disposal yet undisclosed technological inventions enables conspiracy theorists to speculate on devices and procedures worthy of science fiction literature, such as brain manipulation, telepathy, microchip implants or tectonic or meteorological weapons. Within the conspiracist culture, the idea that it may be possible to use advanced technology to affect perceptions and thinking patterns, create or delete memories or control behaviour is not treated as, at best, a futuristic vision, but as a crucial feature of contemporary hidden reality (see Byford, 2002, 2006).

The esoteric and the materialist versions of mass manipulation are not mutually exclusive: it is often the conspirators' wealth that allows them to acquire the secret knowledge and keep it secret, while at the same time, the application of secret technology is often in the service of material wealth. Thus, Alex Jones and David Icke will, for example, seamlessly blend the economic argument (with the emphasis on European 'baron bankers', Wall Street or the 'military industrial complex') with musings about 'Caananite rituals' practiced by the world's elite and their alleged involvement in satanic practices. In the anonymous pamphlet *The Occult Technology of Power*, originally published in 1974, but which still attracts interests from conspiracy theory buffs on the internet (in part because it is another 'secret document' containing a blueprint for world domination) 'occult technology' on which the conspirators' immense power is said to rest is defined almost entirely in financial terms: the control over currency flows, influence over interest rates, the ability to create inflation or destroy national economies are all seen as forms of esoteric knowledge or magic (Thurlow, 1978).

The Manichaean view of politics

Alex Jones's syndicated radio show, broadcast daily across the United States, begins with the sounds of the Imperial March from the soundtrack of the *Star Wars* trilogy. This is the tune that, in the film, accompanies the appearance on screen of the archetypal villain, the lord of the Dark Side, Darth Vader. The choice of the tune signifies not just the malevolent and threatening nature of the conspiracy which Jones claims to be exposing in his show, but also the Manichaean distinction between Good and Evil, which lies at the core of the plot of both *Star Wars* and the conspiratorial narrative: 'conspiracy mentality divides people, things and actions into two classes, one is pure, the other impure. Classes are polar opposites: everything social, national, etc. vs. what is anti-social, anti-national' (Moscovici, 1987: 154). Within this polarised view, the course of history is seen as 'almost exclusively a matter of good or ill will' (Lipset and Raab, 1978: 13), politics is reduced to a struggle between good and bad intentions, while the possibility of negotiation or compromise is dismissed outright.

The dualism of conspiracy theory consists of two inter-related elements. It assumes, first of all, 'the natural unity and cohesiveness of the non-conspiratorial majority: their readiness, if freed from conspiratorial interference, to engage collectively in whatever is the crucial social and moral endeavour of the time' (Cubitt, 1989: 15). At the same time, any individual or organisation that appears to threaten the non-conspiratorial majority is automatically and indiscriminately allocated the role of villain in the unfolding morality play. This is why, as we have seen earlier, communism and capitalism, Freemasonry and the Catholic Church, the Illuminati and the Jesuits can all be seen, within the conspiracy narrative, as different faces of the same plot, pitted against the ordinary person and her or his interests.

Some authors have traced this binary opposition between good and bad in conspiracy theories to the historical link between the conspiracy tradition and Christian theology (Groh, 1987, Hofstadter, 1967). The Christian origins of the conspiracy theory's Manichaeism are sometimes acknowledged by conspiracy theorists themselves. Garry North, a 'historian by training', a 'Christian by conviction', who authored the foreword and the epilogue to Larry Abraham's conspiratorial classic *Call It Conspiracy* (1985), explains that 'biblical religion sees history as the product of cosmic struggle: between good and evil, between God and Satan, between redeemed men and rebellious men'. This struggle is 'inherently *conspiratorial*. The Bible teaches us about a great conspiracy against God. It is a conspiracy which affects every area of life, including politics' (North, 1985: xiii, original emphasis). This means that conspiracy theorists are by their own admission 'moral absolutists' who see 'history as a continuing struggle between the forces of good and the forces of evil' (ibid.: 263).

Manichaeism, as well as being a feature of the conspiracy theory's explanatory style, is also its condition of possibility. Karl Popper (1972) argued that conspiracy theory tends to be characteristic of those belief systems or political ideologies which are concerned with the implementation of fundamental truth, or with the creation of 'heaven on earth'. The unavoidable failure of such projects can only be explained by reference to an evil force that has a vested interest in thwarting this endeavour. This simplistic moral dualism imposes itself as an appealing explanation for why the promised second coming of the saviour, whether literal or metaphorical, has failed to occur (Groh, 1987, see also Cubitt, 1989). What is more, the 'all or nothing' perspective inherent in the Manichaeism of the conspiracy theory makes success virtually impossible, thus increasing the frustration and strengthening the belief in the terrifying qualities of the enemy (Hofstadter, 1967).

Although the division between Good and Evil is believed to be absolute, some exceptions are allowed. Conspiracy theories pay particular attention to the figure of the renegade from the enemy cause – former Freemasons, ex-communists or converted CIA operatives – whose confessions and first-hand accounts are used to reveal the 'real motives' and the mechanics behind the implementation of the devious plot. The defector offers 'the final verification of suspicion which might otherwise have been doubted by a sceptical world' (Hofstadter, 1967: 35). And yet, the role of the renegade in a conspiracy narrative is not merely to provide first-hand proof of the complot, but also to bring 'promise of redemption and victory': in the fight between good and evil, 'the renegade is the living proof that all conversions are not made by the wrong side' and that the conspirators might nevertheless be vulnerable (Ibid.).

Naïve optimism of the conspiracy theory

Conspiratorial Manichaeism gives conspiracy theory a visibly apocalyptic tone. Explanations of events in a conspiratorial narrative often assume that the evil aspirations of the conspirators are coming close to being fulfilled. The present is defined as the time for the final showdown which will determine whether evil will accomplish world domination. The apocalyptic vision is driven by the fact that the conspiracy theorist

> traffics in the birth and death of whole worlds, whole political orders, whole systems of human values. He is always manning the barricades of civilisation. He constantly lives at a turning point: it is now or never in organising resistance to conspiracy. Time is forever just running out. (Hofstadter, 1967: 29–30)

Although conspiratorial apocalypticism runs dangerously near to hopeless pessimism, conspiracy theorists never lose their determination to fight. The conspiracy theory typically envisages a positive outcome, 'a (never-to-arrive) new beginning where secrecy vanishes and power is transparent and utilized by good people for the good of all' (Fenster, 2008: 288). For example, on the very last page of Pat Robertson's *The New World Order*, the reader is assured that 'the triumph of God's world order is certain' and that 'people of the humanistic-occultic sphere' will be defeated by 'people of faith.' The book ends with a quote from the Gospel according to John: 'In the world you will have tribulation; but be of good cheer, I have overcome the world' (Robertson, 1991: 268). Robertson's use of Christian rhetoric is not insignificant here. The theme of decisive confrontation with the evil enemy draws upon the millennial pattern of thinking manifested in the belief that the establishment of Heaven on Earth will follow the inevitable destruction of the current order and the end of the temporary rule of Satan (see Billig, 1978, Barkun, 2006). Millennial eschatology drives the optimism of conspiracy theory because it enforces the belief that success is always the result of good intentions and pure values: positive spirit and the belief in God can and will overcome the technological and economic superiority of the enemy.

Optimism is also apparent in the conspiracy theorist's choice of metaphor. The role of volition and design (at the expense of chance or complex, impersonal forces) is often reinforced through the use of metaphors from the world of puppetry and theatre: conspirators are said to be 'pulling strings', orchestrating, scripting or directing world affairs. However, the 'puppetry and orchestral metaphors' do more than 'imply a non-spontaneous performance according to a script' (Billig, 1978: 323). The image of a hopeless lack of agency and freedom among those in the grip of the conspirators also conceals a message about the latter's intrinsic weakness: 'the puppeteer's strings can be easily cut and the orchestra could easily disarm the conductor of his baton'. Somewhat paradoxically, the stronger the enemy gets, the closer their final defeat is thought to be:

> The more puppets they control, the greater the weight upon flimsy strings. The conspiracy theorist might appear crazily fearful of his imagined enemies, but in his scheme of things these enemies should be just as frightened, lest the secret of their lack of power should become more widely known. (Ibid.: 324)

Therefore, what is needed is a final push which will drive the conspirators over the edge and cause the conspiracy to collapse in a heap.

The optimism of the conspiracy theory is, however, of a naïve kind because it is based on the assumption that dedication to truth and justice is enough to foil the evil plans of the technologically and financially superior enemy (Billig, 1978). The premise of every conspiracy theory is that meticulously collected evidence, packaged in a well-crafted argument and communicated by good people will convince the public to accept the truth, thus rendering the conspiracy powerless (Cubitt, 1989). Gary Allen's alludes to this in *None Dare Call It Conspiracy* when he uses the analogy of the 'hidden picture' puzzle in children's

Figure 4.2 German propaganda poster from Nazi-occupied Serbia (Serbian National Library Digital Collection http://digital.nb.rs)

magazines, which requires the reader to locate an object cleverly concealed by the artist somewhere in the image. Allen points out that once the 'real picture' is located, it sticks out 'like the proverbial painful digit', and the child can no longer look at the picture without seeing it (Allen, 1972: 7). Conspiracy theory is believed to work in the same way: once people learn about the complot and see the truth, they will no longer be susceptible to mass manipulation and deception on which the conspiracy rests. Or, as Pat Robertson (1991: 258) put it, once the truth comes out, 'their house of world order will splinter apart like so many matchsticks.'

The importance of foreknowledge

In addition to the evidence provided by 'secret documents', 'blueprints' or confessions from defectors, conspiracy theorists regularly invoke 'evidence' of foreknowledge about a dramatic event to suggest that its causes may have been different to those found in official explanations. For example, 9/11 Truth movement cites the 'fact' that 'some prominent travellers such as San Francisco mayor Willie Brown and top Pentagon officials' had been warned not to fly on 9/11, as clear evidence of government involvement in the attacks (9/11Truth.org, 2010). Similarly, the claim that Jewish employees failed to turn up for work on 11 September 2001, in anticipation of the attacks, sparked off much of the conspiracy theorising, particularly in the Middle East, about the involvement of Mossad and Israel in 9/11. In the aftermath of the Oklahoma bombing five years earlier, identical claims were made about the employees of the Bureau of Alcohol, Tobacco and Firearms who allegedly left the Federal Building minutes before the bomb blast (Ramsay, 2008: 111, also Keith, 1996). Jon King, author of *Princess Diana: The Hidden Evidence* claims that he obtained information about the plot (by the MI6 and the CIA) to kill the Princess 'one week prior to the crash' (cited in Aaronovitch, 2009: 150). In the aftermath of the terrorist attacks on the primary school in the North Ossetian town of Beslan in September 2004, conspiracy theories included the allegation that, in the words of a survivor, Larisa:

> During the last days of August, all of the Chechen and Ingush patients started to check out of the [Ossetian] hospitals to go home [...] We noticed the same thing happening in the run-up to every terrorist attack there's been here, and just before the Ossetian-Ingush conflict in 1992. There's no denying that they all knew about it before-

hand. They always know if something is going to happen in North Ossetia and they make damn sure to get out. (cited in Phillips, 2007: 248–249)

The emphasis on the importance of foreknowledge is not new. In the classic work of nineteenth-century conspiratorial antisemitism, Gougenot des Mousseaux's *Le Juif: le judaïsme et la judaïsation des peuples chrétiens*, a letter supposedly written by a German statesman, is offered as evidence of the Jewish complicity in the revolution of 1848:

I have had relations with a Jew who, from vanity, betrayed the secret of the secret societies with which he had been associated and who warned me eight or ten days beforehand of all the revolutions which were about to break out at any point in Europe. (cited in Webster, 1924: 410)

The reference to foreknowledge is ubiquitous in conspiracy theories because it is central to the overall argument. The main tenet of the conspiracy theory is that a particular event (9/11, Oklahoma bombing, the Beslan siege, the 1848 revolution) was *planned in advance*, so evidence that someone seemingly unconnected to the event might have had foreknowledge of it presents incontrovertible evidence of prior intent and conspiracy.

Foreknowledge is, however, not the only recurring motif in conspiracy theories. As we shall see in the next chapter, in crafting their argument, conspiracy theorists often draw on the writings of their predecessors in the quest for 'patterns' in the conspirators' actions. Over time, these also become 'patterns' in the conspiratorial argument. For example, in the aftermath of the 1995 Oklahoma bombing, conspiracy theorists offered elaborate accounts of how the home-made explosive made of fertiliser could not have produced a blast strong enough to cause the damage to the Federal Building, especially to its internal supporting pillars. This led to speculation that this was an 'inside job', that military grade explosive was planted within the building, and that Timothy McVeigh was just a 'patsy' framed for the attack. More or less identical themes about the discrepancy between the extent of the damage and the cause of the explosion, even the assumed critical importance of the damage to 'supporting pillars', resurfaced after the 9/11 attacks. Equally, practically every political assassination since Kennedy has been accompanied by claims that the person who fired the shots was just a decoy diverting attention from the real culprits. Robin Ramsay (2008: 114), for example, explicitly states that political assassinations follow a pattern, a 'scenario' which involves 'patsy firing blanks while somebody else does the real shooting'. This is the prism through which the assassinations of Martin Luther King, Norwegian Prime Minister Olof Palme, the Israeli Prime Minister Yitzak Rabin, Serbian Prime Minister Zoran Djindjić, Pakistani politician Benazir Bhutto, and others have been interpreted by conspiracy theorists in different parts of the world.

The rhetoric of scientific inquiry

In addition to the specific features of the conspiracy theory's narrative, and what we might call its dramaturgy, the conspiratorial explanatory style is also defined by the way in which the evidence of the supposed plot and cover-up is presented. For example, an important feature of the conspiratorial explanatory style is the elaborate concern with demonstration and presentation of proof (Hofstadter, 1967). Conspiracy theorists do not see themselves as raconteurs of alluring stories, but as investigators and researchers. That is why the conspiracy thesis will usually be embedded within a detailed exposition of plausible and verifiable historical facts. For example, Barruel's and Robison's late eighteenth-century writing on the machinations of the Illuminati reveals intricate knowledge of Adam Weishaupt's life and work and the history of eighteenth-century French Freemasonry. Contemporary writers of conspiracy literature who focus on the machinations of the Bilderberg group or the Trilateral Commission will also sift through the mainstream media and current affairs literature for clues about the history, structure and membership of these organisations. AIDS denialist material is replete with references to mainstream literature on medicine and molecular biology, while 9/11 conspiracy theories cite sources from the fields of structural and aeronautical engineering or forensic science.

Importantly however, as already noted in Chapter 2, in conspiracy theories, the multitude of arguments placed along factual lines and drawing on mainstream literature usually leads to extraordinary conclusions. 'The most careful, conscientious and seemingly coherent application to detail' apparent in the conspiracy theory turns out to be mere preparation for the 'big leap from the undeniable to the unbelievable' (Hofstadter, 1967: 37–38). The vast amount of the detailed 'evidence' becomes encapsulated into a completely consistent and coherent theory which concludes that the 'unbelievable is the only thing that can be believed' (Ibid.: 36).

The leap of the imagination contains within it an essential paradox. On the one hand, conspiracy theorists are markedly disdainful of orthodoxy: the starting point of the conspiracy theory is that 'any widely accepted belief must necessarily be false' and that 'the forces of orthodoxy will necessarily try to perpetuate error out of self-interest or some evil motive' (Barkun, 2006: 26–27). This creates the situation whereby any 'more widely accepted evidence becomes a sign of the conspirators' power, rejection by authority a sign of the depth of the conspiracy, and consensual denial a sign of public gullibility' (Goodnight and Poulakos, 1981: 307). On the other hand, conspiracy theorists insist on being judged by the same standards that apply in mainstream academia. For example, conspiracy theorists are inherently sceptical towards conventional mechanisms of warranted belief production: peer reviewed journals, judicial investigations, university departments or scientific institutions, and yet they routinely seek to emulate mainstream scholarship and enquiry. The 'high brow' conspiracy theorists will flaunt dubious academic credentials (professor, Dr., MD, etc.) and other markers of institutional respectability. They will publish books with scholarly sounding titles and adopt a style of writing that mimics mainstream academia: they will use the appropriate jargon, graphs, footnotes and extensive bibliographies (Hofstadter, 1967). In the 1970s, Holocaust deniers founded the scholarly sounding 'Institute of Historical Review' and the associated *Journal of Historical Review*, in which the claim that the Holocaust is a Zionist conspiracy is routinely flaunted, in a quasi-intellectual guise. More recently, a group of 9/11 conspiracy theorists founded a 'scholarly' publication, *Journal of 9/11 Studies*, 'a peer-reviewed, open-access, electronic-only journal, covering the whole of research related to the events of 11 September, 2001'. One of the journal's editors, Frank Legge (2009) asserted that in the emerging field of '9/11 studies' authors should 'scrupulously adhere to the scientific method and to promote to the public only those concepts which are shown to be soundly based'. Of the 57 articles published in the journal by 2010, 35 have been written by authors who included their academic credentials in the by-line, but without mentioning that, in most cases, they were writing on topics unrelated to the discipline for which the title was awarded. AIDS denialists also have their own *Journal of Physicians and Surgeons* where fringe theories about HIV/AIDS are regularly published, as well as works on topics such as abortion or 'gay lifestyle' (Kalichman, 2009).

The application of a quasi-academic style, which gives the conspiracy treatise a plausible appearance and an aura of respectability, is apparent also in the affinity for footnotes. Joseph McCarthy who was profoundly disdainful of elitism included 313 footnote references in the 96-page 'manifesto' *McCarthyism*, thereby mimicking the academic genre (Hofstadter, 1967). In David Ray Griffin's *The New Pearl Harbor Revisited* (2008), 250 pages of text on the 9/11 conspiracy are accompanied by 80 pages of notes, some of which are several pages long. The footnote is so valuable to the conspiracy theorist because it gives the impression that claims are corroborated and that behind them lays verifiable evidence, the product of reliable research by trustworthy sources. However, the superscripted number at the end of a sentence obscures as much as it reveals. It conceals, for example, the tendency to cite other conspiracy theorists or the 'fondness for reciprocal citation' (Barkun, 2006: 28). Authors of conspiracy material routinely cite one another, creating the false impression that multiple authors had arrived independently at the same conclusion. Aaronovitch (2009) mentions the example of the French 9/11 conspiracy theorist Thierry Meyssan, who cites an American colleague, Webster Tarpley, who in turn cites David Ray Griffin, whose work refers to – Meyssan.

The conspiracy theorists' endeavour to emulate mainstream scholarship stems from the fact that the conspiracy thesis often addresses 'the failed, or would be intellectuals, and amateurs who dream of intellectual success where the professional fails' (Billig, 1987a: 132). Conspiracy theory instils in the audience the faith that 'a believer can become an expert', a feature that is linked to the participatory approach to conspiracy theory examined in the previous chapter. Crucially however, the conspiracy theory's irrefutable logic means that this belief is illusory. As Michael Billig put it, 'the conspiracy theorist is to the professional historian what the treasure-hunter is to the archaeologist; only in the case of the conspiracy theorist, there is no means of convincing them that their quick dig among the documents has revealed only false gold' (ibid.).

The rhetoric of just asking questions

Another way in which the conspiracy theorist will seek to convince their audience of the veracity of their claims is by promoting what David Aaronovitch (2008) calls *'it's not a theory' theory*. This is where a conspiracy theory is articulated in the form of a question. Rather than purporting to have all the answers, the writer 'merely' poses a set of questions, hinting at some hidden 'truth' that is yet to be uncovered or demonstrated. Most such questions are built around an official explanation, which is perceived to be the product of deception and which the writer sets out to undermine and cast doubt on (Keeley, 1999). For example, the main argument of Jim Keith's book *OKBomb: Conspiracy and Cover-up* (1996) which explores the 1995 Oklahoma bombing is that a set of questions about McVeigh's act of terrorism remain unanswered, and that this in itself casts suspicion on the official account. The reader of Keith's book is then invited to consider alternative (conspiratorial) explanations and decide whether they 'make sense' and whether they are more 'likely', 'plausible', and so on. The same rhetoric underpins 9/11 conspiracy theories. The website 9/11Truth.org contains a downloadable 'factsheet' that poses 14 questions everyone should ask about the attacks on New York and Washington. The German publisher of *The CIA and September 11* (2003), the 9/11 conspiracy theory by Andreas von Büllow, defended the decision to print this work on the grounds that 'Mr. von Büllow poses a number of very interesting and important questions' ('9/11 Conspiracy theory books dominate debate at Frankfurt book fair', 2003). Also, both Holocaust deniers and exponents of AIDS denialism tend to phrase their argument as a call for a 'rational' and 'informed' debate about the number of Jewish victims of Nazism or about the link between HIV and AIDS.

The practice of asking questions is not in itself objectionable. Investigations into real conspiracies usually begin with questions which raise doubts about official explanations. In the case of the Watergate affair, revelations about the Nixon administration's complicity in the bugging of the members of the Democratic National Convention came out after Bob Woodward and Carl Bernstein of the *Washington Post* quite legitimately began to pose questions and proceeded in the quest for the answers (Goodnight and Poulakos, 1981). However, in the case of conspiracy theories, the rhetoric of 'just asking questions' and calls for 'open dialogue' or 'independent inquiry' are for the most part disingenuous. This is, above all, because they involve the continuous moving of goalposts. In the case of AIDS denialism, for example, the conspiracy theorist is challenging scientific research on a complex medical condition which scientists are still working hard to understand and treat. At any point, the denialist simply needs to demand more scientific evidence than is available at that moment, and then interpret its absence as a sign that there is something dubious about the research itself or that there is a conspiracy to conceal the truth (Smith and Novella, 2007). Asking questions is, therefore, no more than the means of undermining competing accounts and opening up a space for the conspiracy theory to fill.

The rhetoric of 'asking questions' is also a form of agenda setting. The questions posed by conspiracy theorists will often focus on what Brian Keeley (1999) calls 'errant data' namely specific details (which are mostly irrelevant, attributable to coincidence, or based on inaccurate information or false premise) that have not been adequately accounted for by the received (non-conspiratorial) explanation. For example, the official, lone gunman theory of the Kennedy assassination cannot (unlike the many variants of the conspiracy theory) account for the fact that a bystander opened the umbrella on the grassy knoll shortly before the shots were fired, or that some witnesses heard three shots rather than two. Conspiracy theories about Elvis faking his own death will claim that official accounts cannot explain why the inscription on the King's grave contains a spelling error (see Coady, 2006). The 9/11 conspiracy theorists claim that the official account of the attacks never produced an answer to what they deem to be a key question, namely why George W. Bush, who was visiting a Florida school at the time, continued 'reading about a goat' to a classroom of children, even after he was told that the first of the towers had been hit. By asking questions which point to such 'errant data', conspiracy theorists present their own alternative account as a more 'complete' and therefore better explanation.

All that this kind of questioning does, however, is to conveniently divert the audience's gaze from the glaring gaps in the conspiracist argument. Conspiracy theorists are highly selective both in their approach to evidence and in deciding what question they want to ask. For example, the questions about the number of shots heard by the witnesses on the day of the Kennedy assassination, pays no attention to the fact that around 88 per cent of almost 200 witnesses heard two shots and that this finding was corroborated by acoustic analysis. The rhetoric of 'asking questions' therefore simply obscures the mountain of 'errant data' hidden in the conspiracy theorists own back yard (Coady, 2006).

The rhetoric of asking questions also serves the purpose of placing the ball in the corner of dissenters. By posing a set of questions, conspiracy theorists throw the gauntlet into the face of the sceptics and challenge *them* to disprove that a conspiracy exists. Seth Payson, the New England pastor who in 1802 published a digest of Barruel's and Robison's work on the Illuminati, poses the following rhetorical question:

> Have any solid, satisfying proofs been exhibited, either that there has not been, or is not now existing, a conspiracy, which has for its ultimate object, the abolition of Christianity and government? Solid

proofs alone ought to satisfy us on a subject so highly interesting to mankind. Such proofs have not, I confess, come to my knowledge. (Payson, 1802: iii)

Similarly, Nesta Webster who, having been rejected by the mainstream academic community in England for her penchant for conspiracy theories, demanded of detractors documentary evidence that her claims are wrong (see Thurlow, 1978). During the time of McCarthyism, an organisation called Constitutional Educational League offered a $10,000 reward 'if *anybody* can prove that one single *innocent* person has been *falsely* accused by Senator Joe McCarthy of being a Communist or pro-Communist when such person had never been involved in any way in the Communist conspiracy to overthrow the government'. Given that, as we have established in Chapter 2, the conspiracy theory is irrefutable, such evidence cannot, of course, ever be produced. The practice of posing questions and directing them, implicitly or explicitly, at representatives of scientific, scholarly and media establishments, is, therefore, merely a way of cajoling the mainstream into a dialogue with the conspiracy theorist, with the view of augmenting the latter's status and esteem.

Conclusion

The common representations of the conspirators, their sinister plans and the means of mass manipulation, the Manichaean moral dualism and the naïve optimism of the conspiracy theory, as well as the whole suite of common motifs and rhetorical tropes which were examined in this chapter, is what makes conspiracy theories sound so much alike. However, when considering conspiracy theories and their narrative and rhetorical composition, it is also important to bear in mind Geoffrey Cubitt's (1993: 2) warning that 'the temptation to pare the paranoid style down to a set of immutable theoretical elements needs to be resisted'. This is, first of all, because conspiracy theories do not always take the form of fully elaborated accounts aimed at intellectual insiders and enthusiasts with an active commitment to a conspiracy theory-based view of the world. They persist also in a diluted, less-detailed form, comprising a much looser pattern of 'interpretative habits, implicit in a stream of assertions or arguments', where the common structures are typically less visible (ibid.). What is more, as we shall see in the next chapter, because of the intellectual presumption against conspiracy theories, conspiracist discourse is continuously evolving so as to present itself as a legitimate view of the world, rather than as an irrational mode of thinking. Engaging in this rhetorical work requires some aspects of the conspiratorial explanatory style to be modified, curtailed or at least temporarily abandoned. Therefore, the extent to which the described anatomical features will appear in any specific conspiratorial account, as well as their precise shape and form, will vary depending on the context within which the account is produced, its level of detail, and a number of other factors. And yet, despite this, the explanatory style outlined in this chapter somehow manages to persist and remains a hallmark of the distinct conspiracist tradition of explanation. The question that needs to be addressed now is *why* this is so, and why is it difficult to construct a theory of world conspiracy that does not, at least inadvertently, draw upon the conspiratorial explanatory style and tradition.

5
Conspiracy Theory and Antisemitism

No critical introduction to conspiracy theories would be complete without a discussion of their strong and longstanding connection with antisemitism. As we have seen in Chapter 3, for a substantial proportion of its history the conspiracy tradition was dominated by the idea of a Jewish plot to take over the world. This connection is not just historical, however. Much of contemporary antisemitism remains inherently conspiratorial. Animosity towards Jews is today seldom expressed in terms of demeaning stereotypes that defined racial antisemitism in the past or as routine 'dislike' of Jews or 'disapproval' of their culture or religion (Smith, 1996, Bauman, 1999, Harrison, 2006). Instead, the biggest 'fault' of Jews in the eyes of antisemites worldwide is that they are in possession of considerable wealth, power and influence and are using it to exercise undue control over democratic governments, international organisations, financial institutions, media corporations and cultural establishments. For those affiliated with the right, whether in the West, in the Middle East or elsewhere, the Jewish elite represents an omnipotent force with almost supernatural powers, intent on the destruction of independent nations and the creation of a secular, Jewish-controlled, New World Order. Sections of the left, on the other hand, see it as united in a powerful Zionist/Israel/Jewish lobby that pulls the strings of American politics and controls Western media. It is also noteworthy that conspiratorial antisemitism appears to be unrelated to the actual presence of Jews. Conspiracy theories with antisemitic motifs are expounded and believed even in cultures that have no Jewish minority, such as in Japan (Goodman and Miyazawa, 2000, Kowner, 1997). Similarly, in Eastern and Central Europe, levels of antisemitism are unconnected to the size of the local Jewish community or the history of relations between Jews and the majority population (Hockenos, 1993). This pattern has led a number of scholars of Eastern European antisemitism to refer to the local manifestations of anti-Jewish prejudice as 'antisemitism without Jews' (Lendvai, 1972, Hockenos, 1993).

The connection between antisemitism and conspiracy theory is also manifested in the fact that the idea of a *Jewish* conspiracy persists as a latent motif in a sizeable proportion of contemporary conspiracy culture. Of course, not all conspiracy theories are unavoidably antisemitic, but it is also true that discernible within many conspiracy narratives, even those that are not explicitly targeting Jews, are worrying, and often subtle, reminders of the conspiracy theory's earlier, overtly antisemitic incarnations.

The present chapter considers the connection between conspiracy theory and antisemitism from two distinct angles. Drawing on the important, but in literature on conspiracy theories often neglected work of Michael Billig (1978, 1989), the first part of the chapter looks at why antisemitism persists within conspiracist culture, or rather, why authors of conspiracy material so often find it difficult to escape subtle allusions to the Jewish dimension within alleged plot. In exploring this question, forthcoming sections address a broader issue that was raised at the end of the previous chapter, namely, what it is about the way in which conspiracy theories are written and communicated that preserves their distinctive rhetorical style and thematic consistency.

As well as looking at the persistence of antisemitism *within* the conspiracy culture, the present chapter considers how the motif of Jewish conspiracy sometimes contaminates ordinary discourse and becomes perceived as a respectable interpretation of reality, even within political cultures which do not have a notable record of antisemitism. This is an important point because what makes conspiracy theories so prevalent in modern society is precisely that they are *not* confined to a closed community of conspiracy enthusiasts, sealed off from the mainstream by the adherence to a dysfunctional 'paranoid' explanatory logic, or to individuals or groups committed to right-wing, or radical Islamist ideologies. Rather, they influence everyday understanding of politics through a loose array of images, motifs and assumptions about the world, which through transmission and communication become part of the shared knowledge and beliefs, and which are then available to people to draw upon as they attempt to make sense of events around them. The second part of the chapter examines this issue using as an example the way in which, in recent years, the conflict in the Middle East provided traditional antisemitic motifs of Jewish power, greed and malevolence with a new mode of expression, but importantly also new advocates, this time on the political left.

Conspiracism as a dynamic and evolving culture

As hinted at in previous chapters, the fluid and dynamic quality of the conspiracy culture was instrumental in its persistence over the past two and a half centuries. The main force behind the permanent process of evolution and change has been the need to make conspiracy theories more plausible, acceptable and pertinent in response to changing social and political circumstances. Conspiracy theorists are and always have been surrounded by sceptics who place them under pressure to modify their theories in the direction of greater plausibility. As early as in 1802, Seth Payson, who popularised European anti-Illuminati literature in the United States, identified 'ridicule and defamation' as 'weapons found to be of great importance in this *age of reason*' (Payson, 1802: iii, original emphasis). The threat of 'ridicule and defamation', which has been hanging over purveyors of conspiracy theories ever since, makes anticipating and reacting to potential or actual charges of irrationality, paranoia or prejudice, an essential feature of the conspiracy theorist's endeavour. This is especially so given that conspiracy theorists always, if only implicitly, address an audience beyond the conspiracist community, all in the hope that they will be recognised and accepted by the very mainstream which they consistently reject and accuse of being in collusion with the nefarious rulers of the world. The evolution of the conspiracy culture, therefore, entails the continuous creation of novel and more convincing ways of stating conspiratorial claims, which implies a sense of *discontinuity* with older versions.

A poignant example of discontinuity, which was noted in Chapter 3, is the post-Second World War shift away from the emphasis on the Jewish conspiracy towards a new variant of secret society mythology. In the aftermath of the Holocaust, when the notion of a Jewish plot to rule the world was relegated to the outer reaches of the political spectrum, those among conspiracy theorists who had mainstream pretentions, turned their attention towards non-ethnic world elite organisations such as the Council on Foreign Relations or the Bilderberg group (Lipset and Raab, 1978, Billig, 1978). The choice of these political groups was not haphazard. What made it possible to promote this new secret society mythology as a serious and informed analysis (rather than as a paranoid or bigoted explanation) is that it dealt with *real life* elite organisations, whose influence was recognised even by political analysts and journalists who do not subscribe to the conspiratorial worldview. In other words, they made their views appear plausible by absorbing, within the conspiracy theory, claims, arguments and evidence from the more conventional discourses of current affairs, international relations and world politics. Focusing on existing organisations coated the basic thesis of conspiracy in a set of otherwise sensible and reasonable representations, thus providing what Michael Barkun (2006: 181) calls a *bridging mechanism* – an organisational device that links the conspiracy theory to an accepted form of political expression.

This rhetorical move was not in itself a new development. The Illuminati too were a real secret society, so even the earliest conspiracy theorists like Barruel and Robison, constructed their argument on foundations based in reality (Hofstadter, 1967). Antisemitic literature of the late nineteenth and early twentieth centuries also cited real institutions – the Zionist Organisation, the Alliance Israélite Universelle, B'nai B'rith and others – as the hub of a Jewish world conspiracy (Cohn, 1967). In each case, however, the assimilation of real life organisations within a conspiratorial explanatory framework preceded the inevitable leap from the 'undeniable to the unbelievable' (Hofstadter, 1967: 37–38) which meant that, in the end, it only helped to reproduce and sustain the conspiratorial view of the world and its explanatory logic.

The incorporation, within the conspiracy theory, of arguments originating from contemporary, mainstream analysis of politics and international relations is not the only strategy at the conspiracy theorist's disposal in the perpetual quest for social acceptance. In the 1990s, at the time when the idea of the New World Order conspiracy was seen by the mainstream in the US as the provenance of far-right movements and various antigovernment militias, a number of writers sought to establish links with other, more popular and politically less-contentious domains of stigmatised knowledge (Barkun, 2006, Goldberg, 2001). UFO citations and alien abduction, 'motifs regarded sympathetically by tens of millions of Americans' proved particularly convenient (Barkun, 2006: 180). While doing little to bring conspiracy theories closer to the mainstream of academic enquiry, the alliance with 'UFOlogy' helped to sanitise the conspiracy culture in terms of its underlying politics and provide it with a route to the 'territory of semi-respectable beliefs' (ibid.: 83). This coming together of conspiracy theories and other domains of stigmatised knowledge was facilitated by the fact that beliefs in extraterrestrial invasion and pseudoscience are, just like conspiracy claims, sustained by a perpetual doubt about the credibility of mainstream sources. This means that, while providing conspiracy theory with an innocuous image and a new audience, the other domains of counterknowledge appropriated, from conspiracism, a ready made framework of conspiratorial mass manipulation, which helped them make sense of their own difficult relations with the dominant regimes of knowledge and truth.

The constant evolution of conspiracy theories is also manifested in the way in which writers often seek to differentiate their views from other variants of conspiracism which are, implicitly or explicitly, set up as crude, naïve, ideologically problematic or just plain wrong (Billig, 1988, Byford and Billig, 2001). As much as conspiracism sometimes appears as a single culture, it is marred by constant rivalry and even animosity among its different exponents, all of whom are eager to be recognised as respectable, both by those within and by those outside the conspiracist community. For example, the US radio host Alex Jones dismissed David Icke's theory about alien lizards ruling the world as 'ridiculous Hollywood stuff', claiming that it discredits 'all the reality we're talking about' (*David Icke, the Lizards and the Jews*, 2001). After the Second World War, this rhetoric of distancing was particularly common among those who sought to dissociate themselves from accusations of antisemitism and create a new politically more palatable version of conspiracy theory. Gary Allen (1972: 11), in outlining the plot by the Council on Foreign Relations and associated organisations, explicitly dismissed those who argue that the conspiracy is Jewish, Catholic or Masonic on the grounds that rather than helping expose the *real* conspiracy, such writings 'play in the hands of those who want the public to believe that all conspiratorialists are screwballs'. Jim Marrs (2000: 61) similarly argues, in his bestselling book *Rule by Secrecy*, that those 'attempting to bring race or religion into a discussion of modern secret societies and conspiracies only serve to confuse the issue and repel conscientious researchers'.

The changes in the conspiracy culture after the Second World War and the frequency with which conspiracy theorists today distance themselves from the idea of a Jewish complot open the possibility that explanations that focus on the machinations of the Council on Foreign Relations, the Bilderbergers and the myriad of other similar groups, need not be linked to the long-standing tradition of antisemitic conspiracy theories. In fact, much of the new secret society mythology belongs to a genre of conspiracy theory that Michael Barkun (2006: 79) calls 'New World Order lite'. In it, most of the themes of the conspiracy tradition and most of the features of its explanatory style are represented in a semi-respectable, seemingly uncontroversial and, most importantly, outwardly unprejudiced way.

A closer inspection of specific texts reveals, however, that in the world of conspiracy theories, the boundaries between the politically palatable and the disreputable are seldom clear cut. While a writer may seek to dissociate him or herself from the 'outdated' trends within the conspiracy tradition, including the focus on the Jewish provenance of the alleged plot, they nevertheless continue to operate in an ideological space with a long antisemitic tradition (Billig, 1978, 1989). The impact of the antisemitic legacy of the conspiracy culture on the contemporary, seemingly non-antisemitic, conspiracy theories is especially visible in the way in which the theorist places the notion of the contemporary and ongoing plot in the appropriate historical context.

Continuities within the conspiracy tradition

One of the key concerns in any conspiracy theory is the origin and the history of the alleged plot. A conspiracy that is believed to be the motive force in history cannot be reasonably conceived as historically isolated. It would be implausible to argue, for example, that before the Council on Foreign Relations was founded in 1921, or before the Bilderberg group was formed in 1954, things happened by chance, while since then everything has been the result of a conspiracy. Just as it cannot be convincingly argued that 9/11, 'the mother of all conspiracies' and a hoax that required the collusions of hundreds of complicit individuals was a singular event hatched by the neoconservatives within the Bush administration in the months between the election victory in November 2000 and September 2001. The conspiracy theory of society is a view of the world not only as it is at present but also as it always was. Hence, specific plots need to be, and invariably are, imagined as links in a longer chain of conspiracies. Even the earliest works of the conspiracy tradition, the books by Barruel and Robison, presented the French Revolution not as a historically isolated scheme but as a continuation, by the Illuminati, of the machinations of the Knights Templar and the Freemasons.

When locating current plots and schemes within the centuries-long line of conspiratorial activity, conspiracy theorists seldom set out to write the history of the conspiracy from scratch. Instead, they draw on the work of their predecessors: they refer to, cite and quote established sources within the conspiracy culture, and in doing so place their own discoveries and revelations about the present within a broader tradition of explanation. In the 1960s, for example, exponents of the new mythology of secret societies, who had their sights on the machinations of the Council on Foreign Relations, revived the late eigtheenth century anti-Illuminati literature as a means of 'contextualising' the contemporary plot. In 1967, more than 150 years after it was first published, Robison's *Proofs of Conspiracy* was reissued in the United States by the John Birch Society. In the introduction to the reprint, an anonymous commentator explicitly acknowledged the continuing relevance of this book and established a direct connection between the Illuminati and the more recent world elite organisations:

> The main habitat [of the Illuminati] these days seems to be the great subsidized universities, tax-free foundations, mass media communication systems, government bureaus such as the State Department, and a myriad of private organisations such as the Council on Foreign Relations. (quoted in Lipset and Raab, 1978: 258)

In the work of Gary Allen, the present-day plot is also presented as a continuation of that orchestrated by the Illuminati: the means of mass manipulation devised by Adam Weishaupt and his henchmen are said to have provided 'models for Communist methodology' (Allen, 1972: 80). Similar acknowledgments of the relevance not only of both Robison's and Barruel's work, but also of other conspiracy 'classics' have become ubiquitous in conspiracy literature. This is why the reference sections of conspiracy books often read like a catalogue of the conspiracy tradition.

This continuity within the conspiracy culture, sustained by the need to place the plot in the appropriate historical context, is facilitated further by the conspiracy theory's inherent problem with proof. Writers of conspiracy material are accountable for the claims they make and the quality of the supporting arguments. And yet, conspiracy theorists, by definition, deal with imperfect evidence: they are concerned with matters that are inherently secret and which the most powerful forces in the world are working hard to suppress. Conspiracy theories can, therefore, never offer incontrovertible proof. As was stated in an editorial published in the 1970s in the British far-right publication *Spearhead*, 'if such a degree of proof was available, there would no longer be a conspiracy' (cited in Billig, 1978: 309).

To address the tricky issue of evidence, conspiracy writers tend to interpret the world around them through the work of other conspiracy theorists, past and present, and invoke their authority as a substitute for direct proof. They do so, of course, without acknowledging that, in an overwhelming number of cases, their source's claims are also reinterpretations of someone else's work. Over time, this compulsion to regurgitate the works of others, and simply adapt it to new circumstances, acquired a momentum of its own, to the point where it has now become difficult to construct a theory of world conspiracy that does not, at least inadvertently, draw upon the cultural heritage of the conspiracy tradition (Billig, 1989). After all, the main criterion for a successful conspiracy theory is that it is recognised as such by the wider community of conspiracy enthusiasts, who will judge it, among other things, according to whether it echoes the motifs and arguments of the conspiracy tradition, and according to how knowledgeable the author appears to be of the canonical works of the genre. This is, ultimately, why conspiracy theories so often sound alike and why the explanatory style examined in the previous chapter remains so persistent and robust.

This continuity of thought within the conspiracy tradition is important in relation to antisemitism. As we have seen in Chapter 3, between the mid-nineteenth century and the end of the Second World War, antisemitism was the dominant motif in conspiracy theories. Much of the conspiratorial literature of that period, but also *about* that period, revolves around the idea of a Jewish conspiracy. This means that, when authors today reflect on the history of the plot – a task that requires them to recognise the relevance of past conspiracies and past conspiracy theories – they invariably come into contact with the antisemitic legacy of the conspiracy culture.

The New World Order and the causes of the Bolshevik Revolution

The interpretations of the origins of the Russian Revolution offer an illustrative example of how, in elaborating on the history of the conspiracy, the theorist is constantly 'battling against the trends of his own political heritage' (Billig, 1978: 159). It is today virtually impossible to find an elaborate account of world conspiracy that does not allege, in one way or another, that understanding the causes of the Russian Revolution of 1917 demands a different explanation to that found in mainstream historiography. The allegation is that the Bolsheviks' rise to power was bankrolled by a group of American financiers and industrialists. In *Rule by Secrecy*, Jim Marrs writes that 'there indeed exists a wealth of documentation indicating that the Russian Revolution – indeed the very creation of communism – sprang from Western conspiracies beginning even before World War I' (Marrs, 2000: 192). In another conspiracy best-seller, *The New World Order* by Pat Robertson, it is alleged that a group of American businessmen, with the aid of the members of 'the British Round Table' and a 'very secret society' operating from Geneva, financed Lenin's and Trotsky's revolutionary endeavours (Robertson, 1991: 71–73, 178). A virtually identical claim appears in Gary Allen's *None Dare Call It Conspiracy* (1972), David Icke's *The Biggest Secret* (1999), John Coleman's *The Conspirators Hierarchy: The Committee of 300* (1992), as well as on countless websites from the United States through Eastern Europe, to the Middle East, and beyond.

In the writing of the likes of Robertson, Allen or Marrs, the involvement of American bankers in the financing of the Bolsheviks is not explicitly discussed as an example of a *Jewish* conspiracy. In fact, all three authors have, in one way or another, sought to distance themselves from the notion of a Jewish plot. However, as soon as one looks more closely into the sources for their claims about a 'Western conspiracies' and 'American businessmen', a different picture emerges. Jim Marrs's *Rule by Secrecy* (2000) is a case in point. In this book, the five-page section in which the true origins of the Russian Revolution are 'exposed' is based on seven sources, most of them books by conspiracy theorists. Among them is the today largely forgotten work *Czarism and the Revolution* by Arsene de Goulévitch (1962). Marrs identifies de Goulévitch as a particularly important source, given that, as a Russian, he was an eyewitness to 'the early days of Bolshevism' (Marrs, 2000: 192). What Marrs omitted to mention, however, is that de Goulévitch – his key 'witness' – was a White Russian general and antisemitic campaigner who fled to Paris after the revolution, where he campaigned against 'Jewish propaganda' about pre-revolutionary Russia. His book *Czarism and the Revolution*, originally published in French in the 1930s, attracted interest from far-right circles in the United States and Britain after a translation was published in California in 1962 (see Billig, 1978). In de Goulévitch's writing (unlike in Marrs's) the revolution is presented as the complot by Jewish bankers, affiliates of the 'Rheine-Westphalian Syndicate', the same mysterious organisation of rich Jews targeted in post-revolutionary antisemitic pamphlets publicised in the West by various Russian émigré organisations. In fact, the main source for de Goulévitch's claims, which Marrs indirectly reproduces, was the antisemitic pamphlet *The German-Bolshevik Conspiracy*, and the writings of Boris Brasol, the man who brought the *Protocols of the Elders of Zion* to the United States, and who was responsible for much of the content of Henry Ford's *The International Jew* (see Chapter 3).

Significantly, when citing Arsene de Goulévitch and acknowledging the significance of his writing as a source of historical knowledge, Marrs does not claim to have first-hand familiarity with de Goulévitch's tract. Instead, he merely reproduces passages from *Czarism and the Revolution* which are quoted in Gary Allen's *None Dare Call It Conspiracy* (1972), where de Goulévitch's motives, political leanings and sources are also concealed. This, in many ways, is precisely the point, one that illustrates perfectly the conspiracy tradition's unstoppable momentum and the subtle, but persistent influence of its antisemitic legacy. As Billig (1978) pointed out in relation to the use of de Goulévitch's work in Gary Allen's book, by drawing upon the conspiracy tradition and citing an antisemitic source, Allen leaves a paper trail that directs his readers to the kind of antisemitism that post-war conspiracy theorists wanted to avoid being associated with. In doing so, Allen (even if inadvertently) legitimises and perpetuates the conspiracy tradition's antisemitic heritage. In some ways, Jim Marrs is nothing more than the representative of the next generation of conspiracy theorists who, although one additional step away from the openly antisemitic literature, remains firmly rooted in the same tradition of thought. With the passage of time, the paper trail might be getting longer, but it still leads to the same end.

In *Rule by Secrecy*, a further and more direct link with the conspiracy culture's antisemitic legacy is apparent in the treatment of the Rothschild family. Ever since the nineteenth century, the Rothschilds, who combined Jewishness, financial wealth and international connections, have been the epitome of the international Jewish conspiracy (Barkun, 2006). The family name continues to feature in conspiratorial narratives to the present day, although writers of the post-1945 era have tended to play down their importance. Gary Allen, for example, while mentioning the Rothschilds, often emphasised the greater role, in the conspiracy, of the manifestly non-Jewish industrialists, the Rockefellers or the Morgans, in part so as to avoid accusations that he is selectively targeting Jews.

In *Rule by Secrecy*, however, the role of the Rothschilds in the world conspiracy is recognised without any distancing or mitigation. In contrast to Gary Allen, Marrs relegates the non-Jewish industrialists, J.P. Morgan and John D. Rockefeller, to the role of mere 'operatives' or 'gofers' who, in early twentieth-century were enlisted as 'fronts for the Rothschild organisation' (Marrs, 2000, 61–62, see also Icke, 1999). Jewish names frequently encountered in conspiratorial accounts of the Russian Revolution – Kuhn, Loeb, Schiff and others – are also said to be linked to the Rothschilds, either through family or through business ties, but always as their subordinates. In fact, Marrs gradually weaves a narrative which quite openly points to the Rothschild dynasty as the

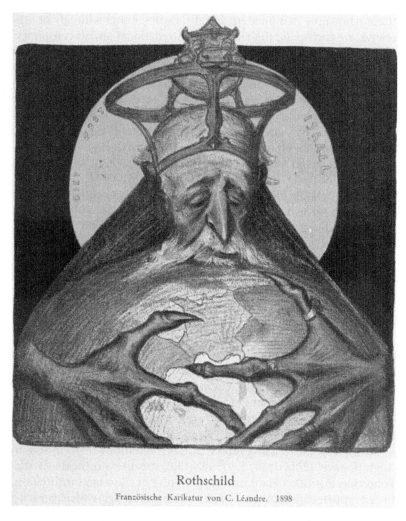

Rothschild

Französische Karikatur von C. Léandre. 1898

Figure 5.1 Antisemitic political cartoon entitled "Rothschild" by the French caricaturist, C. Leandre (1898) (United States Holocaust Memorial Museum)

pinnacle of the conspiratorial hierarchy. He claims for example that the Rothschilds were behind the creation of the Council on Foreign Relations, the Skull and Bones society and all the sinister secret and semi-secret organisations featured in most contemporary New World Order conspiracy theories. In the light of such claims, Marrs's attempts at distancing from antisemitism, evidenced in his apparent rejection of those who argue that 'modern secret societies, either willingly or otherwise, are furthering the aims of an international Jewish conspiracy' (ibid.: 60), suddenly appear less convincing. This is especially so given that the Rothschilds are said to derive power and influence not just from their business acumen and good connections, but also from 'the metaphysical aspects' of their background, especially their knowledge of the 'Cabalistic tradition' and 'deep understanding of ancient mysteries' (ibid.: 80). The source of the family's influence is therefore directly linked with its Jewish heritage, echoing the worst excesses of conspiratorial antisemitism found in the writings of the likes of Gougenot des Mousseaux or Nesta Webster.

Jim Marrs's book is by no means an isolated case. A similar homage to the conspiracy theory's antisemitic past is to be found in William T. Still's *New World Order: The Ancient Plan of Secret Societies* (1990, see Barkun, 2006), Pat Robertson's *The New World Order* (1991) and other similar literature. Robertson's book, for example, reflects on a motif which many contemporary conspiracy theorists argue is central for understanding the workings of the New World Order and the history of the conspiracy: the link which connects the Illuminati and the wealthy bankers, financiers and industrialists who, among other things, financed the Russian Revolution. Perhaps unsurprisingly, the author of *The New World Order* finds this link in the power of the Rothschilds. In 1782, the Illuminati are said to have moved from Ingolstadt to Frankfurt, a city 'controlled by the Rothschild family'. On arrival, the secret society supposedly infiltrated the wealthy local Masonic lodge, of which the Rothschilds were members and polluted the influential family with the 'occultism of Weishaupt's Illuminated Freemasonry'. This, for Robertson, is a key discovery, the 'missing link' that ties the Illuminati 'occultism' to 'high finance' (Robertson, 1991: 181–182). It is not a coincidence that Robertson identified Frankfurt as the centre of Illuminati infiltration: in early nineteenth century, a Frankfurt Masonic lodge, which consisted mainly of Jews (Loge zur aufgehenden Morgenröthe), was frequently targeted by German nineteenth-century antisemitic conspiracy theorists (von Bieberstein, 1977). What is more, the discovery of the so-called missing link was not the result of any painstaking archival research on Robertson's part, or the product of his imagination: it was lifted directly from Nesta Webster's *World Revolution* (1921: 19–20), where the same link is presented as one not between the Illuminati and 'high finance', but between the Illuminati and Jews.

The examples from Marrs's and Robertson's work, which are representative of a pattern that permeates contemporary conspiracy culture, illustrate how, while apparently distancing itself from the dishonourable tradition of the *Protocols of the Elders of Zion*, and while portraying itself as a more reasonable and sound explanation of history and politics, the post-war secret society mythology – the 'New World Order lite' genre of conspiracy theory – is in fact a continuation and refinement of that same tradition. It is interesting, however, that whenever attention is drawn to the presence, in contemporary conspiracy literature, of antisemitic motifs, coded references or innuendos, the debate tends to focus on the issue of intent and whether the authors in questions are antisemites whose prejudices are comparable to those of, for example, Nesta Webster or Boris Brasol (Pipes, 1997, for instance). And yet, it could be argued that whether Robertson, Marrs or indeed any other author of similar mate- rial is an 'antisemite' or not, or what his or her intentions were, is largely immaterial. The issue here is not the antisemitic dispositions or inten- tions (or the lack thereof) of individual conspiracy theorists, but the way in which a tradition of explanation which, for a variety of reasons to do with the way in which conspiracy theories are written and transmitted, and with their internal logic, organisation and epistemology, finds it hard to escape its own disreputable ideological and intellectual history. More important than the authors' intent, therefore, is the *consequence* of their work. By recognising the relevance of antisemitic works of the past and by perpetuating their message (albeit often in a coded or veiled form or through the subtlest of hints), the recent literature ensures the persist- ence of antisemitic themes within the conspiracy culture. Even just the constant repetition of recognisably Jewish names in the context of the narrative of conspiracy, and the allusion to Jewish individuals and fami- lies as the source of longstanding sinister influence in the world, desen- sitises the consumers of these seemingly innocuous conspiracy theories and broadens the boundaries of acceptable opinion to the point where the notion of a Jewish conspiracy becomes recognised as a legitimate explanation of political and historical reality.

Conspiracy tradition and the alternative interpretations of 9/11

Conspiracy theories expounded by the likes of Jim Marrs or Pat Robertson are particularly susceptible to the influence of the conspiracy tradition's antisemitic heritage because they are, above all, historical accounts that specifically set out to link a whole variety of plots, historical as well as contemporary, into a single, continuous narrative of conspiracy. Not all conspiracy theories are like that, however. Some pay far less attention to the plot's historical origins and tend to focus on a single, contemporary event. For example, David Ray Griffin's writing on 9/11 conspiracy theory, or the internet sensation *Loose Change*, contain no allusions to the Illuminati, the Rothschilds or the Bolshevik Revolution (although they do make comparisons between 9/11 and Pearl Harbour and interpret both as 'false flag' incidents). Conspiracy theories about climate change, AIDS or the assassination of John F. Kennedy are also often presented outside the context of the longer chain of sinister plots and machinations of the world's elite. These strands of conspiracy theory stake much of their reputation on the fact that they are primarily concerned with debunking official explanations, rather than looking for the culprits or tracing everything back to the Illuminati. This is especially so given that they are not confined to the right, but include sections of the left, or very often a fusion of the two (Berlet, 2009).

And yet, even these explanations cannot escape the influence of the conspiracy tradition. As already indicated, a conspiracy theory which does not situate the plot within the appropriate historical context, or which does not purport to provide a comprehensive, all-encompassing account is, at best, an incomplete explanation. There are, of course, those who argue that the World Trade Centre was destroyed through a controlled demolition, masterminded by the neoconservative elite and carried out by government agents, but unless this claim is adequately contextualised, it opens more questions than it answers. How could a plot of that size and complexity be realised without there being a single leak, mistake or a whistleblower? How could the required amount of explosives be planted in an office block without anyone noticing? Who has the necessary will and power to orchestrate an atrocity of that scale? Questions such as these do not remain unanswered for long, however. The explanatory vacuum left behind by incomplete accounts, generated as part of the 'it is not a theory theory' (see previous chapter) is filled by writers, broadcaster and activists who already 'know' who has both the motive and the wherewithal to perform fiendish acts of unprecedented magnitude. In other words, the single event conspiracy theories are instantly absorbed within, and influenced by, the broader conspiracist culture.

On the websites affiliated with the different branches of the 9/11 Truth movement, one does not need to dig deep to find evidence of such influence. An article published in 2009 on 911Truth.org mentions, among the whole list of 'curious coincidences' about the attacks, the fact that the plane that struck the North Tower hit the offices of a brokerage company whose senior executives are members of the Bilderberg

Group, the Trilateral Commission, a 'secret society called Quill and Dagger, the membership of which includes Paul Wolfowitz, Sandy Berger and Stephen Hadley' (Ryan, 2009). This revelation is supposed to provide the answer to the question about who planted the military grade explosives that brought down the Twin Towers, and how they could do so inconspicuously. On the same website, the 9/11 Truth movement's apparent failure to mobilise public opinion in the United States is also attributed to the machinations of the Bilderbergers, the Council on Foreign Relations and the Trilateral Commission, whose purpose 'is to manipulate world governments and economies to promote a global, capitalist agenda commonly referred to as the "New World Order"' (Shaw, 2005).

As well as attracting ideas, motifs and arguments from the conspiracy tradition, the 9/11 Truth movement acts as a magnet for the wider conspiracist community. Jim Marrs, for example, joined the Scholars for 9/11 Truth and contextualised the movement's claims by linking 9/11 to the machinations of the Council on Foreign Relations (see Taibbi, 2009). The internet documentary *9/11 – The Great Illusion*, written and produced by George Humphrey, articulates the same doubts about the official version of 9/11 as the much more popular *Loose Change*, but places them in the context of the longstanding Illuminati conspiracy. Furthermore, exponents of 9/11 conspiracy theories, including David Ray Griffin, routinely feature on Alex Jones's radio show and public events organised by Jones's franchise, where their ideas are, even if only by association, placed within the overall narrative of Illuminati-led, New World Order conspiracy involving greedy 'baron bankers' and other ubiquitous protagonists of the conspiracy tradition.

Crucially, from the idea of a New World Order to the wilder reaches of the conspiracy culture and its antisemitic variants is usually a short (although not inevitable) step. In 2007, in an article published on the Scholars for 9/11 Truth website, the organisation's founder James H. Fetzer, confidently asserted that over the years the 9/11 Truth movement had successfully refuted the official account of the attacks, but that what remains to be explained is 'how it was actually done' (Fetzer, 2007). He went on to state that 'if it turns out that only unconventional methods are able to account for the depth and breadth of devastation at the WTC, this points in the direction of the military-industrial complex, since – apart from Israel – it is the sole likely source of those means'. This sentence contains a curious allegation that might be overlooked by the casual visitor to Fetzer's website. It suggests that only two entities in the whole world have at their disposal the 'unconventional methods' required to destroy the Twin Towers and cover their tracks: the omnipotent 'military industrial complex' and the state of Israel. Although the phrasing of the sentence suggests that Fetzer considers the former to be the more likely culprit, in a later elaboration on this theme he reveals that, in his mind, the distinction between the 'military industrial complex' and Israel might not be all that clear-cut. In the article '9/11 and the neo-con agenda', Fetzer insists that the question about Israel's connection to 9/11 is a perfectly reasonable one to ask, given that among the most influential people in American establishment, including the neoconservatives, are Jews whose loyalties lie with Israel, rather than with the United States (Fetzer, 2008). Fetzer's article is, therefore, both about the culpability of Israel, which is said to have American foreign policy in its grip, and about the dual loyalty of American Jews, who are responsible for America finding herself in the hands of an alien power and a victim of the hitherto unexplained terrorist attack. This is little more than a contemporary variant of the old antisemitic, conspiracist canard about the disloyalty of Jews and their usurpation of power in the name of communal interests and the accumulation of wealth. Fetzer's argument was, of course, not particularly original. In the weeks following the 9/11 attacks, David Duke, the neo-Nazi activist and former Grand Wizard of the Ku Klux Klan, offered an interpretation of 9/11, which although cruder and coated in overtly racist language, was not dissimilar to Fetzer's. He too blamed the destruction of the Twin Towers on the 'Jewish bosses of American foreign policy' acting in the name of 'world wide Jewish Supremacism' (cited in Stern, 2006: 44).

Of course, not all 9/11 conspiracy theorists would follow Fetzer in implicating either Jews or Israel in the 9/11 attacks. Some would probably seek to dissociate themselves from such antisemitic innuendos and even accuse Fetzer (who is considered something of an oddball within the world of 9/11 Truth movement) of discrediting the movement and diverting attention from the important work of uncovering the 'truth' about 11 September 2001. However, once again, the issue is not about specific authors but about the way in which a conspiracy based explanation of a significant event – even if it does not explicitly situate itself within the conspiracy tradition – leaves itself vulnerable to contamination by the latter's antisemitic element.

Israel, the Left and 'new antisemitism'

So far, the discussion of the connection between conspiracy theories and antisemitism focused on the writing by authors associated with the right-wing of politics. However, recent years have witnessed an increased awareness of a seemingly new brand of conspiratorial antisemitism propagated mainly by sections of the left. The phenomenon, which has become known as 'new antisemitism', or anti-Zionism, is defined by the fact that the central object of disparagement and prejudice are not Jews as such, but Israel as the Jewish state (Chesler, 2003, Iganski and Kosmin, 2003, Foxman, 2004, Taguieff, 2004). Rather than viewing Israel as a country whose policies and actions, like that of any other, can (and indeed should be) criticised on merit, sections of the political left have come to view it as the source of uniquely harmful influence in the world. Israel's actions, and even its very existence, are believed to be an expression of the uniquely iniquitous nationalist ideology (Zionism), which is considered to be comparable to Nazism: it is racist, imperialist, expansionist and tyrannical. Transgressions of the Israeli state – from human rights violations to military actions that are deemed, by critics, to be disproportionate – are seen as inherently more sinister than those committed by any other state in history, with the exception of Nazi Germany. Furthermore, Israel's policies are seen as sufficiently egregious to undermine its basic legitimacy: exponents of 'new antisemitism' often go as far as to call for the dismantlement of Israel. This makes Israel the only member of the United Nations whose very existence is routinely brought into question and Jews the only people whose right to self-determination, it is argued, should be retrospectively revoked. Crucially, as David Cesarani (2004: 72) notes, the definitive crossing of the boundary between criticism of Israel and antisemitism occurs at the point where the former becomes articulated in language typically associated with antisemitism, that is, when it 'intentionally or unintentionally uses or echoes long-established anti-Jewish discourse, characterising Jews inside Israel or in the Jewish diaspora as singularly wealthy, powerful, conspiratorial, treacherous and malign.' In other words, when it is embellished with the motifs of a Jewish conspiracy.

The conspiracist element of 'new antisemitism' is most obvious in discussions about the existence and the machinations of what has become known as the Israel/Zionist/Jewish lobby. A common assumption of left-wing anti-Zionist critique is that Israel commits its fiendish acts with the unwavering political, military and financial support from America and to a lesser extent Britain, whose governments are in the grip of the menacing and all-powerful pro-Israel lobby. When the sinister influence of 'the Lobby' is discussed in the context of US politics, the focus of attention is on organisations which campaign for the interests of the American Jewish community and Israel, such as the

American Israel Public Affairs Committee (AIPAC), the Anti-Defamation League (ADL) or the American Jewish Committee (AJC). Although these institutions differ in terms of their legal status, agenda, means of operating and degree of influence, for the critics of 'the Lobby', they are a single, 'hugely powerful, coherent, covert, and therefore conspiratorial political agent' (Hirsh, 2007: 50, see also Fine, 2006). What is more, the Israel lobby is seen as distinct from all other lobby groups campaigning on different political issues in the US; it is believed to have virtually unlimited financial resources, which it deploys cunningly to purchase political influence on an unprecedented scale. According to critics, 'the Lobby' has nothing short of 'a stranglehold' over the US Congress (Fisk, 2006); it can 'eliminate' any politician critical of Israel through disparagement or withdrawal of funds (Avnery, 2003: 45) and even has the power to destroy the career of American presidents (Blankfort, 2003). Over the past decade, it has been blamed not just for America's support for Israel but also for the rise to power of the neoconservatives, for the American-led invasion of Iraq and Afghanistan and even for any future confrontation between the United States and Iran.

'The Lobby' is also said to be active in Britain, where it functions through a less-organised network of politicians, advisers and media moguls. The former British Labour Party MP Tam Dalyell was alluding to the power of 'the Lobby' when he stated that Tony Blair's foreign policy was 'unduly influenced by a cabal of Jewish advisers' who have infiltrated the government (cited in Cesarani, 2004: 75). In the left-wing British media, journalists and commentators have on occasions gone as far as to count the number of Jews among Tony Blair's advisers and have even scrutinised who has had breakfast with, or may be married to a Jew or a 'Zionist', all with the view of uncovering the manoeuvrings of 'the Lobby' at the heart of government (see Cesarani, 2004, Hirsh, 2007, Rosenfeld, 2004).

The direct manipulation of political elites is, however, only part of 'the Lobby's' modus operandi. Where 'the Lobby' is said to be the most powerful, and the most sinister, is in its control over public opinion. It manages the press, television, mainstream publishers and Hollywood, and, as a result, is able to silence all those who dare to criticise it. Its main weapon is the label of antisemitism: anyone casting a critical eye on the sinister, covert operations of 'the Lobby' is immediately branded an 'antisemite' by the powerful Zionist media machinery. Having been falsely and permanently tarnished by this incriminating label (which is said to be incriminating in part because 'the Lobby' made it so), victims become ostracised from polite company and the mainstream of society

(Cockburn and St Clair, 2003, Ingrams, 2001, Mearsheimer and Walt, 2006).

Accounts of the machinations of 'the Lobby' formulated by those aligned with the political left contain many features of the classic, right-wing conspiracy theory, including the preoccupation with an anonymous and elusive Jewish collective that skilfully directs the foreign policy of Western democracies, the routine exaggeration of the

Figure 5.2   'The Zionist Lobby' by Carlos Latuff, 2007 (with author's permission)

financial and political influence of the Jewish diaspora, particularly in America, and the assumption about the essential disloyalty of Jews. In fact, accounts of 'the Lobby' are so blatantly conspiratorial that their exponents on occasions candidly admit that what they are alleging *is* essentially a Jewish plot, one that resembles the classic antisemitic conspiracy theory. Writing in the magazine *Tikkun*, Paul Buhle (2003) writes, for example, that when one looks at the power of the pro-Israel lobby 'it is almost as if the anti-Semitic *Protocols of Zion*, successfully fought for a century, have suddenly returned with an industrial sized grain of truth'. The British historian Tony Judt has also admitted that claims about the sinister power of the 'Israel lobby' sound 'an awful lot like, you know, the *Protocols of the Elders of Zion* and the conspiratorial theory of the Zionist Occupational Government and so on' but that, while 'unfortunate', this cannot be helped as this is 'just how it is' (cited in Hirsh, 2007: 86). Such comparisons are rhetorically significant, because writers use the notoriety of the *Protocols* to accentuate the sinister influence of 'the Lobby', while at the same time forestalling any accusations of antisemitism by implying that, despite the resemblances, their claims are distinguishable from those of the right. As Tony Judt put it, 'you can't help it if idiots [on the right], once every 24 hours, with their stopped political clock are on the same time as you' (ibid.). Thus, following the pattern examined already in Chapter 2, a distinction is drawn between disreputable (and false) conspiracy theories of the right and the accounts of *real* conspiracies uncovered by the left, although, in this case at least, it is admitted that both lines of inquiry have arrived at the same conclusion.

The presence of antisemitic motifs in left-wing writing cannot be explained in terms of the continuities within the conspiracy tradition that are so easily discernible in the literature of the right. Exegeses of 'the Lobby' theory of American politics, such as John Mearsheimer's and Stephen Walt's 500-page book *The Israel Lobby and U.S. Foreign Policy* (2007) or the different contributions on Israel published in periodicals such as *Tikkun* or *CounterPunch* (e.g. Cockburn and St. Clair, 2003) do not situate the machinations of the AIPAC within a longer history of (Jewish) conspiracy. The likes of Kuhn, Loeb or the Rothschilds are, similarly, not identified as the precursors of 'the Lobby'. When the latter's origins are commented on, they tend to be traced to the actions of individuals who rarely feature in contemporary right-wing conspiracy theories, such as the Supreme Court Justice Louis D. Brandeis or Rabbi Stephen Wise, two public figures who are said to have influenced Woodrow Wilson to support the Balfour Declaration in 1917

(Mearsheimer and Walt, 2007). Equally, although some of the central tenets of 'new antisemitism' – including the tendency to equate Israel with Nazism and South African apartheid or the calls for the abolition of Israel – date back to the late 1960s, when they were disseminated around the world by the Soviet anti-Zionist propaganda (see Chapter 3), there is no straightforward link between the latter's overtly antisemitic rhetoric and contemporary conspiratorial accounts of the Israel lobby. The mainstream of the European left never had any truck with the crude antisemitism of Soviet 'Zionologists'. The motif of a Jewish/Israeli conspiracy played a marginal role even in the writing of radical Trotskyite groups that peddled Soviet-style anti-Israeli rhetoric in western Europe and the United States in 1960s and 1970s (see Billig, 1987a).

Also, the preoccupation with the machinations of the Israel lobby is not ubiquitous in contemporary criticism of Israel. There are large sections on the left that are highly critical of Israel but which nevertheless downplay the role of the AIPAC and other organisations constitutive of 'the Lobby'. Noam Chomsky (1983: 13), for example, has dismissed the insinuation that America's support for Israel is attributable to the 'effectiveness of the American Jewish community in political life and influencing opinion', on the grounds that such a view 'overestimates the role of political pressure groups in decision making'. He argued that the likes of the AIPAC are a 'paper tiger' that appears powerful only when its interests happen to coincide with those of the policy makers in Washington (see Blankfort, 2003). For Chomsky (2002: 117), Israel is 'utterly dependent on the United States and hence dependable, serving US needs as a local "cop on the beat" and as a mercenary state employed for US purposes'. The view of Israel as America's stooge has a longer tradition within left-wing thought. In Soviet propaganda up to the late 1960s, Israel was mostly conceptualised as a tool of Western imperialism, its 'shock detachment', 'gendarme', 'Trojan horse' or 'puppet' in the Middle East (Hirszowicz, 1979, Wistrich, 1979). This interpretation of America's relationship with Israel gained wider currency among left-wing circles in the West at the time of the Vietnam War, when the conflict in the Middle East was viewed through the lens of the broader critique of American interventionism, which Chomsky's generation helped to articulate.

How does this predominant view of Israel as America's 'colony' morph, within the writing of the political left, into its opposite, namely the claim that those whose loyalty is ultimately with Israel control the United States? Moreover, what is it that leads writers who belong to a political tradition that has in the past been opposed to expression of antisemitism to adopt the motifs of antisemitic conspiracy theory? The answer to these questions lies in a particular pattern of thought that contributes to the widespread appeal of conspiracy theories. It is a well-established fact that conspiratorial explanations tend to flourish in response to unusual, dramatic and unforeseen events, such as wars, revolutions, major accidents, terrorist attacks or assassinations. The breakdown of existing explanations that often accompanies such events makes people more susceptible to causal accounts based on the existence of a hidden and deliberate plan, formulated in secret by powerful enemies (Groh, 1987, Byford and Billig, 2001). Or, as Young (1990: 104) put it, the 'human desire for explanation' always aids the conspiracy theory in its 'quest for public acceptance'. After the onset of Second Intifada in 2000, and even more so in the aftermath of 9/11 and the invasions of Afghanistan and Iraq, elements of the left began to question the common sense view that America's support for Israel stems from the desire to protect her own vital interest in the Middle East. They argued that the continuing financial and military support for Israel goes against the country's own economic, political and foreign policy interests, to the point of making the United States vulnerable to disastrous terrorist attacks and getting it embroiled in two bloody conflicts thousands of miles from American soil. Evidently, everything was not as it seems and the reasons why the only remaining superpower would forego its own interests was sought in the possibility that someone with their own agenda and motive was pulling the strings of American politics (see Fine, 2006). The ubiquitous 'Cui bono?' question lead to the so-called 'Israel connection', and once claims about the lobbying power of the AIPAC and similar organisations was added to the mix, only a short 'leap of imagination' was required before the left-wing criticism of American foreign policy in the Middle East slipped into the full blown theory about Jewish power.

The influence of the conspiracy tradition in this process was subtle and indirect. As already noted, conspiracy theorists have always coveted a place on the boundaries between the fringe and the mainstream, one that allows them to claim distance from the conventional wisdom while at the same time satisfying the craving for public recognition. This means that while feeding off the mainstream and seeking alliances with it, purveyors of conspiracy-based explanations also feed *into* it the notions that not everything is as it seems and that hidden forces might be at work. The century-long dominance of conspiratorial antisemitism has left behind it a rich inventory of images, motifs and tropes about

Jewish financial power and questionable loyalty, which although largely ostracised from polite conversation, nevertheless circulate in public discourse and colour the perceptions of events involving Jews, whether in Israel or in the diaspora. Thus, the suspicion that there *is* a conspiracy and that it involves Jews, which is apparent in some contemporary left-wing interpretations of America's foreign policy, created the necessary preconditions for the resurfacing of the 'underground repertoire of stereotypes, instinctively understood by both the utterer and the recipient' (Pulzer, 2003: 101). The 'antisemitic atmosphere' on the left is therefore sustained not through a whole-scale endorsement of the conspiracy tradition, but by 'the drip-drip-drip of argument, coded and implicit, clothed in allusion and wrapped in innuendo, always with a pre-emptive disavowal of any antisemitic intent' (ibid.). Lukasz Hirszowicz (1979: 62) made a similar observation about the emergence of antisemitic motifs in Soviet anti-Zionist conspiracy theory in the 1960s: once it was accepted that a shadowy elite within the Jewish diaspora might be the force behind the 'bogey' of Zionism, the next logical step was 'the application of traditional antisemitic notions of Jewish world power'.

The 'slippage from criticism of American foreign policy to wild eyed conspiracy theory' (Fine, 2006) apparent in the discussions of 'the Lobby' should not occur so easily, however. Left-wing thought is marked by long tradition of opposition to racism and a standing commitment to equality and social justice, which means that its contemporary exponents should be resistant to ideas traditionally peddled by their ideological opponents. And yet, as we have seen, among critics of 'the Lobby', this sensitivity is often lacking. This is at least in part because their ideological position is sustained by another key feature of the conspiracy theory, namely its essential *irrefutability*. As noted in Chapter 2, conspiratorial explanatory logic comprises a number of interpretative devices that makes the conspiracy theory immune to conventional cannons of proof and testing (e.g. by transforming disconfirming evidence into proof of the conspiracy). These devices protect the conspiracy theorist not just from challenges related to evidence or proof, but also from those made on *moral* grounds. Moral criticism, just like disconfirming evidence, can be attributed to the conspiracy and thus rendered invalid. This is an essential feature of the writing on 'the Lobby'. The very reason why the idea of a Jewish plot should be resisted – namely antisemitism – is perceived as a distraction, a label deliberately manufactured, manipulated and used by 'the Lobby' for silencing opponents, de-legitimising criticism of Israel and controlling public opinion. Thus, antisemitism ceases to be a danger to be avoided by all those discussing the sensitive issue of Jewish influence in politics, and is perceived, instead, exclusively as a weapon of Zionist self-legitimisation. This stance towards antisemitism goes hand in hand with the so-called Holocaust industry argument, popularised by Norman Finkelstein (2000). According to Finkelstein and his followers, the Holocaust has been exploited and instrumentalised by powerful Jews to justify Israel's aggression against the Palestinians and build a taboo around antisemitism (see Laqueur, 2006, Cesarani, 2004). The effect of this stance on antisemitism and the Holocaust, but also its underlying psychological function, is to undermine any sympathy for Jews that would normally foster resistance to antisemitic motifs. In other words, by persuading their audience, and, importantly, also themselves, that the moral standpoint from which their arguments can be criticised is consciously imposed by 'the Lobby' – and therefore an essential part of its sinister method – writers can pre-empt, destabilise and render unfounded any criticism of their ideological position. This places 'the Lobby' theory of America's foreign policy beyond moral reproach, removes the taboo surrounding antisemitism, reinforces the believers' conviction in the absolute truth of their views and inoculates them from any awareness of where the boundaries lie between acceptable and unacceptable opinion. The belief that everything, including the definition of what is acceptable, is manipulated by the sinister lobby not only shields the anti-Zionist worldview from the effects of disconfirming evidence, but also makes it vulnerable to the malign influence of motifs and stereotypes rooted in the conspiracy tradition.

Conclusion

The continuing presence of antisemitic motifs in conspiracy theories propagated by the right and the theorising about the machinations of the Zionist/Israel/Jewish lobby by sections of the political left are not unrelated phenomena. In sharing the motif of a Jewish plot, conspiracy theories propagated by both sides of the political spectrum are locked in a relationship of mutual reinforcement. A number of writers on the far-right of American politics have greeted the recent writing on 'the Lobby' as a long-awaited vindication of their views and have embraced it as a convenient source of 'respectable vocabulary for the articulation of antisemitic conspiracy theory' (Hirsh, 2007: 57). David Duke, for example, claimed that Mearsheimer's and Walt's work (which he describes as 'excellent') proves that his theory of 'Jewish Supremacism' has been correct all along (Lake, 2006) and has expressed similar admiration for the views of other anti-Zionists, including Tony Judt (see Hirsh, 2007). One can expect, therefore, that the writing of these respected mainstream academics will make its way into the footnotes of right-wing conspiracy literature, where it will be exploited as a source of much coveted credibility. At the same time, by persevering with their subtle allusions to the Jewish conspiracy, writers on the right (many of whom, incidentally, claim to be pro-Israel) continue to keep alive the gamut of stereotypes, motifs and tropes which will occasionally seep into the discourse of the left, especially in response to events which involve Israel, America's foreign policy in the Middle East or the Jewish community in the United States. In fact, this cooperation across the traditional ideological divides has already produced the 'routine stereotype' of twenty-first century antisemitism, namely the claim about the Jewish/Zionist dimension of the neoconservative elite in the United States and its role in taking America to war in Iraq. This motif is so prevalent today that it is threatening to become as robust a feature of conspiracy culture as that about the Jewish origins of Bolshevism (Cesarani, 2004).

Finally, understanding the link between conspiracy theory and antisemitism is noteworthy also because it says something about the complex causal relationship between the two phenomena. The commonly found emphasis on the intentions and dispositions of individual conspiracy theorists vis-à-vis antisemitism is underpinned by the assumption that conspiracy theories emerge as a manifestation or rationalisation of a more basic or profound feeling of animosity and hatred towards Jews. However, this is not necessarily the case. The belief in the existence of a Jewish plot can, and often does, emerges as a *consequence* of the endorsement of conspiracism, a tradition of explanation and a way of seeing the world that has, for reasons examined in this chapter, failed to exorcise the ghost of antisemitism from its past.

6
Psychology and Conspiracy Theory

In everyday discourse, believers in a conspiracy-based explanation are often labelled lunatics, kooks or paranoiacs. They are perceived as having 'an essential character weakness predisposing them to paranoia or gullibility' or as 'buffeted by forces not only beyond their control but beyond their ken' (Husting and Orr, 2007: 140). In literature on conspiracy theories written by historians, philosophers, sociologists or political scientists, one also frequently encounters explanations which are essentially of a psychological nature. Writers talk of conspiracy theories as manifestations of 'paranoia', 'anxiety', 'fantasy', 'hysteria', 'projection' and 'aggression', or, more recently, as fulfilling a profound psychological need for certainty in the precarious (post-) modern age.

Even though conspiracy theories are often recognised as being of intrinsic psychological interest, there has been comparatively little work specifically on the psychology of conspiracy theories. In recent years, a number of psychologists have commented on this dearth of empirical research and have lamented the fact that the phenomenon has been left, almost entirely, at the mercy of scholars from other disciplines (Abalakina-Paap et al., 1999, Leman, 2007, Swami and Coles, 2010, Graumann, 1987). And yet, this does not mean that psychology has had nothing to say about conspiracy theories. Over the years a number of research paradigms within psychology have been applied, directly or indirectly, to this phenomenon. Especially since the resurgence of public interest in conspiracy theories in the 1990s, there has been a burst of studies looking at different psychological factors that might account for the susceptibility of some people to conspiracist thinking.

The present chapter offers an overview of this research, beginning with probably the most overused psychological concept in literature on conspiracy theory, namely *paranoia*. Ever since Richard Hofstadter

(1967) published his seminal essay on the 'paranoid style' in American politics, conspiracy theories have been associated with this term whose provenance is in clinical psychiatry. The link between conspiracy theories and paranoia has become so strong that the two terms are now treated as almost synonymous: those who believe in conspiracy theories are said to do so because they are paranoid, while at the same time, paranoia is often defined by the belief in conspiracy theories (Knight, 2000). After a critical examination of the relationship between the two phenomena, the chapter surveys other, predominantly social psychological research that looked into a range of psychological factors that might account for why some people believe in conspiracy theories while others do not. As will become apparent, much of this work conceptualises conspiracy theories as a manifestation of *individual* beliefs and attitudes independent of social and interactional context in which they are produced. By identifying a number of shortcomings of this approach, the chapter argues that psychological aspects of conspiracy theories can be more productively investigated if conspiracy theories are approached as a *social phenomenon* and an evolving set of historically bound discourses and stories that people can draw upon, debate, challenge and modify as they collaboratively make sense of the world around them.

Conspiracy theories and paranoia

When psychological terms enter the vernacular, their meaning is usually much broader than what psychologists would deem appropriate. In everyday conversation, when a person is said to be 'hysterical', 'depressed', 'anxious' or 'obsessive', these terms are not used in the formal, clinical sense. The psychological label is applied in order to accentuate the strength of particular emotions or behaviours ('depression' rather than 'sadness', 'anxiety' rather than 'worry') or to mark them out as in some way excessive or disproportionate. Equally, when a person is said to be 'paranoid' this is, in most instances, an allusion not to the full set of clinical symptoms listed in diagnostic manuals, but to some feeling of persecution that is deemed by the speaker to be extreme or unwarranted. Since the middle of last century the word 'paranoia' has been widely used in this colloquial sense, to signify any excessive 'tendency to suspect or distrust others or believe oneself unfairly used' (Brown, 1993: 2097).

In non-psychological literature on conspiracy theories, the term 'paranoia' is mostly used in this broader sense. In his classic analysis of the 'paranoid style' in American politics, Richard Hofstadter (1967) openly asserted that his use of the term 'paranoid' to refer to the rhetorical style of the conspiracy theory is only analogous to the conventional, clinical meaning. Hofstadter was not interested in classifying conspiracy theorists as 'certifiable lunatics', but sought instead to analyse 'paranoid modes of expression' which share with clinical paranoia the excessive suspicion, aggression and fear of persecution (Hofstadter, 1967: 4). He was, in his own words, merely 'borrowing a clinical term for other purposes' (ibid.: 3). Nevertheless, the choice of analogy was not haphazard. Hofstadter's essay was not a disinterested description of a political style, but a well-crafted critique of an aspect of American political culture which he believed was dysfunctional. A term borrowed from psychology or psychiatry was crucial in setting up the beliefs, feelings or behaviours associated with the 'paranoid style' as in some sense irrational, unreasonable and dysfunctional. The same rhetorical use of the term 'paranoia' is apparent in the work of other authors who followed in Hofstadter's footsteps in their critique of conspiracy theories (e.g. Pipes, 1997).

Importantly however, the sense in which the term 'paranoia' is used in literature on conspiracy theories has the tendency to slip from the realm of metaphor to the original, clinical meaning. In Hofstadter's work, for example, the discussion of a paranoid political *style* occasionally drifts into the discussion of personal attributes and dispositions of individuals who subscribe to it. Exponents of conspiracy theories are referred to, at times, as 'the paranoid', in possession of unreasonably 'angry' or 'suspicious minds', or as susceptible to 'sadomasochistic fantasies' (e.g. Hofstadter, 1967: 1, 31, 34). This kind of language led Robert Goldberg (2001: xi) to suggest that, when examining conspiracy theorists, Hofstadter 'donned the while coat of a clinician'. A similar focus on the psychopathology of believers in conspiracies is observable in Daniel Pipes's (1997) work where, within a predominantly historical analysis of the conspiracy culture and 'political paranoia', instances of individual, paranoid behaviour are occasionally resorted to as the means of accounting for the beliefs of a number of pioneers of conspiracy theory. Thus Nesta Webster is said to have never opened her front door without a revolver in her hand, while the pro-Nazi Russian émigré and notorious antisemite Grigorii Schwartz-Bostunich believed that his Gestapo bodyguards were Masonic agents plotting against him.

This blurring of the boundaries between the clinical and the cultural meaning of paranoia is not limited to non-psychological literature. In *Political Paranoia: The Psychopolitics of Hatred*, Robert Robins and Jerrold

Post (1997: 5) use 'paranoia' to 'subsume both clinical paranoid illnesses and paranoid style and outlook' thereby effectively obliterating the distinction between the cultural and the clinical meaning of the term. Marvin Zonis and Craig Joseph (1994: 450), while retaining a distinction, in principle, between conspiracist thinking and paranoia, go on to suggest that the former could also be characterised as a 'disorder' and that the 'deficits and stressors that predispose an individual to conspiracy thinking are similar to, if less intense than, those involved in the aetiology of paranoid psychosis'.

So, what *is* 'paranoia' and how is it related to the belief in conspiracy theories? According to diagnostic criteria set out in the American Psychiatric Association's *Diagnostic and Statistical Manual of Mental Disorders* (DSM) 'paranoia' is not a mental disorder in its own right, but a common form of delusion found in patients suffering from schizophrenia and two specific types of delusional and personality disorders – persecutory delusional disorder and paranoid personality disorder (see Cromby and Harper, 2009, Freeman et al., 2002, Bentall et al., 2001). The DSM defines a delusion as 'a false personal belief based upon incorrect inference about external reality and firmly sustained in spite of what almost everyone else believes and in spite of what constitutes incontrovertible and obvious proof to the contrary' (APA, 1994: 765). Delusions classified as paranoid or persecutory include persistent and incorrigible beliefs about some form of unjustified persecution, usually involving individuals or powers conspiring to damage the sufferer's reputation or wellbeing, to cause them physical or psychological injury or to bring about their death.

Symptoms of paranoia described in the DSM are, however, not limited to those who are certified by the medical profession as suffering from some form of psychosis or personality disorder. Epidemiological research conducted over the years has found that symptoms associated with different types of mental disorders exist also in the general population, on a continuum of severity (e.g. Strauss, 1969, van Os et al., 2000, Johns and van Os, 2001). Paranoid and persecutory delusions have been shown to be present in up to 10 per cent of the population, a much higher proportion than will ever receive a formal diagnosis of a disorder associated with the symptom (Eaton et al., 1991). This suggests that even 'normal' thinking can, occasionally and often temporarily, take on 'a paranoid colouring' (Bell, 2003: 6, see also Kramer, 1998). Conspiracy theorists, even if not clinically paranoid, might therefore suffer from some milder form of 'paranoid cognition' of the kind found in non-clinical populations.

Even though paranoid ideation and conspiratorial beliefs appear to share a number of common features, including the feeling of persecution or suspicion of others, a closer comparison reveals a number of crucial differences which are often overlooked. First, the defining features of paranoid thought, both in terms of clinical diagnostics and in terms of measures used in epidemiological research, is the *immediacy of threat* and its *personal* nature (Mirowsky and Ross, 1983, Fenigstein and Vanable, 1992, Wagner-Egger and Bangerter, 2007). In paranoia, the target of the persecutors' evil intentions is the belief holder, and in a minority of cases, their immediate circle of family or friends (Freeman and Garety, 2000, Fenigstein and Vanable, 1992). In conspiracy theory, this personalisitic or self-referential interpretation of others' behaviour (also known as *delusion of reference*) is usually absent: the conspiracy theorist does not view him or herself, individually, as the main target of the nefarious scheming by the Illuminati, the CIA or the Jews. It is the whole world that is believed to be under threat. Put differently, an individual's fear that someone is trying to infect them with AIDS (a paranoid idea) is qualitatively different to the belief that AIDS has been created by the US government as an instrument for population control (conspiracy theory). Just as believing that one is being persecuted by government agents (one of the most frequent motifs in paranoid ideation among psychiatric patients in the US, see Gaines, 1988) is not the same as believing that the CIA killed John F. Kennedy (conspiracy theory). Although egocentric, self-referential ideation typical of paranoia might, of course, coexist with conspiratorial beliefs (as was the case with Nesta Webster or Schwartz-Bostunich) fears about personal safety are not a typical or the defining feature of conspiracy theories.

Second, paranoia and conspiracy theories differ in terms of the role that *fear* is assumed to play. As David Harper (2004) notes, both psychiatrists and patients place particular emphasis on fear as a characteristic of paranoia. The frightening nature of paranoid beliefs leads to isolation and contributes to individuals becoming obsessed with the supposed threat. Such fear is notably absent in conspiracy theories. Although as we have seen in Chapter 4, conspiracy theories often have a strong apocalyptic tone, terror is not the main emotion and withdrawal not the principal reaction that they provoke in those who subscribe to them. On the contrary, conspiracy theories are underpinned by the kind of naïve optimism about the ultimate vulnerability of the evil forces that instils a desire to resist and to fight the conspirators. This kind of optimism is difficult to find among individuals affected by paranoid delusions.

Finally, paranoia, in stark contrast to conspiracy theories, is characterised by *idiosyncratic thought*. In psychiatric practice, in order for a patient to be diagnosed with paranoid delusions, their persecutory beliefs need to be shown to be considered 'by other members of that individual's cultural or subcultural group as being unsupportable, as lacking in credibility' (Gaines, 1988: 231–232). Therefore, no matter how irrational or implausible a belief might seem to outsiders, it will not be considered a 'delusion' as long as it has relevance for others (Heise, 1988). This is why, for example, the *Diagnostic and Statistical Manual of Mental Disorders* makes exceptions for any kind of religious belief: what makes a belief a 'delusion' is not its content per se, but rather, its complete lack of social currency or validation from at least a proportion of the outside world.

Idiosyncratic thought is certainly not a feature of conspiracy beliefs. Evidence presented in previous chapters suggests that, if anything, conspiracy theories have *too much* social currency. Conspiracy theorists have syndicated radio shows, they publish bestselling books and some occupy high positions in government. From the perspective of psychiatric diagnostics, the fact that conspiracy theories are based on a shared (even if often stigmatised) body of knowledge and the fact that their exponents engage in some meaningful social activity (forging a movement, organising a convention, creating a website or making an internet documentary) is enough to distinguish them from paranoia and make them 'the object of sociological study rather than psychiatric treatment' (Heise, 1988: 269). This, of course, does not mean that paranoiacs will not sometimes incorporate, into their paranoid ideation, motifs from the conspiracy culture, for instance, by having delusions that some character or organisation featured in a relevant conspiracy theory is out to get them. However, in such instances, the egocentric nature of the paranoid delusion will generally prevent the afflicted person from seeking the company of others. Put differently, certified paranoiacs seldom make successful conspiracy theorists: the inherent egocentricity of their delusions leaves no space for a common reality that can serve as the foundation for social interaction with others (see Wulff, 1987).

The *social* and *shared* nature of beliefs, which is a defining feature of conspiracy theories, but absent in paranoid delusions, is crucial also because no matter how tempting it might be to explain personal beliefs of well-known conspiracy theorists in terms of paranoia, such an account cannot explain their fame and widespread following among the non-delusional population. No psychiatric interpretation of the clinical profiles of for example Nesta Webster, David Icke or Pat Roberston – all of whom, in addition to being 'paranoid' conspiracy theorists, claimed to have experienced some sort of delusion-like epiphany (see Thurlow, 1978, Ronson, 2000, Goldberg, 2001) – can adequately explain the enduring popularity of their work and the fact that it attracted the praise of hundreds of thousands of their (sane) contemporaries, including, in the case of Webster, from Winston Churchill.

Paranoia as a collective phenomenon

Although traditional psychiatry conceptualises paranoia almost exclusively as a form of *individual* pathology, the social nature of conspiracy theories has led to suggestions that conspiracism constitutes a collective form of paranoid disorder, which affects mass movements, or even entire nations or cultures (Robins and Post, 1997, Zonis and Joseph, 1994, 1996). For example, in their study of conspiracy theories in the Middle East, Zonis and Joseph (1994, 1996) conceptualised conspiracy theory as a manifestation of a shared 'neurotic' ideational style that constitutes a milder, collective version of paranoid personality disorder.

The tendency to treat conspiracy theories as a manifestation of collective pathology is particularly common among authors who subscribe to the psychoanalytic tradition. The leaning towards Freudian theory dates back to the 1950s, when psychoanalysis emerged as the prism through which many social scientists and historians observed social phenomena believed to lie in the domain of the irrational. This reasoning led Adorno et al. (1950) to resort to psychoanalysis when explaining the phenomenon of the authoritarian personality. Bettleheim and Janowitz (1950), Ackerman and Jahoda (1950) and others have explored the persistence of conspiratorial fantasies about Jews in the context of repressed desires and the resolution, in early childhood, of the Oedipus complex. Even Norman Cohn's (1967: 284–285) inherently historical analysis of the *Protocols of the Elders of Zion* ended with the suggestion that antisemitic conspiracy theories are 'bizarre phenomena indeed' which, therefore, cannot be explained 'unless one takes unconscious mechanisms into account'.

The employment of psychoanalytic principles to explain collective phenomena is, however, fraught with problems. Zonis's and Joseph's (1994) study of conspiracy theories in 'Arab-Iranian-Muslim culture' is a case in point. In their analysis, the authors postulated that what makes conspiracy thinking 'an especially familiar form of reasoning' in Muslim countries of the Middle East are two specific aspects of child rearing practices (ibid.: 446). First, in infancy and early childhood, boys are reared almost exclusively by women, before being separated from the familiar feminine environment and immersed into the world of men. This 'emotionally violent experiential discontinuity' is said to create a pattern whereby what is real and what is unreal needs to be continuously re-evaluated, something that later becomes projected also onto the world of politics (ibid.: 456). Second, drawing on the long history of psychoanalytic writing which assumes a link between repressed homosexuality and paranoia, Zonis and Joseph (1994) argue that the fact that in the Middle East sexuality (and in particular homosexuality) is shrouded in secrecy makes people susceptible to unconsciously homo-erotic 'paranoid or paranoid-like ideation'. Conspiracy thinking, as a collective phenomenon, is conceptualised as a response to the combined effect of these 'intense or chronic psychosocial stressors' in childhood which 'predispose' people to adopt the conspiracist 'ideational style' (ibid.: 445–446).

The first problem with this interpretation is its tendency to view conspiracy theories as reducible to long-term and seemingly inflexible cultural practices and traditions. Conspiracy theories are a global phenomenon which persists in a variety of cultural contexts with very different child-rearing customs. What is more, as we have seen in Chapter 3, conspiracy thinking persisted in Europe and the United States over the past two centuries, even though during that time childrearing practices and associated 'stressors' changed dramatically. Equally, conspiratorial beliefs tend to ebb and flow within the lifetime of a single generation, which undermines the assumption that any culture or cohort is predetermined to succumb to this particular type of explanation. Psychoanalytically informed literature has generally struggled to explain the pattern of continuity and change in the prevalence of conspiracy theories and link these to specific aspects of childhood development.

Second, when looking at the aetiology of a collective 'paranoid' psyche, psychoanalytic explanations exhibit a pronounced male bias: the susceptibility of certain cultures to conspiracist thinking is seen exclusively in the context of the psychosexual development of boys. Questions about 'intense or chronic psychosocial stressors' to which women in the Middle East might be subjected and how these impact on their susceptibility to conspiracy theories are sidelined. This is an important issue because an essential tenet of psychoanalytic theory is that there are crucial differences between boys and girls in terms of early psychosexual development, and yet there is no evidence that men are more susceptible to conspiracy theorising than women. Also, underpinning psychoanalytic explanations is the assumption that the collective paranoid mind is determined solely by what happens to boys. Why the collective mind is necessarily a male mind is never explicitly addressed (see Blee, 2002). This limitation hints at the inherently speculative nature of psychoanalytic accounts of social phenomena: a huge leap of faith is required before concepts derived from clinical practice with individual patients can be, in such a straightforward and seemingly unproblematic way, applied to whole societies and cultures.

Finally, what makes the approach of Zonis and Joseph (1994) and others especially problematic is the fact that this kind of interpretation tends to be applied selectively in a way that stigmatises and pathologises certain cultures. Even though in sociological literature, conspiracy theories are so often perceived as an aspect of popular culture in the United States – indeed most of the conspiracy theories in circulation in the Middle East have been imported from the West (see Pipes, 1996) – psychoanalytic accounts of paranoia have rarely been applied to the mainstream of American culture and society. It is somehow deemed acceptable to speak of the Middle East as a place where social, political and economic problems trigger mass 'regression in mental processes', provoke an onset of 'infantile narcissism' or cause a collective 'eruption of more primitive ideation' typical of conspiracy theories (Zonis and Joseph, 1994: 447, see Dorn, 1996). Similarly, when explaining the popularity of conspiracy theories among African Americans, Robins and Post (1997: 61) draw a parallel between the whole community and 'abused children [who] may themselves become abusers'. Such selective application of psychoanalytic insights, which creates false dichotomies that split humanity into 'us' (the normal) and 'them' (the pathological), undermines the validity of the psychoanalytically informed approaches to collective paranoia.

Psychological 'profiling' of conspiracy theorists

In contrast to the writing that looks at conspiracy theories as a manifestation of individual or collective psychopathology, psychologists have, in recent years, turned their attention to other, non-clinical factors which predispose certain individuals to endorse conspiracy theories. Given that opinion polls clearly show that not everyone believes in conspiracy theories, a number of psychological studies have examined what distinguishes believers from non-believers. Abalakina-Paap et al. (1999: 646) captured the essence of this strand of psychological research when they wrote that 'history may well be a conspiracy, but apparently only certain types of people endorse this view'. The goal has been, therefore, to uncover who these 'certain types' are, and to create a 'profiling model of conspiracist individuals' (Swami et al., 2010: 751).

Research looking at differences between believers in conspiracy theories and sceptics typically consists of lengthy questionnaires which are distributed to a sample of the population, often university students. The questionnaire is composed of different measures, or scales, one of which usually assesses the participant's belief in conspiracy theories, while others measure whatever variables the researcher hypothesises might explain the difference in susceptibility to conspiracy-based explanations. Statistical procedures, such as structural equation modelling, are then used to analyse the data and assess the strength of the relationship between different variables, all with the view of uncovering factors that underpin what is often referred to as the 'conspiracy mentality' (Moscovici, 1987).

In developing specific hypotheses about the kind of things that might account for the differences between believers and sceptics, researchers have tended to rely on the work of non-psychologists, or in some case simply on 'intuition' (Swami et al., 2010: 752). For example, apart from exploring the relevance of more general demographic factors like gender, socio-economic status, educational level, or ethnic background, psychologists have set out to test empirically a variety of assumptions which appear regularly in sociological literature. These include the claim that conspiracy theories provide a way of simplifying a complex world, that they offer a convenient scapegoat or an outlet for hostility, or that they reflect a more general distrust of authority. The fact that in the classic essay 'The paranoid style in American politics' Richard Hofstadter (1967) mentioned that people who feel alienated and powerless are particularly susceptible to conspiracist beliefs has led to 'anomie' becoming a ubiquitous variable in this strand of psychological research.

The principal finding of the studies in this area has been that belief in conspiracy theories is associated with general disenchantment with political authority, a sense of powerlessness, political cynicism, and more generally, 'the feeling of alienation and disaffection from the system' (Goertzel, 1994: 739, see also Abalakina-Paap et al., 1999). Those who feel dispossessed, alienated and disenchanted with politics are believed to be attracted to conspiracy theories because such beliefs confirm the person's sense that the world is beyond their control, while also protecting self-esteem by offering a simple explanation for existential and status-related problems. It has also been found that susceptibility to conspiracy theorising is not related to gender, educational level or occupation, but is linked to minority status: members of minority groups tend to be more susceptible to conspiracy theorising. The nature of the relationship between minority status and conspiracist thinking remains unclear, however. Abalakina-Paap et al. (1999) suggest that the tendency among minority groups to believe in conspiracy theories might be a secondary effect of anomie, distrust and powerlessness, which tends to be more apparent among minorities. By contrast, Crocker et al. (1999) found that members of the African American minority appear to be more susceptible to conspiracy theories than whites even when things like socio-economic status – a factor that has been associated more generally with external locus of control or suspicion of authorities – is controlled for. In any case, the very fact that conspiracy theorising is not equally distributed across different minority groups suggests that culturally specific factors are also involved.

More recently, Swami et al. (2010) set out to explore whether in addition to anomie and attitudes to authority, personality variables might also account for individual differences in conspiracy beliefs. Focusing specifically on beliefs about 9/11 in a British sample, and using Goldberg's 'Big Five' personality test (which measures five different dimensions of human personality), they found that the only trait that appears to be linked (although marginally) to belief in 9/11 conspiracy theories is Agreeableness. The lower the score on this trait, the more likely a person is to believe the 9/11 conspiracy theories. This is said to be because suspicion of others (typical of conspiracy theories) is one of the features of people who score low on the Agreeableness scale. Swami et al. (2010) also found that those who scored highly on another personality trait, Openness, were more likely to believe in conspiracy theories generally (but not specifically those about 9/11) and were more likely to have been exposed to conspiracy material. The authors see this as a consequence of the fact that 'proclivity for new ideas', characteristic of those who score high on Openness, makes people more receptive to conspiracy claims and leads them to seek out conspiracy material.

Another variable which psychologists have looked at is authoritarianism. In their pioneering work on the authoritarian personality, Adorno et al. (1950) postulated a link between authoritarianism and conspiracy theories, primarily because the latter were seen as a manifestation of scapegoating, a dynamic which is central to the notion of authoritarian personality. However, while some studies found evidence of a correlation between belief in conspiracy theories and authoritarianism

(Abalakina-Paap et al., 1999, Grzesiak-Feldman and Irzycka, 2009) others did not (McHoskey, 1995). The study by McHoskey (1995) found that participants who were authoritarian were in fact more likely to be swayed by arguments in support of the official, *non-conspiratorial* explanation of the Kennedy assassination, which contradicts Abalakina-Paap et al.'s (1999) assumption that authoritarian individuals have a fundamental tendency to seek scapegoats for social problems and are therefore predisposed to believe in conspiracy theories. Also, Swami et al. (2010) have recently found a link between adherence to democratic principles and beliefs in conspiracy theories, which suggests that the latter are not, as is traditionally believed, a prerogative of right-wing authoritarians, but rather a feature of all those who are disenchanted with the mainstream of politics, regardless of whether they see the solution in authoritarianism or in democracy.

Studies seeking to establish what differentiates believers in conspiracy theories from sceptics have also looked at a range of cognitive factors. Because conspiracy theories are so often seen as an outcome of faulty reasoning (resistance to disconfirming evidence, circular way of thinking, etc.), there is a tendency to see them as a manifestation of some perceptual or cognitive deficit which leads to a misunderstanding or misinterpretation of causal relations in the world. The question for psychologists has been, in the words of Arie Kruglanski (1987: 220), whether or not 'conspiracy theories represent gross distortions of reality' and if they should be considered 'cognitive illusions paralleling the widely documented perceptual illusions'.

As conspiracy theories are essentially about ascribing causes to historical and political events, it is unsurprising that the susceptibility to conspiracy theorising has been interpreted as a problem of causal attribution. Ever since the 1950s, psychologists have emphasised the tendency to ascribe causes to events as one of the most fundamental social cognitive processes and therefore as a key, and universal, aspect of human psychological functioning (Heider, 1958; Kelley, 1972; Hewstone, 1989, Försterling, 2001). According to attribution research, in trying to understand the world around them and make sense of the behaviour of others, people act as 'naïve' or 'intuitive scientists' (Heider, 1958, Kelley, 1973). They use different, quasi-rational strategies – a form of 'causal calculus' – to continuously process incoming information, test specific 'hypotheses' about causal relations in the world and arrive at an inference about the causes of events (Heider, 1958, Harrison and Thomas, 1997, Kramer, 1998). Two types of attribution are typically made: events are attributed either to the actions, dispositions or intentions of the actors involved (*personal attribution*) or to situational factors, which lie beyond the motives, intentions and behaviour of specific individuals (*situational attribution*). Much of attribution research examines different factors which affect the type of causal inference made (such as mood, personality or political beliefs) as well as the biases which affect the attribution process.

Given that conspiracy theories are marked by a blatant disregard for the possible causal implications of historical accident, or the broader social, economic and political conditions, they can be said to be an expression of a specific 'causal schemata' or 'attributional style' (Kruglanski, 1987; Zukier, 1987) defined by an overreliance on intentionality and personal attribution. From the perspective of attribution research, however, the excess of personal causal inference is not, in itself, particularly remark-able (Billig, 1978, 1989). It is generally recognised that, in Western socie-ties at least, when observing the behaviour of others, there is a preference for personal attributions over situational ones. This widespread trend is known as the 'fundamental attribution error' (Nisbett and Ross, 1980). However, the one thing that does make conspiracy theory cognitively distinct is that it is often the *same* causal attribution which is made for disparate events. A conspiracy theorist will come back, over and over again, to the same cause and will account for every event in terms of the same conspiracy (Lipset and Raab, 1978). It is as if the conspiracy theory involves an additional layer of attribution. Not only are individual his-torical or political events (the Russian Revolution, the assassination of John F. Kennedy, 9/11 attacks) attributed to someone's intention or voli-tion, but a further attribution is made for these attributions: the different conspiracies are attributed to the machinations of a higher order power: the New World Order, world Jewry, the 'military industrial complex', the Illuminati or some other entity. In explaining political and social events, therefore, conspiracy theory will 'push the personal attribution to the point of absurdity' (Billig, 1989: 161).

This monomaniacal attributional tendency goes against a general trend noted in attribution literature. Research suggests that complex events, especially those of high magnitude or significance, tend to be explained using multicausal explanations (Cunningham and Kelley, 1975). According to this finding 'the more extreme the effect to be attributed, the more likely the attributor is to assume that it entails multiple necessary causes' (Kelley, 1972: 6). Conspiracy theorists seem to suffer from a particular cognitive bias which leads them to aban-don the multicausal explanatory schema. Instead, they 'see simplicity in complexity' and construct a causal explanation for wars, historical changes or economic crises on the basis of the recognisably straightfor-ward conspiratorial narrative (Billig, 1978: 319).

A related cognitive factor which is believed to account for beliefs in conspiracy theories is the bias towards seeking big causes to explain big effects (McCauley and Jacques, 1979, Leman and Cinnirella, 2007). The assumption here is that an intrinsic need for consistency between the magnitude of a cause and its consequence will lead people faced with a dramatic event to seek a cause 'that is commensurate with the effect – seek, in other words, large and global explanations that thereby imbue the event with appropriate meaning' (Bethel, 1975: 39, see also Keeley, 1999). In a study using a scenario describing a hypothetical presiden-tial assassination, McCauley and Jacques (1979) found that participants were more likely to attribute the event to a conspiracy if the assassina-tion attempt results in death, compared to a less-dramatic scenario in which the shooter misses his target. Crucially however, a more recent study by Leman and Cinnirella (2007), while confirming McCauley and Jacques's (1979) principal finding, also found that the 'major event – major cause' heuristic is not confined to believers in conspiracy theo-ries: people are susceptible to this inference-making bias even if they are skeptical towards conspiracy theories. Therefore, this bias explains what kind of *event* is likely to become the object of conspiracist specula-tion rather than what kind of *people* will be susceptible to it. What is more, 'the major event – major cause' heuristic does not always lead to a conspiracy-based explanation: a conspiracy is not always seen as a 'major cause'. As Richard Pipes (1992) points out, one reason why the Russian Revolution is so often perceived as a 'bottom up' event, a spon-taneous revolution initiated and driven by a mass movement involving millions, is precisely because of the assumption that great events in his-tory cannot be attributed to a relatively simple cause – a *coup d'état* car-ried out by a small number of well-organised revolutionaries. Therefore, just as in some instances the 'major event – major cause' heuristic might lead to the endorsement of a conspiracy theory, it can also work the other way and lead to a preference for a non-conspiratorial explanation even when a conspiratorial one might be more appropriate (see Coady, 2006).

Finally, given that writers of conspiracy materials are notorious for their tendency to gather evidence selectively, they have also been said to be susceptible to what is known as *biased assimilation* – the kind of motivationally based information processing which leads individuals to uncritically accept evidence supporting a pre-existing view, while rejecting any disconfirming information (Lord et al., 1979). Butler et al.

(1995) found that the stronger a person's belief in a conspiracy theory, the more confident they will be about the veracity of the evidence on which their belief is based. However, just as with the 'major event – major cause' heuristic, biased assimilation is by no means a privilege of believers in conspiracy theories (McHoskey, 1995). It is also present among sceptics, who are just as susceptible to systematic privileging of confirmatory evidence. In fact, people who hold very different, even diametrically opposite views on a particular issue (in this case, a conspiracy theorist and a sceptic) will process and evaluate the same body of information differently, in a way that confirms their initial position. This appears to suggest that, with the exception of the monomaniacal attributional bias, conspiracy theorists might not be as cognitively distinct as it is sometimes tempting to think. As Harrison and Thomas (1997:115) put it, 'beliefs in conspiracies rest less on emotional upheaval and gross distortions of reality [...] than on normal, primarily rational information processing strategies that are accountable also for other beliefs'.

Conspiracy theories: individual beliefs or social phenomena?

The distinguishing feature of the research on psychological factors underpinning the 'conspiracy mentality' is that it approaches conspiracy theories as *individual beliefs*. Adherence to conspiracy-based explanations is seen as an aspect of individual differences and something that can be explained by reference to individual information processing biases, identity maintenance strategies or personality characteristics. The treatment of conspiracy theory as an individual belief is reflected also in the use of attitude scales to measure the extent to which a person endorses conspiracy-based explanations. A number of such scales have emerged in recent years consisting of anywhere between 10 and 22 items. Some require respondents to rate the extent to which they believe specific conspiracy theories to be true (ranging from fluoridisation of water to the causes of 9/11), while others contain more abstract questions about the role of conspiracies in world history. Most have been designed in the United States, although a number of culturally specific scales have been created also in the UK (Leman and Cinnirella, 2007, Swami et al., 2010), Poland (see Grzesiak-Feldman and Ejsmont, 2008, Kofta and Sędek, 2005) and France (Wagner-Egger and Bangerter, 2007).

The use of attitude scales to tap into conspiracy beliefs raises important theoretical and methodological questions. Regardless of the type of item included in a scale, the belief in conspiracies is conceptualised as a *continuous* dimension. Rather than asking participants to give a 'yes' or a 'no' answer, the questions require them to rate items on a sliding scale typically from 1–5 or 1–7, with numbers representing level of agreement (from 'strongly disagree' to 'strongly agree') or probability that a conspiracy theory is true ('highly unlikely to 'highly likely'). Therefore, although the research seeks to tap into the factors that differentiate 'believers' from 'sceptics', the scales do not produce a clear dichotomy: everyone in the population is assumed to fall somewhere on the continuum between complete credulity and radical scepticism.

One issue with the continuous scales is that it is not entirely clear what it is that they measure. They certainly do not measure the same thing as questionnaires or surveys inviting a simpler 'yes' or 'no' answer (Crocker et al., 1999). In the case of continuous scales, a very low score might usefully point to a definite sceptic just as high score could help identify a hard-line credulist, but the meaning of scores in the middle range is more difficult to interpret. If, in response to the item 'The Mafia killed JFK', someone chooses '3' or '4' on a scale from 1 (totally disagree) – 7 (totally agree), what does this score mean in practical terms? Is this person a believer or a sceptic? A similar problem arises in research which asks people to make a specific choice between different explanations (rather than rate their level of agreement) but which include also a neutral, 'I don't know' option. The 2008 World Public Opinion survey conducted in 17 countries around the world asked respondents to indicate who was behind the 9/11 attacks on New York and Washington. The choices were 'Al Qaida', 'The US government', 'Israel', 'Other Arabs/ Saudis/Egyptians', 'Other', or 'I don't know'. As many as 26 per cent of British and 23 per cent of French respondents answered 'I don't know' (WorldPublicOpinion.org, 2008). For research seeking to distinguish believers and sceptics, this section of the population represents a problem. Are those who 'don't know' whether Al Qaida destroyed the Twin Towers conspiracy theorists because they do not accept the official explanation, or are they sceptics because they do not endorse any of the obviously conspiracist options? The same can be asked about 25 per cent of respondents in a Russian poll conducted in the early 1990s, who were 'undecided' about whether there is a 'global Zionist plot' against Russia (cited in Smith, 1996: 204). In psychological research using attitude scales, this category of response is never subjected to theoretical interpretation, even though most participants tend to choose the more 'neutral' responses in the middle of the scale, rather than those at the extremes. Instead, it is simply assumed that belief in conspiracies is a continuous dimension, ranging from radical scepticism to complete endorsement.

An important problem with this assumption, however, is that questionnaire-based measures do not necessarily measure *belief* in the conventional sense of the word. For one thing, participants' scores might reflect familiarity with, rather than the level of endorsement of, conspiracy theories. It has been found, for example, that people are generally less likely to dismiss explanations with which they are familiar, even if they do not agree with them (Crocker et al., 1999). This is in part due to an effect that Sunstein and Vermeule (2009) refer to as *conspiracy cascades*. In making inferences about events in the world, people often look to others for clues. A claim which is believed to be shared by a significant proportion of the population will often, for that reason alone, be recognised as being in the realm of possibility, even if it is not believed to be unequivocally true. People simply tend to assume, sometimes misguidedly, that others' beliefs or actions are based on evidence that might not be available to them. This element of trust means that reports about the widespread nature of belief in, for example, 9/11 conspiracy theories or the human origins of the HIV virus (which incidentally, are themselves often based on polls using continuous attitude scales) can have the effect of a self-fulfilling prophecy: the more people learn about how many others supposedly believe in these theories, the more likely they will be to recognise them as beliefs that cannot be discounted as being beyond the pale. This, in turn, might translate into near-neutral (as opposed to negative) responses on the scales. Conspiracy cascades are especially important when interpreting findings about higher rates of conspiratorial beliefs among certain populations, such as the African American community. The greater tendency to agree that a conspiracy theory about the victimisation of the black population is true, or the failure to dismiss it outright, could be a side-effect of the greater familiarity with such a theory among African American respondents, compared to whites (Crocker et al., 1999).

Also, research that uses scales to measure belief in conspiracies does not recognise the possibility that engaging with conspiracy theories comprises a complex set of phenomena involved in taking a position in a matter of controversy, one that cannot be reduced to a single dimension of judgment or unproblematically mapped on the continuum between strong belief and strong scepticism. For example, even among the self-proclaimed hard-line sceptics, there may be those who, while wholeheartedly rejecting the conspiracy based explanations, nevertheless recognise them as a legitimate view for others to hold (Billig, 1987).

This category of the population is important because what enables conspiracy theories to persist in contemporary society is not just that a certain proportion of the population believes in them, but also that a much larger proportion (including mainstream publishers, sections of the media and public figures) recognises them as a view that deserves to be heard. This gives conspiracy theories an air of respectability, contributing to the aforementioned cascading effect. Equally, conspiracy theories sometimes manifest themselves as 'quasi beliefs', namely beliefs that are of relatively little consequence and might even be 'fun' to hold, but which, in most cases, do not lead to action or guide behaviour in any significant way (Sunstein and Vermeule, 2009). People who engage with conspiracy theories might do so with the kind of 'suspicion of phoniness' commonly found among those who read astrology columns (Adorno, 1994: 49). Studies using one-dimensional scales clearly do not distinguish between the different kinds of engagement with conspiracy theory, or examine how these interact to ensure the continuing presence of conspiracism in society.

Finally, psychological research on conspiracy beliefs tends to be based on samples from the general population (or undergraduate students), among whom there are usually very few hard-line conspiracy theorists. It might seem obvious that an inquiry into factors that differentiate sceptics from believers would be based on comparisons between a smaller subset of the population who firmly believe in conspiracy theories (those scoring at the top end of a conspiracy theory scale) and another subset comprising the biggest sceptics (a subset at the lower end of the scale). However, this has not been the case. The supposition that belief in conspiracy theories is a continuous dimension of judgment and that everyone in the population falls somewhere between fundamental belief and radical scepticism means that it is simply taken for granted that factors that differentiate between, for example, a strong and a moderate sceptic are same as those that account for the difference between a strong believer and a strong sceptic. And yet, given the aforementioned points about the possibility that the near neutral responses might be accounted for by considerations other than simply the belief in, or attitude towards, conspiracy theories, this is clearly not a straightforward assumption for researchers to make.

In addition to the supposition that conspiracy beliefs are a continuous dimension, studies into the differences between believers and sceptics are based on the vital assumption that, when faced with a dramatic event, people engage in a complex interpretative process which guides them towards some kind of causal inference, conspiratorial or otherwise.

This process is thought to be vulnerable to different kinds of biases, but these are seen as properties of the individual's information processing system or disposition. Conspiracist *explanations*, of the kind examined in detail in previous chapters, are ultimately seen as a manifestation of, and as following from, some underlying (dysfunctional) inference-making, attributional or identity maintenance process.

It is, however, questionable to what extent invoking any kind of systematic (even if biased) inference-making process is either useful or necessary when accounting for how people arrive at an explanation in real-life situations. When faced with a dramatic event, people tend to instantly 'know' what could have caused it. This is because they have at their disposal 'reservoirs of available explanations' or 'common sense theories' about causal relations in the world (Moscovici and Hewstone, 1983: 121–122). For example, the accusations which surfaced in the 1940s, that Franklin D. Roosevelt deliberately allowed the attacks on Pearl Harbour to happen in order to overcome domestic opposition to America's involvement in the Second World War was not the outcome of a 'cognitive bias' among a section of the population, which yielded a 'personal attribution' in the form of conspiracy theory. It was an explanation that came naturally to those who already saw Roosevelt as a would-be dictator intent on taking over America, and who had the isolationist discourse of the 1910s to draw on. In the aftermath of 9/11, when exponents of the 9/11 Truth movement started to pose questions about the causes of the attacks, they were also not exercising some intrinsic aversion towards 'complex causal schemata', but were drawing on an established tradition of explanation and a pattern set by responses to Pearl Harbour, the 1995 Oklahoma bombing and other events from the past that 9/11 was compared to for different reasons. This opens the possibility that conspiracy theories are not the product of individual information processing, but one of a number of available 'collectively (ideologically) conditioned patterns of misinterpretations' (Ichheiser, 1943: 145) that people can draw on as they attempt to make sense of events in the world. Put differently, it is not the (biased) process of attribution that generates conspiracy theories; rather, the extreme form of personal attribution is constituted within a particular, conspiracy-based, shared social explanation (see Edwards and Potter, 1992).

Reducing conspiracy beliefs to individual cognitive or attribution processes is problematic also because it cannot account for the cultural differences and periodic fluctuations in the popularity of conspiracy theories. It was already noted that African American community in the US has been found to be more receptive to conspiracy theories, especially those whose content is linked to the history of racial oppression and discrimination. And yet, no systematic differences have been found between ethnic groups with regards to inference-making and attribution, or other potentially significant variables like locus of control (Graham, 1994). The key difference between black and white Americans lay not in some cognitive deficit among the former, or a systematic difference with regards to some personality variable, but to the difference in exposure to culturally specific and historically contingent ways of interpreting the world and the power relations within it.

Most importantly, psychological accounts looking at conspiracy theories as an aspect of individual information processing cannot account for the *content* of conspiracy theories (Billig, 1978, 1989). In fact, such explanations do not even engage with conspiracy theories *as explanations* which, apart from attributing causes to a global plot, consist also of a distinct and persistent explanatory style examined in Chapter 4. By stripping conspiracy theory down to a one-dimensional attitude, psychologists have ignored what is, arguably, the most important aspect of this phenomenon: its persistence as a dynamic set of stories and *shared* assumptions about the world embedded in a tradition of explanation. After all, conspiracism is least interesting as an individual attitude and much more so as an array of accounts which are continuously exchanged, debated, evaluated and modified and on the basis of which movements are established, political projects forged and power relations challenged and sustained.

Conspiracy theory and the value of being 'in the know'

There is an area of psychological research that is rarely acknowledged in the literature on the psychology of conspiracy theories, which has been more attentive to the communicative, interpersonal dimension of conspiracism. It is the research on rumour. Ever since the first psychological studies on the topic were carried out in the 1940s, stories of conspiracies, plots and subversion were identified as notable examples of rumour and hearsay (Allport and Postman, 1947; Rosnow and Fine, 1974; Shibutani, 1966; Turner, 1993; Neubauer, 1999, Nkpa, 1975, 1977, Campion-Vincent, 2005). This is unsurprising given that many conspiratorial claims began as rumours and were only later incorporated in a formal conspiratorial account, which, in turn, fuelled further rumour mongering, initiating an endless cycle of mutual reinforcement. The idea of Jewish ritual abuse of children, for example, was part of medieval antisemitic folklore which was passed on by means of rumour, until it become incorporated into the conspiracy culture in the nineteenth century (Cohn, 1967; Billig, 1989). In the same way, the claim that Jews employed in the World Trade Centre failed to turn up for work on 11 September 2001 because they had foreknowledge of what was about to happen, began as a rumour on the internet, before it became a motif of more elaborate conspiracy theory.

Although rumours are often assumed to be of temporary interest and transmitted by word of mouth, it is today widely recognised that they can be the topic of more systematic and organised dissemination through mass media, including the internet, and that they can take the form of unusually persistent claims which are transmitted through generations. These 'solidified rumours' (Allport and Postman, 1947: 167) have been shown to contain cyclically reappearing symbolic themes (Rosnow, 1980, Rosnow and Fine, 1974, Shibutani, 1966), which, a bit like legends, 'become part of the verbal heritage of a people' and can be drawn upon in the face of events to which they appear to apply (LaPierre and Farnsworth, 1936: 322). The recurring motifs and themes of the conspiracy culture, which were examined in Chapter 4 and even the notion of conspiracy *per se*, can be productively examined as manifestations of such 'solidified' and inveterate rumours. Research on rumour has also been highly sensitive to the fact that it is dealing with an inherently dynamic phenomenon, one that constantly changes through transmission. This is because rumours are always part of some social action and are shaped by the need to attract the attention of the audience, to meet its expectations, manage the speaker's identity as a credible source and someone who is 'in the know'. Conspiracy theories are the outcome of the same complex process of adaptation and fine-tuning geared at meeting the conspiracy theorist's needs in the specific communicative context. This, after all, is the dynamic that underpins the continuous evolution of conspiracy theories explored in the previous chapter.

The contribution that research on rumour has made to understanding conspiracy theories lies, therefore, in the fact that, unlike other approaches in psychology, it is actually concerned with conspiracy theories as stories that people tell, and as rhetorically complex and situated accounts which perform certain social functions. Moreover, because the transmission of rumours is seen as a 'collective problem solving process' (Bordia and Difonzo, 2005: 88), it also points to important socially produced *motivational* factors in conspiracy theories.

Psychologists have long argued that the adherence to a rigid, and seemingly simplistic, cognitive style characteristic of conspiracy theories might be maintained by the psychological benefits that it brings to those who subscribe to it (see Billig, 1978). Traditionally, emphasis has been on what Kruglanski (1987) calls 'defensive attributions', that is, the assumption that through scapegoating, conspiracy theories allow a group's self-esteem, threatened by negative events, to remain protected from potentially damaging inferences. Kruglanski (1987: 219) goes as far as to suggest that conspiracy theories are ' "kissing cousins" of various scapegoating constructions, persecutionary belief-systems, and so forth' (see also Moscovici, 1987, Allport, 1954, Goertzel, 1994). The key idea behind 'scapegoating' is that in frustrating situations, when the causes of some social strain are unclear or out of reach, groups tend to displace their aggression onto outgroups, typically minorities (Hovland and Sears, 1940). In this context, conspiracy theories (particularly those involving minority ethnic communities) are seen as the rationalisation of the majority group's displaced aggression and a means of externalising feelings of hostility and avoiding self-blame (Young, 1990, Goertzel, 1994).

A further and arguably more important motivational factor is the *illusion of control* (Bains, 1983). Rumours of conspiracy have been shown to flourish in times of war, social crises or economic disasters, when previously established 'social machinery' breaks down and available canons of explanation prove inadequate for explaining the causes and the implication of a social strain (Nkpa, 1975, 1977). The driving force behind such rumour-mongering is the desire to bring relief to those among whom they are circulated (Allport and Postman, 1947, Shibutani, 1966). This includes reclaiming the sense that the world is ordered. Because they attribute causes to someone's volition and design, conspiracy theories imply that events are ultimately controllable and are not contingent upon random or unforeseeable events (Bains, 1983, Keeley, 1999, Kalichman, 2009). What is more, they imply a straight-forward (although not always easy) solution: all that is needed is for the conspiracy to be exposed and its architects eliminated, and good will prevail over evil. This assumption of controllability underpins the naïve optimism of the conspiracy theory explored in Chapter 4. Also, one should not discount the *emotional* aspect of conspiracy theories either. Conspiracism derives much of its appeal from the emotion it awakens in the audience. The conspiracy theory seduces not through its arguments, but by the intensity of the judgement inherent in its Manichaean narrative of praise and blame, good and evil (Miller, 2002).

The most important and the most obvious benefit that conspiracy theories bring to those who believe in them is, however, the feeling of 'self assurance and superiority towards the non-initiated' (Heins, 2007: 792). Because conspiracy theorists deal in arcane knowledge and 'facts' disbelieved by all those who have fallen victims of the orchestrated campaign of mass manipulation, 'adherence to a conspiracy theory allows a person to see himself or herself as perfect and infallible in comparison to others who are seen as evil and defective' (Young, 1990: 156). The participatory approach to conspiracy theory mentioned in Chapter 3, whereby consumers of conspiracy theories are invited to take part in gathering 'evidence' and exposing the plot, is in fact underpinned by the belief that the dissenter, through sheer hard work and fortitude, can uncover some truth that has eluded, or has been suppressed by, the specialist (Billig, 1987, see also Clarke, 2002). The resulting conviction that one is in possession of an unprecedented insight into the working of the world is a huge generator of esteem, because it offers compensation for 'what might otherwise be insupportable feeling of powerlessness' (Barkun, 2006: 35). Crucially, being 'in the know' has its own interpersonal, social dimension: it becomes especially important when it is recognised by others. As research on rumour-mongering points out, the knowledge about how the world works operates as the 'currency of power and influence' and brings prestige and esteem in and through communication with others (Bordia and Difonzo, 2005: 93). This is why conspiracy theories are never just individual beliefs; they are pieces of communication to be traded and exchanged, debated and contested.

The fact that conspiracy theories are shared, especially among communities of believers, means that self-enhancement generated through engagement with conspiracy theories has a *collective* dimension. Conspiracy theorising is increasingly becoming a communal endeavour, performed through organisations, movements, campaigns or through jointly produced websites or internet forums. The personal rivalries notwithstanding, conspiracy theorists tend to perceive themselves, as a collective, to be resourceful and competent, and 'part of a genuinely heroic elite group who can see past the official version duplicated for the benefit of the lazy and inert mass of people by the powers that be' (Aaronovitch, 2009: 10). This sense of a shared mission and common enemy underpins the over-reliance on the work of other conspiracy theorists that was examined in the previous chapter and helps sustain the conspiracy tradition of explanation.

Conclusion

The image of conspiracy theories that emerges at the end of this discussion is a far cry from that implicit in traditional psychological approaches which conceptualise conspiracy beliefs as an attitude reflecting biased or faulty individual reasoning, or a symptom of individual or collective paranoid delusion. It is the image of the conspiracy theory as a socially and historically bounded explanatory discourse, composed of a dynamic and evolving set of arguments, images, interpretations and assumptions about causal relations in the word. These are flexibly drawn upon, modified, debated and applied to novel circumstances in everyday social interaction, in the course of the ongoing process of making sense of the world and negotiating one's place within it. The key implication of such a conceptualisation is that looking for stable psychological characteristics or cognitive biases that differentiate believers from sceptics may not be the most productive avenue of research for psychologists interested in conspiracy theories. 'Faulty reasoning' is not what *causes* people to endorse conspiracy-based explanations, but something that is constituted within those explanations, within their thematic configuration, narrative structure and explanatory logic. As a number of social psychologists have argued over the years, psychology ought to be more attentive to the historical contingency of psychological phenomena and turn its interest to the issue of how specific ideologies, worldviews and cultural traditions produce particular patterns of thinking and behaviour, not the other way around (Gergen 1973, Moscovici 1984, Tajfel 1981, 1984, Billig, 1996, 2008). In relation to conspiracy theories, this means that specific explanations and accounts of conspiracy, and the ideological tradition within which they are situated, should become the central object of study, with the view of explaining why conspiracism persists in modern society, and how it sustains distinct forms of individual and collective thought and action.

7
Conclusion

The critical enquiry undertaken in the preceding chapters, and the exploration of the historical, political and psychological dimensions of conspiracy theories, yielded an unflattering portrait of this surprisingly persistent, global social phenomenon. Since the late eighteenth-century conspiracy theories played a notable role in shaping public perceptions of history and politics, and all too often as a feature of political ideologies and projects whose role in history has been far from positive. Conspiracism has been the staple ingredient of discriminatory, anti-democratic and populist politics, a trademark of the rhetoric of oppressive regimes, and, as we have seen in Chapter 5, a faithful companion to antisemitism. Conspiracy theories remain the refuge of every dictator and authoritarian leader in the world, from Mahmoud Ahmadinejad in Iran and Robert Mugabe in Zimbabwe, to Hugo Chavez in Venezuela and Alexander Lukashenko in Belarus. The tried and tested alliance between conspiracy theory and totalitarian politics is unsurprising, not just because the idea of conspiracy presents a potent tool for legitimising tyranny and oppression, but also because the two share the view of the people as a collection of dupes susceptible to manipulation and control, who need a strong leader to guide them and protect them from malign outside influences. This is why, as Karl Popper (1972) rightly pointed out, conspiracy theorists, when they take over the reins of power, invariably end up governing by conspiracy.

The harmful social implications of conspiracy theories are not restricted to the sphere of politics. Because they harbour suspicion about any official source of knowledge, conspiracy theories stand in opposition to science, medicine and other forms of mainstream academic enquiry. This suspicion of scientific and medical knowledge translates into regrettable lifestyle choices with serious implications for public health provision and sometimes lethal consequences. The death-toll which AIDS-related conspiracy theories and the resulting rejection of antiretroviral medication leave in their wake is the most obvious example. Likewise, resistance to flu or MMR vaccination is often sustained by the view of 'Big Pharma' and (mainly Western) governments as a menacing force conspiring against ordinary people.

And yet, in recent years it has become increasingly fashionable – not only in scholarly writing, but also in everyday discourse and in the media – to advocate a more sympathetic and permissive stance towards conspiracy theories and their role in society. Rather than being viewed as politically suspect, conspiracy theories are treated as an almost rational response to the uncertainties of the modern world or as an interpretative framework with a playful and ironic side, one whose political dimensions should not be overplayed. In the context of this argument, those who continue to draw attention to conspiracism's darker side and point to its historical ties with radical politics are viewed as narrow-minded curmudgeons and intellectual diehards incapable of grasping the true essence of the contemporary conspiracy culture and appreciating its more light-hearted and innocuous character.

In scholarly literature, this emerging perspective on conspiracy theories is articulated in a sizeable body of work published over the past 10 years, much of which is situated within the field of critical cultural studies (Fenster, 2008, Melley, 2000, Knight, 2000, 2002a, Parish and Parker, 2001, and others). In drawing this critical introduction to conspiracy theories to a close, the present chapter provides a brief overview of this alternative and increasingly popular approach to conspiracy theories. It considers some of its key shortcomings and in doing so revisits some of the main conclusions of the book as a whole.

From the *Protocols* to the *X-Files*

The central assumption of some of the more recent writing on conspiracy theories is that conspiracy-based accounts of history and politics which are in circulation today constitute a different breed to those that defined the nineteenth or early twentieth-century conspiracy culture. The assassination of President John F. Kennedy in November 1963 in particular is seen as a turning point in the history of conspiracism. In the aftermath of the assassination, the argument goes, conspiracy theories ceased to be the prerogative of the 'obsessive-minded right-wing, paranoid nut' or 'the dangerous proponent of extremist politics' and became part of the 'American vernacular' and 'the default view for a countercultural generation' (Knight, 2000: 3, 25). Also conspiracy theories are no longer confined to manifestos of radical political movements, conspiracist websites, or books about the advent of the New World Order, but are present in a much broader range of forms, including novels by writers such as Don DeLillo, Thoman Pynchon and William S. Burroughs, the TV series *X-Files* and the hundreds of Hollywood films whose plot revolves around conspiracist doubt and suspicion of political or scientific authority.

Conspiracy theories are said to owe their newly found mainstream status, especially in American society (on which much of the recent literature is focused), to the fact that they provide an all-encompassing response to contemporary challenges, including globalisation, increased surveillance, insecurities of a global economy, the onset of the information age and the crisis of post-modern knowledge and politics. The perceived loss of agency in particular, and the pervasive sense of being dispossessed and alienated from society, are compensated for 'by the imagination of *surplus* of intentionality on the part of scary behind-the-scenes actors' (Heins, 2007: 795, also Melley, 2000, Spark, 2002). In the words of Frederic Jameson (1988: 356), conspiracy theory constitutes the 'poor person's cognitive mapping in the postmodern age', a 'degraded figure of the total logic of late capital' which helps make sense of the inherently disorienting, fragmented and alienating nature of late capitalism. It individualises impersonal forms of control and regulation and attributes to them the human capacities of volition, intent and agency (see also Jameson, 1991).

While undergoing this far-reaching transformation, conspiracy theories are said to have developed new features which distinguish them from those which Richard Hofstadter analysed in his seminal treatise on the 'paranoid style', and which, in the present volume, were identified as constitutive of the conspiracy tradition. First and foremost, conspiracy culture is said to have acquired a distinct 'self-ironising', reflexive, self-conscious, almost playful, quality. It has become a 'half-serious, half-cynical' cultural commodity, one that consumers can purchase, engage with and discard, without necessarily fully buying into it (Knight, 2002b). This makes conspiracism today a 'hobby', defined not by ideological certainty and an obsession about the existence of a nefarious complot involving minorities, but by perpetual doubt about everything, including the existence of a conspiracy (Spark, 2002: 59). Rather than providing certainty, conspiracy theories are believed to operate as a form of radical scepticism prevalent among those who feel excluded from the mainstream of society (Fenster, 2008). Silverstein

(2000) captured the essence of this assumed change in the conspiracy culture and the onset of the playful and ironic 'popular paranoia', when he wrote that 'if the previous paradigm of conspiracy was the *Protocols of the Elders of Zion*, the new model is the *X-Files*'.

An important implication of the conceptualisation of conspiracy theories as 'a form of pop sociology cobbled together on the fly as people try to gain a handle on the complexities of social and economic causation in an era of rapid globalisation' (Knight, 2002b: 8), is that it goes some way towards releasing the term from its negative political connotations. In fact, one of the explicit aims of the recent re-evaluation of conspiracy theories has been to 'complicate simplistic assumptions about conspiracy theory's politics' and 'rescue the study of conspiracy theory from those who would condemn it as an inevitable threat to civilised discourse and democratic order' (Fenster, 2008: 280–281). Traditional approaches are censured for being overly dismissive of conspiracy theories and for seeking to delegitimise them as a form of political or intellectual dissent, and for rejecting 'as pathological any challenge or resistance to consensus' (ibid.: 42). This means that conspiracy theories are viewed not just as playful and ironic, but often also as a response to real structural inequalities and genuine problems, and a reaction to a world that is in fact becoming more secretive and conspiratorial. Peter Knight (2000: 3, 8), for example, considers conspiracy theories to be 'a creative response to the rapidly changing condition of America since the 1960s', one that, in the aftermath of the Kennedy assassination, Watergate, the Iran-Contra affair and other scandals encapsulates 'permanent uncertainty about the fundamental issues of causality, agency, responsibility, and identity' and 'a not entirely unfounded suspicion that the normal order of things itself amounts to a conspiracy' (see also Fenster, 2008, Melley, 2000, Harper, 2008). Willman (2002) goes as far as to claim that in modern society, power relations are based, more and more, on malicious design, to the point where the 'contingency theory of society' (the opposite of Karl Popper's notion of the 'conspiracy theory of society') can no longer adequately account for what is 'really going on'. Therefore, while conspiracy theories may be based on 'dizzying leaps of logic' and can sometimes drift into an anti-democratic, racist or antisemitic discourse, they nevertheless have the potential to 'correctly identify present and historical wrongs' (Fenster, 2008: 9, 11), encourage critical attitudes towards political elites, and, through vigilance, prevent excessive secretiveness of agencies of the state (see Basham, 2003, also Husting and Orr, 2007 and Olmsted, 2009).

However, the extent to which conspiracy theories really changed over the past four decades, and whether the transformation has been as profound as the recent literature suggests is open for discussion. As we have seen throughout this book, the rhetorical style and explanatory logic of the conspiracy tradition persist in both the United States and elsewhere around the world. Over the past 40 years, conspiracy theories undoubtedly adapted to new circumstances and to emerging political and social realities (as they had done throughout history), just as they undoubtedly made the most of new technologies, especially the internet and cable television. They also unquestionably benefited from the more general rise in suspicion of authority and revelations about political corruption and real conspiracies. But whether this is anything new is a different question. Conspiracy theorists today may pander to distinctly new fears associated with identity theft, surveillance, or developments in biotechnology or genetic engineering, but they do so in much the same way as they had done in the past in relation to social reform, the rise of international finance, the threat of communism or the prospect of war. Conspiracy theories abandoned neither the established explanatory logic and narrative style, nor the traditional ideological links with reactionary politics. After all, the protean nature of conspiracy theories, which accounts for their longevity and persistence, has always relied on a combination of continuity and change.

It is therefore enough to glance at any contemporary conspiracy theory purporting to explain 9/11, the origins of HIV and AIDS, the New World Order, or the machinations of 'the Lobby', to realise that post-modern tongue-in-cheek playfulness and the 'self-reflexive' ironic tones are few and far between. On the contrary, the ideological single-mindedness of the conspiracy tradition, whether expounded on Russia Today, in yet another best-seller from Jim Marrs or on the pages of *CounterPunch* remains firmly entrenched in the realm where tales of clashes between civilisations, the implementation of truth, and battles between moral extremes are elaborated without even the smallest dose of post-modern irony.

Also, the contention that conspiracy theories are today somehow more of a 'hobby' than an 'obsession', 'frisson' rather than 'faith' (Spark, 2002: 59), implies that in the past, consumers of conspiracy theories were all intensely devoted to the notion of a sinister plot, with an unwavering ideological commitment to the conspiracist cause. There is, however, no evidence that this was ever the case. In fact, as was argued in the previous chapter, conspiracy theories, past and present, are best understood as a set of motifs, claims, patterns of interpretation and rhetorical tropes that people can dabble in, draw upon, modify and propagate as they make sense of the world, individually and collectively. For the majority of consumers of conspiracy theories – from the readers of Barruel's and Robison's counter-revolutionary literature, through the subscribers to Henry Ford's *Dearborn Independent* to television viewers in Syria or Egypt who follow one of several dramatisations of the *Protocols of the Elders of Zion* – engagement with the notion of a conspiracy has *always* been 'transitory and passing, with elements being forgotten and remembered, sampled and retained' (Spark, 2002: 59). Of course, thanks to developments in technology and the proliferation of the conspiracy theory industry, people today generally have a quicker and easier access to a broader range of conspiracy claims and can engage with them in more diverse ways, but this does not mean that the essential nature of that engagement has changed beyond recognition.

The reasoning behind the increasingly common assumption that over the past 40 years conspiracy theories underwent deep-seated qualitative and quantitative changes becomes clearer when one considers more closely how its exponents define conspiracy theories. In Peter Knight's work, for example, the term 'conspiracy culture' covers 'a broad spectrum of conspiratorial representations, from fully elaborated theories to passing suspicions about hidden forces' (Knight, 2000: 11). It encompasses everything from the ideologies of far-right militias and New World Order conspiracy theories (which in the cultural studies literature are typically accorded secondary importance), through anxieties about real political conspiracies, to cultural products such as the *X-Files*, Oliver Stone's film *JFK* and a range of fictional works that express suspicion about agency, power and control. In fact, Knight himself acknowledges that 'some of these forms of everyday conspiracy culture are barely recognisable as conspiracy theories by traditional definitions' (ibid.). In the writing of other authors too, including Mark Fenster and Timothy Melley, it is not always easy to see how some of the phenomena they discuss relate to conspiracy theory in the conventional sense of the term. With this in mind, it could be argued that it is not conspiracy theories that have changed radically in recent decades, but that the definition of what a conspiracy theory is has been stretched beyond recognition.

There is, of course, nothing particularly remarkable about the fact that multiple and competing definitions of conspiracy theories circulate in scholarly literature. As we have seen in Chapter 2, 'conspiracy theory' is, and always has been, a contested category, so it should not come as a surprise that debates about its boundaries are to be found in academic discourse, as well as in everyday language. What is more,

by expanding its focus to a broader range of phenomena, critical cultural studies literature has usefully drawn attention to a number of
important features of contemporary social reality – widespread disenchantment with, and alienation from, the mainstream of politics, the rising concerns about the unequal distribution of financial
power, anxieties about security and risk, or the widespread suspicion
towards, and mistrust of, conventional forms of authority – scientific,
political or religious (see Giddens, 1990, Beck, 1992, 2000, Furedi,
1997) – which might lie beyond the scope of the conspiracy tradition,
but which nevertheless help to sustain it. At the same time, there is a
strong argument to be made in favour of maintaining a conceptual
distinction between broader discourses of suspicion (or 'routinised
paranoia', Knight, 2000:73) and conspiracism as a specific tradition of
explanation. This is not just a question of analytical precision. One
consequence of subsuming the worldview considered in the preceding
chapters under a much broader class of phenomena is that attention
gets diverted away from the conspiracy tradition's distinctive features
and political impact. The uniqueness of its rhetorical style and explanatory logic passes virtually unnoticed, but more importantly, its cultural
and ideological roots and political implications become relativised,
downplayed or in some instances completely overlooked. For example,
in some of the recent literature, the belief in the Zionist Occupational
Government – an antisemitic myth perpetuated by anti-government
conspiracy theorists in the United States – or the worldview expounded
in *The Turner Diaries* – the bible of right-wing militias in the 1990s – are
discussed as manifestations of the same 'agency panic' which under-
lies the fictional writing of Thomas Pynchon and Joseph Heller, while
Timothy McVeigh and the Unabomber are treated as symptoms of the
same pervasive fear of technology evident in fictional works such as
Ken Kesey's *One Flew Over the Cuckoo's Nest* or Ralph Ellison's *Invisible
Man* (Melley, 2000). Peter Knight (2000: 38), while acknowledging that
the New World Order conspiracy theory 'can easily shade into tedi-
ous and vicious scapegoating which often contains a barely concealed
antisemitic strain', nevertheless considers *The Turner Diaries* 'a homage to the value of skilled labour' which laments 'the way those skills
have begun to be redundant in post-war America' (Knight, 2000: 40).
He also discusses Nation of Islam's antisemitic rhetoric exclusively as
a reaction to contemporary race relations in the United States, rather
than as the legacy of the conspiracy tradition. Lewis and Kahn (2005:
45) see David Icke's claim that the world is run by alien lizards along
similar lines, as no more than a manifestation of the pervasive 'fears

and discontents that have arisen around contemporary issues such as global imperialism and transnational capitalism.'

By considering contemporary manifestations of the conspiracy tradition solely in the context of recent cultural trends and in terms of the 'routinised paranoia' of the post-modern age, the recent literature somehow misses the central point of conspiracy theories. There is no doubt that the conspiracy tradition and the broader discourses of suspicion exist side by side, that they may even address similar concerns and to some extent play off each other, but they are nevertheless very different phenomena in terms of both substance and consequence. After all, nobody blew up a government building or planted a bomb in a supermarket after reading *One Flew over the Cuckoo's Nest* or the *Invisible Man*. Just as it is unlikely that *The Turner Diaries* appealed to Timothy McVeigh as a piece of social commentary on labour relations, or that it would have captured the attention of cultural studies scholars had it not inspired an act of terrorism motivated by a sentiment that has been in circulation for several centuries. Also, the more affirmative and even sympathetic stance towards conspiracy theories is contingent on *not* engaging with the aetiology of conspiracy narratives and their ideological roots. David Icke's work might indeed seem like a fairly innocuous piece of 'quintessentially dystopian literature concerned with providing pathways towards a less repressive future' (Lewis and Kahn, 2005: 50), if one does not look at the ideological sources of his claims and treat as noteworthy the fact that his books, lecture tours and internet films are introducing new generations of readers to the antisemitic writings of Eustace Mullins or Nesta Webster.

In providing a critical introduction to conspiracy theories, the present book offered an argument in favour of preserving the narrower and more clear-cut definition of conspiracy theories. Conceptualising the object of analysis as a historically rooted and continuously evolving tradition of explanation, brings with it the much needed emphasis on historical enquiry when investigating the form, content and evolution of conspiracy-based explanations and accounting for their continuing, global appeal. As we have seen, much can be learned about conspiracy theories by locating specific explanations within the appropriate ideological and cultural context, scrutinising their logic and rhetoric against the backdrop of the broader historically situated patterns of thought and analysing them as manifestations of a longer tradition of political explanation (Billig, 1988). Such an approach also helps to build resistance against taking conspiracy theories seriously or recognising them as a view of the world that might be worth listening to.

Combating conspiracy theories

Given the conspiracy tradition's long legacy of harmful influence, and its noted 'affinity' for bad causes (Hofstadter, 1967), it might be worthwhile concluding with a brief discussion about how one should go about the task of undermining its presence in modern society. One approach that has been proposed focuses on the specific conditions within which conspiracism flourishes. If conspiracy theories are understood as a response to a particular model of power based on secrecy, concentration of authority and the lack of transparency and accountability, then creating a more transparent and responsible government would indeed foster a political environment where there would be fewer questions to which conspiracy theorists can offer appealing and comforting answers. If, as Christopher Hitchens (1993: 14) argues, conspiracy theories are 'the white noise that moves in to fill the vacuity of the official version' of social and political events, then it might indeed be the case that providing more complete, honest and authoritative non-conspiratorial, official explanations would leave less scope for rampant conspiracy theorising (Clarke, 2002).

It has also been suggested that we should resist the temptation to seek to suppress, persecute, pathologise or psychologise conspiracy theorists, but should instead refute their claims with rational arguments in the context of a 'free and open debate' (Garton Ash, 2008). Arie Kruglanski (1987: 224), for example, proposes that 'what we could do is confront [the conspiracy theorist's] beliefs with ours, battle them by our evidence, fight against them and try to uproot them via the best techniques of persuasion we can muster'. Kruglanski is keen to point out, however, that 'we cannot hope to disprove [conspiracy theories] objectively to everyone's total and everlasting satisfaction. Nor may we hope that somehow miraculously Truth shall prevail, for what Truth is does not appear readily knowable.' Nevertheless, because the human belief system is thought to have an inherently 'deductive structure', confronting a conspiracy theory 'with hard to deny evidence (e.g. ascribed to experts, credible eyewitnesses or consensus of intelligent peers) may be an efficient way of undermining its credibility' (ibid.: 230). More recently, Sunstein and Vermeule (2009) have recommended that this war of ideas might be conducted covertly, rather than in open debate. The 'crippled epistemology' of the conspiracy theory, marked by a lack of insight into alternative explanations or disconfirming evidence could be combated through 'cognitive infiltration' whereby government agents, or even scientists and experts enlisted by the authorities would, either anonymously or openly, infiltrate online communication among conspiracy theorists (e.g. forums and internet chats), introduce 'informational diversity' into the proceedings, and in doing so 'expose indefensible conspiracy theories as such' (Ibid.: 204, 211).

In the light of the argument considered in this book, one might question the plausibility and the effectiveness of both approaches. First, openness and transparency of government and the accountability of those in power are desirable goals in their own right, and they are not causes that should be pursued with conspiracy theorists in mind. Society should be able to go about its business without having to respond to real or anticipated challenges from conspiracy theorists, especially as the latter operate according to standards of evidence and proof that can never be met. As we have seen in previous chapters, an essential feature of the conspiracy theory is the continuous shifting of goalposts and the constant demand for new evidence, in an endless and insatiable spiral of suspicion and mistrust of official sources. As Philip Zelikow, executive director of the government sponsored 9/11 Commission argued in 2004, one should avoid at all costs engaging in an endless game of 'Wack-a-mole' with conspiracy theorists, as the incessant stream of challenges and questions popping up all over the place, makes it a game that can never be won (Morello, 2004). What is more, engaging conspiracy theorists in debate imbues their views with legitimacy: it presents conspiracy theories as a valid (even if not normative) stance in a matter of public controversy and an opinion that deserves to be heard. Doing so only increases the likelihood of conspiracy theories being accepted as a view that cannot, or should not, be rejected outright.

Similarly, it is difficult to see how the creation of a more transparent government would ever successfully drive out conspiracy theories. After all, governments in democratic societies, including the United States, are far-more transparent today than they have ever been, and yet conspiracy theorists remain undeterred. In fact, important institutions of governmental transparency introduced over the past 40 years, such as the freedom of information legislation, have not rendered conspiracy theories obsolete. On the contrary, as Burr et al. (1998: 471) conclude, 'it is an irony that the greater disclosure of classified information can have the immediate impact of increasing mistrust'. This is not just because, by revealing that there *is* secrecy in government, such disclosures act as a launch pad for wide-eyed conspiracy theorising (an issue considered in Chapter 2) but also because the conspiracy theory views any revelation about the government, official or unofficial, through the prism of its skewed interpretative logic impervious to disconfirming evidence.

To show that this is so, it is enough to peruse the reactions from conspiracy theorists to the publication, in late 2010, of confidential US diplomatic correspondence by the internet site Wikileaks. The central inference that can be drawn from the Wikileaks affair – namely, that the American government security is so inadequate that a low-ranking official was able to get hold of, copy and pass on to outsiders the complete database of confidential diplomatic cables – contravenes the conspiracy theorist's essential argument and exposes the importance of contingency, coincidence and error in world affairs. And yet, the conspiracy theorists were left unscathed by this disconfirming argument: in fact, they offered it as proof that there *is* a conspiracy. Within days of the announcement of the Wikileaks scoop, or, more precisely, as soon as it was clear that the leaked diplomatic cables would not confirm that a global government is in the making, that the world is run by the Bilderberg group or the Illuminati, or that 9/11 was orchestrated by US security services, right-wing conspiracy theorists around the world overwhelmingly dismissed the whole affair as a diversion, a piece of 'psychological operations' aimed at the naïve public which, unlike the community of seasoned conspiracy theorists, remains oblivious to what is 'really going on'. As one writer put it, in typical conspiracist style, 'the ascent and timing of the Wikileaks phenomenon could not be more scripted and perfect' (Henningsen, 2010). Conspiracy theorists on the left were similarly suspicious. One contributor to the *CounterPunch* magazine noted that the fact that 'Israel, a nuclear-power with ongoing military adventures was spared much of the embarrassment' (in other words because the leaks did not instantly confirm what anti-Zionists on the left already 'know' to be true about Israel's sinister influence in the Middle East) makes the whole affair seem 'particularly suspicious' (Baroud, 2010). What is more, one of the more interesting revelations made by Wikileaks, namely that a number of Arab countries in the Middle East (including Saudi Arabia) urged the US to intervene against the Iranian nuclear programme, was interpreted as proving the exact opposite: that 'someone, or some entity' keen to meddle in the affairs of the Middle East, was planting stories of this kind so as to divert attention from its own misdeeds. The entity in question remained nameless, but from the overall drift of the article many readers of *CounterPunch* undoubtedly recognised the allusion as referring to Israel and 'the Lobby' as the mysterious force behind Wikileaks.

Therefore, and this is a key point made throughout this book, conspiracy theories are, and always have been, more than just a worldview centred on the notion of intentionality and collusion, or an explanation marked by excessive suspiciousness towards mainstream institutions. They also consist of a warped explanatory logic that is not amenable to rational debate. This is why conspiracy theories cannot be eradicated either through the creation of a more transparent government, or through any conventional means of persuasion or 'cognitive infiltration'. The latter strategy in particular (especially when it is announced in a mainstream scholarly journal) only strengthens the conspiracy theorists' conviction that some sinister force is engaging in 'information war' against them, thus exacerbating the already excessive mistrust and suspicion. In fact, as soon as Cass Sunstein – who, in 2009, was appointed Administrator of the Office of Information and Regulatory Affairs (a US government body tasked with overseeing policy related to information technology and privacy in the US) – publicised his idea about 'cognitive infiltration' as a method that can be used to combat conspiracy theories, the high-priest of the 9/11 Truth movement, David Ray Griffin, sat down and wrote a whole book about the sinister plans by the criminal state and one of its appointed officials to suppress the truth and stifle dissent about the most elaborate hoax in the country's history (Griffin, 2010).

It could be argued, therefore, that no approach to combating conspiracy theories is likely to succeed in changing the opinions of fervent believers, the writers, radio hosts, bloggers and campaigners who disseminate conspiracy material through the various electronic and printed media, or their army of dedicated followers. This is why this category of conspiracy theorists should be ignored, rather than flattered by being engaged in any kind of 'open and honest' debate. These individuals are, to paraphrase Jim Garrison's character in Oliver Stone's film *JFK*, already beyond the 'looking glass', in a world in which 'white is black and black is white'. Instead, attention should be directed at the much broader constituency of people for whom conspiracy theories are a mere resource, a set of culturally available discourses and assumptions about power and governance, that can be called upon, evaluated and deployed selectively and strategically in the context of making sense of the world and dealing with the challenges of modern society, especially in the context of unforeseeable or traumatic events. The question, therefore, is how to make conspiracist ideas less appealing as an interpretative framework to resort to and how to prevent everyday reasoning from being contaminated by the explanatory logic and narrative structure of the conspiracy tradition. Given the arguments presented in this book, a three-pronged approach can be proposed. First, it is important to maintain a clear distinction between three different phenomena: (1) conspiracy theories as tradition of explanation; (2) accounts of (or investigations into) real conspiracies that can be verified using conventional standards of evidence and proof; and (3) the broader discourses of suspicion about politics and government that do not postulate the existence of conspiracy as a motive force in history or which do so in a deliberately playful, ironic and reflexive way. Second, apart from seeking to disconfirm conspiracist claims on factual or logical grounds, it is also necessary to engage in the kind of critical practice undertaken in this book, which involves deconstructing the logic and rhetoric of conspiracy theories, demonstrating their historical contingency and exposing their problematic history and disreputable ideological and political roots. As already noted, this might not succeed in transforming existing believers into sceptics, but it will help infuse public discourse with arguments about why conspiracy theories should not be believed, and in doing so inoculate everyday sense-making practices against the appeal of the conspiracist view of the world. Finally, without necessarily doubting the motives (patriotic, progressive or any other) of those who succumb to the appeal of conspiracy theories, it is also important to draw attention to the fact that a conspiracy theory, regardless of its promises, can never be a force of genuine social change or emancipatory politics. As Daniel Bell (1960: 121) observed, conspiracy theory effectively converts 'concrete issues into ideological problems' and 'invests them with moral colour and high emotional charge'. By focusing all of its resources on exposing the sinister activities and pathological disposition of a small group of conspirators – the Bilderbergers, the 'military industrial complex', or 'the Lobby' – conspiracy theorists commit to the 'politics of the illusory' over the 'politics of the possible' (Fenster, 2008: 288). While there is no doubt that conspiracy theories offer a certain amount of comfort – that, after all, is the source of much of their appeal – they invariably lead to a dead-end, away from genuine solutions to problems of society. The causes of the latter are, without a shadow of a doubt, more diverse and more complex than any conspiracy theorist can imagine.

References

'9/11 Conspiracy theory books dominate debate at Frankfurt Book Fair' (2003). Radio Deutche Welle, 10 October, [online] http://www.dw-world.de/dw/article/0,,993523,00.html (accessed 1 December 2010).

'US base leads poll's top conspiracy theories' (2008). *The Guardian*, 31 July, 9.

'What we were reading' (2009). *The Guardian*, Features and reviews section, 5 December, 2.

9/11Truth.org (2010). Connecting the dots: unanswered questions (leaflet), [online] http://www.911truth.org/flyers/connectingdots.pdf (accessed 1 December 2010).

Aaronovitch, D. (2009). *Voodoo Histories: The Role of the Conspiracy Theory in Shaping Modern History*. London: Vintage.

Abalakina-Paap, M., Stephan, W.G., Craig, T., and Gregory W.L. (1999). Beliefs in conspiracies. *Political Psychology* 20 (3): 637–647.

Abraham, L. (1985). *Call It Conspiracy*. Seattle, Washington: Double A Publication.

Ackerman, N.W. and Jahoda, M. (1950). *Anti-Semitism and Emotional Disorder: A Psychoanalytic Interpretation*. New York: Harper and Brothers.

Adorno, T.W. (1994). *The Stars Down to Earth and Other Essays on the Irrational in Culture*, ed. S. Cook. London: Routledge.

Adorno, T.W., Frenkel-Brunswik, E., Levinson, D.J. and Sanford, R.N. (1950). *The Authoritarian Personality*. New York: Harper and Brothers.

Allen, G. (1972). *None Dare Call It Conspiracy*. Rossmoor, CA: Concord Press.

——. (1987). *Say 'No!' to the New World Order*. Seal Beach, CA: Concord Press.

Allport, G.W. (1954). *The Nature of Prejudice*. Reading, MA: Addison-Wesley.

Allport, G.W. and Postman, L.J. (1947). *The Psychology or Rumor*. New York: Holt, Reinhart and Winston.

Alter, J. (1997). The age of conspiracism, *Newsweek*, 24 March, 47.

American Psychiatric Association. (1994). Diagnostic and statistical manual of mental disorders (4th ed.). Washington, DC: APA.

Anti-Defamation League. (2003). *The Talmud in Anti-Semitic Polemics* (pamphlet), [online] http://www.adl.org/presrele/asus_12/the_talmud.pdf (accessed 1 December 2010).

Avnery, Y. (2003). Manufacturing anti-Semites. In A. Cockburn and J. St. Clair (Eds.), *The Politics of Anti-Semitism*. Petrolia, CA: CounterPunch and AK Press, 43–47.

Bailyn, B. (1975). The logic of rebellion: Conspiracy fears and the American Revolution. In R.O. Curry and T.M. Brown (Eds.), *Conspiracy: The Fear of Subversion in American History*. New York: Holt, Rinehart and Winston, 21–41.

Bains, G. (1983). Explanations and the need for control. In M. Hewstone (Ed.), *Attribution Theory: Social and Functional Extensions*. Oxford: Blackwell, 126–143.

Bale, J.M. (2007). Political paranoia v. political realism: On distinguishing between bogus conspiracy theories and genuine conspiratorial politics. *Patterns of Prejudice* 41 (1): 45–60.

Barkun, M. (2006). *A Culture of Conspiracy: Apocalyptic Visions in Contemporary America*. Los Angeles: University of California Press.

Baroud, R. (2010). Leaking the Obvious?, *CounterPunch*, 10–12 December [online] http://www.counterpunch.org/baroud12102010.html (accessed 20 December 2010).

Barruel, A. (1797). *Mémoires Pour Servir À L'Histoire Du Jacobinisme*. London: French Press.

———. (1799). *Memoirs, Illustrating the History of Jacobinism. Second edition, revised and corrected*. London: T. Burton.

Basham, L. (2003). Malevolent global conspiracy. *Journal of Social Philosophy* 34 (1): 91–103.

———. (2006). Afterthoughts on conspiracy theory: Resilience and ubiquity. In D. Coady (Ed.), *Conspiracy Theories: The Philosophical Debate*. Aldershot: Ashgate, 133–137.

Bauman, Z. (1999). *Modernity and the Holocaust*. New York: Cornell University Press.

Beck, U. (1992). *Risk Society: Towards a New Modernity*. London: Sage.

———. (2000). Risk society revisited: Theory, politics and research programmes. In B. Adam, U. Beck and J. Van Loon (Eds.), *The Risk Society and Beyond: Critical Issues for Social Theory*. London: Sage, 211–229.

Bell, D. (1960). *The End of Ideology*. New York: Free Press.

———. (1962). The dispossessed. In D. Bell (Ed.), *The Radical Right*. New York: Anchor Books, 1–45.

———. (2003). *Ideas in Psychoanalysis: Paranoia*. Cambridge: Icon Books.

Bennett, B. (2007). Hermetic histories: Divine providence and conspiracy theory. *Numen* 54: 174–209.

Bentall, R.P., Corcoran, R., Howard, R., Blackwood, N., and Kinderman P. (2001). Persecutory delusions: A review and theoretical integration. *Clinical Psychology Review* 21 (8): 1143–1192.

Benz, W. (2007). *Die Protokolle der Weisen von Zion. Die Legende von der Jüdischen Weltverschwörung*. München: Beck.

Berlet, C. (1994). Right woos Left: Populist Party, LaRouchian, and Other Neo-fascist overtures to progressives and why they must be rejected (revised report). Cambridge, MA: Political Research Associates, [online] http://www.publiceye.org/rightwoo/rwooz9.html (accessed 1 December 2010).

———. (2009). *Toxic to Democracy: Conspiracy Theories, Demonization, and Scapegoating*. Somerville, MA: Political Research Associates.

Berlet, C and Lyons, M.N. (2000). *Right-wing Populism in America: Too Close for Comfort*. New York: Guilford Press.

Bernstein H. (1921). *The History of a Lie*. New York: J.S. Ogilvie Publishing Company.

Bethell, T. (1975). The quote circuit. *Washington Monthly*, December issue, 34–39.

Bettleheim, B. and Janowitz, M. (1950). *Dynamics of Prejudice*. New York: Harper and Brothers.

Billig, M. (1978). *Fascists: A Social Psychology of the National Front*. London: Academic Press.

———. (1987a). Anti-Semitic themes and the British far Left: Some social-psychological observations on indirect aspects of the conspiracy tradition. In

C.F. Graumann and S. Moscovici (Eds.), *Changing Conceptions of Conspiracy.* New York: Springer-Verlag, 115–136.

Billig, M. (1987b). *Arguing and Thinking: A Rhetorical Approach to Social Psychology.* Cambridge: Cambridge University Press.

———. (1988). Methodology and scholarship in understanding ideological explanation. In C. Antaki (Ed.), *Analysing Everyday Explanation: A Casebook of Methods.* London: Sage, 199–215.

———. (1989). Extreme Right: Continuities in anti-Semitic conspiracy theory in post-war Europe. In R. Eatwell and N. O'Sullivan (Eds.), *The Nature of the Right: European and American Politics and Political Thought since 1789.* London: Pinter.

———. (1996). Remembering the particular background of social identity theory. In W.P. Robinson (Ed.), *Social Groups and Identities – Developing the Legacy of Henri Tajfel.* Oxford: Butterworth-Heinmann, 337–357.

———. (2008). *The Hidden Roots of Critical Psychology.* London: Sage.

Bird, S.T. and Bogart, L.M. (2005). Conspiracy beliefs about HIV/AIDS and birth control among African Americans: Implications for the prevention of HIV, other STIs and unintended pregnancy. *Journal of Social Issues* 61 (1): 109–126.

Blankfort, J. (2003). The Israel Lobby and the Left. In A. Cockburn and J. St. Clair (Eds.), *The Politics of Anti-Semitism.* Petrolia, CA: CounterPunch and AK Press, 99–117.

Blee, K.M. (2002). *Inside Organized Racism: Women in the Hate Movement.* Berkeley: University of California Press.

Bloomberg Business Week (2009). China's most powerful people 2009, [online] http://images.businessweek.com/ss/09/11/1113_business_stars_of_china/ index.htm (accessed 1 December 2010).

Booker, C. (2010). 'The Met Office gives us the warmest weather'. *Daily Telegraph,* 2 January, [online] http://www.telegraph.co.uk/comment/columnists/ christopherbooker/6924898/The-Met-Office-gives-us-the-warmist-weather. html (accessed 1 December 2010)

Bordia, P. and DiFonzo, N. (2005). Psychological motivations in rumor spread. In G.A.Fine, V. Campion-Vincent and C. Heath (Eds.), *Rumor Mills: The Social Impact of Rumor and Legend.* New Brunswick, NJ: Transaction, 87–101.

Boym, S. (1999). Conspiracy theories and literary ethics: Umberto Eco, Danilo Kiš and The Protocols of Zion. *Comparative Literature* 51 (2): 97–122.

Bratich, J.Z. (2008). *Conspiracy Panics: Political Rationality and Popular Culture.* New York: State University of New York Press.

Bronner, E.S. (2000). *A Rumor About the Jews: Reflections on Antisemitism and the Protocols of the Learned Elders of Zion.* New York: St Martin's Press.

Brown, D. (2000). *Angels and Demons.* New York: Pocket Books.

———. (2003). *The Da Vinci Code.* New York: Doubleday.

———. (2009). *The Lost Symbol.* New York: Doubleday.

Brown, L. (ed) (1993). *The New Shorter Oxford English Dictionary on Historical Principles.* Oxford: Clarendon Press.

Buhle, P. (2003). The civil liberties crisis and the threat of 'too Much Democracy', *Tikkun,* May/June issue [online] http://www.tikkun.org/article.php/may2003_ buhle (accessed 1 December 2010).

Burr, W., Blanton, T.S. and Schwartz, S. (1998). *Atomic Audit: The Cost and Consequences of U.S. Nuclear Weapons since 1940*. Washington, DC: Brookings Institutions Press.

Bush, G.W. (2001). Remarks by the President to United Nations General Assemby, UN Headquarters, New York, USA, 11 November 2001. [online] http://www.whitehouse.gov/news/releases/2001/11/20011110-3.html (accessed 1 December 2010)

Butler, L.D., Koopman, C. and Zimbardo, P.G. (1995). The psychological impact of viewing the film 'JFK': Emotions, beliefs, and political behavioral intentions. *Political Psychology* 16 (2): 237–257.

Byford, J. (2002). Anchoring and objectifying neocortical warfare: re-presentation of a biological metaphor in Serbian conspiracy literature. *Papers on Social Representations*, 3.1–3.14.

———. (2006). *Teorija Zevere: Srbija protiv 'novog svetskog poretka'*. [Conspiracy theory: Serbia vs. the 'New World Order']. Belgrade: BG Centar.

Byford, J. and Billig, M. (2001). The emergence of antisemitic conspiracy theories in Yugoslavia during the war with NATO. *Patterns of Prejudice* 35 (4): 50–63.

Campion-Vincent, V. (2005). From evil others to evil elites: A dominant pattern in conspiracy theories today. In G.A.Fine, V. Campion-Vincent and C. Heath (Eds.), *Rumor Mills: The Social Impact of Rumor and Legend*. New Brunswick, NJ: Transaction.

Cesarani, D. (2004). *The Left and the Jews / The Jews and the Left*. London: Labour Friends of Israel.

Chesler, P. (2003). *The New Antisemitism*. San Francisco, CA: Jossey-Bass.

Chesterton, A.K. (1975). *The New Unhappy Lords*. Liss Forest: Candour.

Chigwedere, P., Seage, G.R., Gruskin, S., Lee, T.H. and Essex, M. (2008). Estimating the lost benefits of antiretroviral drug use in South Africa. *Journal of Acquired Immune Deficiency Syndrome* 49, 410–415.

Chomsky, N. (1983). *The Fateful Triangle: The United States, Israel and the Palestinians*. Cambridge, MA: South End Press.

———. (2002). *Pirates and Emperors, Old and New: International Terrorism in the Real World*. Cambridge, MA: South End Press.

———. (2004). On historical amnesia, foreign policy and Iraq. American Amnesia [online] http://www.chomsky.info/interviews/20040217.htm (accessed 1 December 2010).

———. (2006). 9-11: Institutional Analysis vs. Conspiracy Theory. Zblog, [online] http://www.zcommunications.org/9-11-institutional-analysis-vs-conspiracy-theory-by-noam-chomsky (accessed 1 December 2010).

Churchill, W. (1920). Zionism vs. Bolshevism: The struggle for the soul of the Jewish people, *Illustrated Sunday Herald*, February 8, 5.

Clarke, S. (2002). Conspiracy theories and conspiracy theorizing. *Philosophy of the Social Sciences* 32 (2): 131–150.

Coady, D. (2003). Conspiracy theories and official stories. *International Journal of Applied Philosophy* 17 (2): 197–209.

———. (2006). An introduction to the philosophical debates about conspiracy theories. In D. Coady (Ed.), *Conspiracy Theories: The Philosophical Debate*. Aldershot: Ashgate, 1–11.

Cockburn, A. and St. Clair, J. (2003). *The Politics of Anti-Semitism*. Petrolia, CA: CounterPunch and AK Press.

Cohn, N. (1967). *Warrant for Genocide: The Myth of the Jewish World Conspiracy and the Protocols of the Elders of Zion.* London: Secker and Warburg.

Coleman, J. (1992). *The Conspirators Hierarchy: The Committee of 300.* Carson City, NV: America West.

Connolly, P. (2003). German Sept 11 theory stokes anti-US feeling. *Daily Telegraph,* 20 November, [online] http://www.telegraph.co.uk/news/world news/europe/germany/1447232/German-Sept-11-theory-stokes-anti-US-feeling.html (accessed 1 December 2010).

Cooper, A. (1984). *Portraits of Infamy: A Study of Soviet Antisemitic Caricatures and Their Roots in Nazi Ideology.* Los Angeles: Simon Wiesenthal Center.

Crocker, J., Luhtanen, R., Broadnax, S. and Blaine, B.E. (1999). Belief in U.S. government conspiracies against Blacks among Black and White college students: Powerlessness or system blame? *Personality and Social Psychology Bulletin* 25 (8): 941–953.

Cromby, J. and Harper, D.J. (2009). Paranoia: A social account. *Theory and Psychology* 19 (3): 335–361.

Cubitt, G. (1989). Conspiracy myths and conspiracy theories. *Journal of the Anthropological Society of Oxford* 20 (1): 12–26.

———. (1993). *The Jesuit Myth: Conspiracy Theory and Politics in Nineteenth Century France.* Oxford: Clarendon Press.

Cunningham, J.D. and Kelley, H.H. (1975). Causal attributions for interpersonal events of varying magnitude. *Journal of Personality* 43 (1): 74–93.

Dark Secrets: Inside Bohemian Grove (2000). Documentary by Alex Jones. Austin, TX: InfoWars.com.

David Icke, the Lizards and the Jews (2001). TV. Channel 4, UK. 6 May.

Davis, D.B. (1972). Some themes of countersubversion: An analysis of anti-Masonic, anti-Catholic and anti-Mormon literature. In D.B. Davis (Ed.), *The Fear of Conspiracy: Images of Un-American Subversion From the Revolution to the Present.* Ithaca, NY: Cornell University Press.

des Mousseaux, H.R.G. (1869). *Le Juif: Le Judaïsme et la Judaïsation des Peuples Chrétiens.* Paris: Henri Plon.

Disraeli, B. (1844). *Coningsby; or, The First Generation.* London: Henry Colburn.

Dorn, R.M. (1996). To the editor ["Conspiracy Thinking in the Middle East"]. *Political Psychology* 17 (2): 353–356.

Douglas, J.D. and Waksler, F.C. (1982). *The Sociology of Deviance: An Introduction.* Boston: Little Brown.

Dunbar, D. and Reagan, B. (2006). *Debunking 9/11 Myths: Why Conspiracy Theories Can't Stand Up to the Facts.* New York: Hearst Communications.

Eaton, W.W., Romanoski, A., Anthony, J.C., and Nestadt, G. (1991). Screening for psychosis in the general population with a self-report interview. *Journal of Nervous and Mental Disease* 179 (11): 689–693.

Edwards, D. (1997). *Discourse and Cognition.* London: Sage.

Edwards, D. and Potter, J. (1992). *Discursive Psychology.* London: Sage.

Encyclopaedia Judaica (2007). 'United States of America', Second Edition, Vol. XX, 302–404.

Farber, C. (2006). Out of control: AIDS and the corruption of medical science. *Harper's Magazine,* March Issue, [online] http://harpers.org/archive/2006/03/0080961 (accessed 1 December 2010).

Fenigstein, A. and Vanable, P.A. (1992). Paranoia and self-consciousness. *Journal of Personality and Social Psychology* 62 (1): 129–138.

Fenster, M. (2008). *Conspiracy Theories: Secrecy and Power in American Culture (Revised and updated edition)*, Minneapolis: University of Minnesota Press.

Fetzer, J.H. (2007). Philosophy 9/11: What Could a Professor Contribute? Scholars for 9/11 Truth website [online] http://twilightpines.com/images/phil911.pdf (accessed 1 December 2010).

———. (2008). 9/11 and the neo-con agenda. Scholars for 9/11 Truth website [online] http://twilightpines.com//index.php?option=com_content&task=view&id=123&Itemid=67 (accessed 1 December 2010).

Fine, R. (2006). The Lobby: Mearsheimer and Walt's conspiracy theory. www.EngageOnline.org.uk, March 21 [online] http://www.engageonline.org.uk/blog/article.php?id=310 (accessed 1 December 2010).

Finkelstein, N. (2000). *The Holocaust Industry: Reflections on the Exploitation of Jewish Suffering*: London: Verso.

Fisk, R. (2006). United States of Israel?, *The Independent*, 27 April [online] http://www.independent.co.uk/opinion/commentators/fisk/robert-fisk-united-states-of-israel-475811.html (accessed 1 December 2010).

———. (2007). Even I question the 'truth' about 9/11. *The Independent*, August 25 [online] http://www.independent.co.uk/opinion/commentators/fisk/robert-fisk-even-i-question-the-truth-about-911-462904.html (accessed 1 December 2010)

Försterling, F (2001). *Attribution: An Introduction to Theories, Research, and Applications*. Hove: Psychology Press.

Foxman, A. (2004). *Never Again? The Threat of the New Antisemitism*. New York: Harper Collins.

Freeman, D., Garety, P.A., Kuipers, E., Fowler, D. and Bebbington, P. (2002). A cognitive model of persecutory delusions. *British Journal of Clinical Psychology* 41 (4): 331–347.

Freeman, D., and Garety, P.A. (2000). Comments on the content of persecutory delusions: Does the definition need clarification? *British Journal of Clinical Psychology* 39 (4): 407–414.

Friedan, B. (1992/1963). *The Feminine Mystique*. Harmondsworth: Penguin.

Furedi, F. (1997). *Culture of Fear: Risk-Taking and the Morality of Low Expectations*. London: Cassell.

Gaines, A.D. (1988). Delusions: Culture, psychosis and the problem of meaning. In T. Oltmanns and B. Maher (Eds.), *Delusional beliefs*, New York: Wiley, 230–258.

Garton Ash, T. (2008). The freedom of historical debate is under attack by the memory police. *The Guardian*, 16 October, 27.

Gentzkow, M.A. and Shapiro, J.M. (2004). Media, education and anti-Americanism in the Muslim world. *Journal of Economic Perspectives* 18 (3): 117–133.

Gergen, K. (1973). Social psychology as history. *Journal of Personality and Social Psychology* 26 (2): 309–320.

Giddens, A. (1990). *The Consequence of Modernity*. Oxford: Polity.

Gillan, A. (2006). Full house as leading 9/11 conspiracy theorist has his say. *The Guardian*, 9 September, 13.

Glass, J.M. (1988). Notes on the paranoid factor in political philosophy: fear, anxiety, and domination. *Political Psychology* 9 (2): 209–228.

Goertzel, T. (1994). Belief in conspiracy theories. *Political Psychology* 15 (4): 731–742.

Goldberg, R.A. (2001). *Enemies within: The Culture of Conspiracy in Modern America*. New Haven, CT: Yale University Press.

Goodman, D.G. (2005). Japan. In R.S. Levy (Ed.), *Antisemitism: A Historical Encyclopaedia of Prejudice and Persecution*. Santa Barbara, CA: ABC Clio, 364–366.

Goodman, D.G. and Miyazawa, M. (2000). *Jews in the Japanese Mind: History and Uses of a Cultural Stereotype*. Lanham, MD: Lexington Books.

Goodnight, G.T. and Poulakos, J. (1981). Conspiracy rhetoric from pragmatism to fantasy in public discourse. *Western Journal of Speech Communication* 45 (4): 299–316.

Goulévitch, Arsene de (1962). *Czarism and the Revolution*. Hawthorn, CA: Omni.

Graham, S. (1994). Motivation in African Americans. *Review of Educational Research* 64 (1): 55–117.

Graumann, C.F. (1987). Conspiracy: History and social psychology – a synopsis. In C.F. Graumann and S. Moscovici (Eds.), *Changing Conceptions of Conspiracy*. New York: Springer-Verlag, 245–251.

Griffin, D.R. (2008). *The New Pearl Harbor Revisited: 9/11, The Cover-Up, and the Exposé*. Moreton-in-Marsh: Arris Books.

———. (2010). *Cognitive Infiltration: An Obama Appointee's Plan to Undermine the 9/11 Conspiracy Theory*. New York: Olive Branch Press.

Groh, D. (1987). The temptation of conspiracy theory, or: Why do bad things happen to good people? Part I: Preliminary draft of a theory of conspiracy theories. In Graumann, C.F. and Moscovici, S. (Eds.), *Changing Conceptions of Conspiracy*. New York: Springer-Verlag, 1–13.

Grzesiak-Feldman, M. and Ejsmont, A. (2008). Paranoia and conspiracy thinking of Jews, Arabs, Germans, and Russians in a Polish sample. *Psychological Reports* 102: 884–886.

Grzesiak-Feldman, M. and Irzycka, M. (2009). Right-wing authoritarianism and conspiracy thinking in a Polish sample. *Psychological Reports* 105 (2): 389–393.

Gwynne, H.A. (1920). *The Cause of World Unrest*. London: Grant Richards.

Hagemeister, M. (2008). *The Protocols of the Elders of Zion:* Between history and fiction. *New German Critique* 35 (1): 83–95.

Hari, J. (2009). Voodoo Histories, By David Aaronovitch. It all adds up to paranoia, *The Independent* 1 May, [online] http://www.independent.co.uk/arts-entertainment/books/reviews/voodoo-histories-by-david-aaronovitch-1676707.html (accessed 1 December 2010).

Harper, D.J. (1996). Deconstructing "paranoia": Towards a discursive understanding of apparently unwarranted suspicion. *Theory & Psychology* 6 (3): 423–448.

———. (2004). Delusions and discourse: Moving beyond the constraints of the modernist paradigm. *Philosophy, Psychiatry & Psychology* 11 (1): 55–64.

———. (2008). The politics of paranoia: Paranoid positioning and conspiratorial narratives in the surveillance society, *Surveillance & Society* 5 (1): 1–32.

Harrison, A.A. and Thomas, J.M. (1997). The Kennedy assassination, unidentified flying objects, and other conspiracies: Psychological and organizational factors in the perception of 'cover-up'. *Systems Research and Behavioural Science* 14 (2): 113–128.

Harrison, B. (2006). *The Resurgence of Anti-Semitism: Jews, Israel and Liberal Opinion*. Lanham, MD: Rowman and Littlefield.

Heider, F. (1958). *The Psychology of Interpersonal Relations*. New York: John Wiley.

Heins, V. (2007). Critical theory and the traps of conspiracy thinking. *Philosophy & Social Criticism* 33 (7): 787–801.

Heise, D.R. (1988). Delusions and the construction of reality. In T. Oltmanns and B. Maher (Eds.), *Delusional beliefs*. New York: Wiley, 259–272.

Henningsen, P. (2010). Wikileaks: Corrupted Oracle or Cointelpro Asset of the Establishment? [online] http://21stcenturywire.com/2010/12/08/is-wikileaks-a-cointelpro-operation-for-the-establishment/ (accessed 20 December 2010).

Herf, J. (2006). *The Jewish Enemy: Nazi Propaganda during World War II and the Holocaust*. Cambridge, MA: Harvard University Press.

Herman, A. (1999). *Joseph McCarthy: Reexamining the Life and Legacy of America's Most Hated Senator*. New York: Free Press.

Herman, E.S. and Chomsky, N. (1988). *Manufacturing Consent: The Political Economy of the Mass Media*. New York: Pantheon Books.

Hersh, S. (1974). Huge CIA operation reported in US against antiwar forces, other dissidents during Nixon years, *New York Times*, December 22, 1.

Hewstone, M. (1989). *Causal Attribution: From Cognitive Processes to Collective Beliefs*. Oxford: Basil Blackwell.

Hirsh, D. (2007). Anti-Zionism and Antisemitism – Cosmopolitan Reflections. *Yale Initiative for the Interdisciplinary Study of Antisemitism Working Papers*. New Haven, Yale University.

Hirszowicz, L. (1979). Soviet perceptions of Zionism. *Soviet Jewish Affairs* 9 (1): 53–65.

Hitchens, C. (1993). *For the Sake of Argument*. London: Verso.

Hitler, A. (1992/1926). *Mein Kampf*. London: Pimlico.

Hockenos, P. (1993). *Free to Hate: The Rise of the Right in Post-Communist Eastern Europe*. London: Routledge.

Hofman, A. (1988). The origins of the theory of the 'Philosophe' conspiracy. *French History* 2 (2): 152–172.

Hofstadter, R. (1967). *Paranoid Style in American Politics and Other Essays*. New York: Vintage Books.

Holland, M. (2001). The demon in Jim Garrison. *Wilson Quarterly* 25 (2): 10–17.

Holsti, O.R. and Rosenau, J.N. (1984). *American Leadership in World Affairs: Vietnam and the Breakdown of Consensus*. Boston: Allen and Unwin.

Hovland, C. and Sears, R. (1940). Minor studies in aggression, VI: correlation of lynching with economic indices. *Journal of Psychology* 9: 301–310.

Husting, G. and Orr, M. (2007). Dangerous machinery: 'Conspiracy theorist' as a transpersonal strategy of exclusion. *Symbolic interaction* 30 (2): 127–150.

Ichheiser, G. (1943). Misinterpretations of personality in everyday life and the psychologist's frame of reference. *Journal of Personality* 12 (2): 145–160.

Icke, D. (1999). *The Biggest Secret*. Ryde, Isle of Wight: David Icke Books.

Iganski, P. and Kosmin, B. (2003). *A New Antisemitism?* London: Profile.

Ingrams, R. (2001). Who will dare damn Israel? *The Observer*, 16 September [online] http://www.guardian.co.uk/world/2001/sep/16/september11.usa19 (accessed 1 December 2010).

IRIB [Islamic Rerepublic of Iran Broadcasting] (2010). Haiti Earthquake, Consequence of Usage of HAARP Weapon by US, [online] http://english.irib.ir/index.php/news/political/30078-haiti-earthquake-consequence-of-usage-of-haarp-weapon-by-us (accessed 1 December 2010).

Jameson, F. (1988). Cognitive mapping. In Nelson, C and Grossberg, L. (Eds.), *Marxism and the Interpretation of Culture*. Urbana: University of Illinois Press.

———. (1991). *Postmodernism: Or, The Cultural Logic of Late Capitalism*. London: Verso.

Jin, Z. (2009). Pulling the strings of the world economy. *Beijing Daily*, 20 August, [online] http://www.beijingtoday.com.cn/?tag=song-hongbing (accessed 1 December 2010).

Johns, L.C. and van Os, J. (2001). The continuity of psychotic experiences in the general population. *Clinical Psychology Review* 21 (8): 1125–1141.

Jones, J.H. (1981). *Bad Blood: The Tuskegee Syphilis Experiment – A Tragedy of Race and Medicine*. New York: Free Press.

Kalichman, S.C. (2009). *Denying AIDS: Conspiracy Theories, Pseudoscience, and Human Tragedy*. New York: Springer-Verlag.

Keeley, B.L. (1999). Of conspiracy theories. *Journal of Philosophy* 96 (3): 109–126.

Keith, J. (1996). *OKBomb: Conspiracy and Cover-up*. Lilburn, GA: Illuminet Press.

Kelley, H.H. (1972). *Causal Schemata and the Attribution Process*. New York: General Learning Press.

———. (1973). The process of causal attribution. *American Psychologist* 28 (2): 107–123.

Kellner, D. (2003). *Media Spectacle*. London: Routledge.

Kellogg, M. (2005). *The Russian Roots of Nazism: White émigrés and the Making of National Socialism, 1917–1945*. Cambridge: Cambridge University Press.

Klaehn, J. (2002). A critical review and assessment of Herman and Chomsky's 'Propaganda Model'. *European Journal of Communication* 17 (2): 147–182.

Knight, P.G. (1997). Naming the problem: Feminism and the figuration of conspiracy. *Cultural Studies* 11 (1): 40–63.

Knight, P. (2000). *Conspiracy Culture: From Kennedy to X-Files*. London: Routledge.

———. (2002a) *Conspiracy Nation: The Politics of Paranoia in Postwar America*. New York: New York University Press.

———. (2002b). Introduction: A nation of conspiracy theorists. In P. Knight (Ed.), *Conspiracy Nation: The Politics of Paranoia in Postwar America*. New York: New York University Press, 1–17.

———. (2008). Outrageous conspiracy theories: Popular and official responses to 9/11 in Germany and the United States. *New German Critique* 35 (1): 165–193.

Kofta, M. and Sędek, G. (2005). Conspiracy stereotypes of Jews during systemic transformation in Poland. *International Journal of Sociology* 35 (1): 40 – 64.

Korey, W. (1984). The Soviet *Protocols of the Elders of Zion*. In T. Freedman (Ed.), *Anti-Semitism in the Soviet Union: Its Roots and Consequences*. New York: Freedom Library Press of the Anti-Defamation League of B'nai B'rith, 151–160.

Kosmala, H. (1978). *Studies, Essays and Reviews, Volume Three: Jews and Judaism*. Leiden, Netherlands: E.J. Brill.

Kowner, R. (1997). On ignorance, respect and suspicion: Current Japanese attitudes toward Jews. *Analysis of Current Trends in Antisemitism* 11, [online] http://sicsa.huji.ac.il/11kowner.htm (accessed 1 December 2010).

Kramer, R.M, (1998). Paranoid cognition in social systems: Thinking and acting in the shadow of doubt. *Personality & Social Psychology Review* 2 (4): 251–275.

Kruglanski, A.W. (1987). Blame-placing schemata and attributional research. In C.F. Graumann and S. Moscovici (Eds.), *Changing Conceptions of Conspiracy.* New York: Springer-Verlag, 219–229.

Küntzel, M. (2007). *Jihad and Jew-Hatred: Islamism, Nazism and the Roots of 9/11.* New York: Telos Press.

Lake, E. (2006). David Duke claims to be vindicated by a Harvard dean, *New York Sun,* 20 March [online] http://www.nysun.com/national/david-duke-claims-to-be-vindicated-by-a-harvard/29380/ (accessed 1 December 2010).

LaPierre, R.T. and Farnsworth, P.R. (1936). *Social Psychology.* New York: McGraw-Hill.

Laqueur, W. (2006). *The Changing Face of Anti-Semitism: From Ancient Times to the Present Day.* Oxford: Oxford University Press.

Legge, F. (2009). What hit the Pentagon? Misinformation and its effect on the credibility of 9/11 Truth. *Journal of 9/11 Studies* 26, 1–20, [online] http://www.journalof911studies.com/volume/2009/WhatHitPentagonDrLeggeAug.pdf (accessed 1 December 2010).

Leman, P.J. (2007). The born conspiracy. *New Scientist* 195, Issue 2612: 35–37.

Leman, P.J. and Cinnerella, M. (2007). A major event has a major cause: Evidence for the role of heuristics in reasoning about conspiracy theories. *Social Psychology Review* 9: 18–28.

Lendvai, P. (1972). *Anti-Semitism in Eastern Europe.* London: MacDonald.

Levy, R.S. (1996). Introduction: The political career of the *Protocols of the Elders of Zion.* In B.W. Şegel, *A Lie and a Libel: The History of the Protocols of the Elders of Zion.* Lincoln, NE: University of Nebraska Press.

Lewis, J.E. (2008). *The Mammoth Book of Cover-ups.* Philadelphia, PA: Running Press Book.

Lewis, T. and Kahn, R. (2005). The Reptoid hypothesis: Utopian and dystopian representational motifs in David Icke's alien conspiracy theory. *Utopian Studies* 16 (1): 45–74.

Lipset, S.M. and Raab, E. (1978). *The Politics of Unreason: Right-wing Extremism in America, 1790–1977.* Chicago: University of Chicago Press.

Lomnitz, C. and Sánchez, R. (2009), United by hate. *Boston Review,* July/August, [online] http://www.bostonreview.net/BR34.4/lomnitz_sanchez.php (accessed 1 December 2010).

Lord, C.G., Ross, L., and Lepper, M.R. (1979). Biased assimilation and attitude polarization: The effects of prior theories on subsequently considered evidence. *Journal of Personality and Social Psychology* 37 (11): 2098–2109.

Marrs, J. (2000). *Rule by Secrecy: The Hidden History that Connects the Trilateral Commission, The Freemasons and the Great Pyramids.* New York: Harper Collins.

———. (2008). *The Rise of the Fourth Reich.* New York: William Morrow.

McCauley, C. and Jacques, S. (1979). The popularity of conspiracy theories of presidential assassination: A Bayesian analysis. *Journal of Personality and Social Psychology* 37 (5): 637–644.

McConachie, J. and Tudge, R. (2008). *The Rough Guide to Conspiracy Theories.* London: Rough Guides.

McGregor, R. (2007). Chinese buy into conspiracy theories. *Financial Times*, 25 September [online] http://www.ft.com/cms/s/0/70f2a23c-6b83-11dc-863b-0000779fd2ac.html (accessed 1 December 2010).

McHoskey, J.W. (1995). Case Closed? On the John F. Kennedy assassination: Biased assimilation of evidence and attitude polarization. *Basic and Applied Social Psychology* 17 (3): 395–409.

Mearsheimer, J. and Walt, S. (2006). The Israel Lobby. *London Review of Books* 28 (6): 3–12.

———. (2007). *The Israel Lobby and U.S. Foreign Policy*. New York: Farrar, Straus and Giroux.

Melley, T. (2000). *Empire of Conspiracy: The Culture of Paranoia in Postwar America*. Ithaca, NY: Cornell University Press.

Meyssan, T. (2002). *11 Septembre 2001: L'effroyable imposture*. Paris: Editions Carnot.

Miller, S. (2002). Conspiracy theories: Public arguments as coded social critiques. A rhetorical analysis of the TWA Flight 800 conspiracy theories. *Argumentation and Advocacy* 39 (1): 40–56.

Mirowsky, J. and Ross, C.E. (1983). Paranoia and the structure of powerlessness. *American Sociological Review* 48 (2): 228–239.

Morello, C. (2004). Conspiracy theories flourish on the Internet. *Washington Post*, October 7, B1.

Moscovici, S. (1984). The myth of a lonely paradigm. *Social Research* 51 (4): 939–967.

———. (1987). The conspiracy mentality. In C.F. Graumann and S. Moscovici (Eds.), *Changing Conceptions of Conspiracy*. New York: Springer-Verlag, 151–169.

Moscovici, S. and Hewstone, M. (1983). Social representations and social explanations: From the 'naïve' to the 'amateur' scientist. In M. Hewstone (Ed.), *Attribution Theory: Social and Functional Extensions*. Oxford: Blackwell, 99–125.

Nattrass, N. (2008). AIDS and the scientific governance of medicine in post-Apartheid South Africa. *African Affairs* 107 (427): 157–176.

Neubauer, H.J. (1999). *The Rumour: A Cultural History*. London: Free Association Books.

Nisbett, R.E. and Ross, C. (1980). *Human Inference*. New Jersey: Prentice Hall.

Nkpa, N.K.U. (1977). Rumors of mass poisoning in Biafra. *Public Opinion Quarterly* 41 (3): 332–346.

Nkpa, N.K.U. (1975). Rumor mongering in war time. *Journal of Social Psychology* 96 (1): 27–35.

North, G. (1985). Prologue and Epilogue. In L. Abraham, *Call It Conspiracy*. Seattle, Washington: Double A Publication, xi–xix and 241–292.

North, R. (2010). It has a gigantic supercomputer, 1,500 staff and a £170m-a-year budget. So why does the Met Office get it so wrong?, *Daily Mail*, 3 January, [online] http://www.dailymail.co.uk/news/article-1240082/It-gigantic-supercomputer-1-500-staff-170m-year-budget-So-does-Met-Office-wrong.html (accessed 1 December 2010).

Olmsted, K.S. (2009). *Real Enemies: Conspiracy Theories and American Democracy, World War I to 9/11*. Oxford: Oxford University Press.

Oushakine, S.A. (2009). "Stop the invasion": Money, patriotism and conspiracy in Russia. *Social Research* 76 (1): 71–116.

Palmer, P. (1989). *Contemporary Women's Fiction: Narrative Practice and Feminist Theory.* Hemel Hempstead: Harvester Wheatsheaf.

Pantin, T. (2008). Hugo Chávez's Jewish Problem. *Commentary,* July/August, [online]   http://www.commentarymagazine.com/viewarticle.cfm/hugo-chvez-s-jewish-problem-11455 (accessed 1 December 2010).

Parenti, M. (1996). *Dirty Truths.* San Francisco: City Lights Books.

Parish, J. and Parker, M. (2001). *The Age of Anxiety: Conspiracy Theory and the Human Sciences.* Oxford: Blackwell.

Payson, S. (1802). *Proofs of the Real Existence and Dangerous Tendency of Illuminism.* Charlestown, MA: Samuel Etheridge.

Pérez Hernáiz, H.A. (2009). The uses of conspiracy theories for the construction of a political religion in Venezuela. *International Journal of Social Sciences* 3 (4): 241–252.

Phillips, T. (2007). *Beslan: The Tragedy of School No. 1.* London: Granta UK.

Pidgen, C. (1995). Popper revisited, or what is wrong with conspiracy theories. *Philosophy of the Social Sciences* 25 (1): 3–34.

Pilkington, E. (2009a). The former British police officer who wants to bring down Barack Obama, *The Guardian,* 23 November, 20.

Pilkington, E. (2009b). UN general assembly: 100 minutes in the life of Muammar Gaddafi. *Guardian Online,* 23 September, [online] http://www.guardian.co.uk/world/2009/sep/23/gaddafi-un-speech (accessed 1 December 2010).

Pipes, D. (1996). *The Hidden Hand: Middle East Fears of Conspiracy.* London: Palgrave Macmillan.

———. (1997). *Conspiracy: How the Paranoid Style Flourishes and Where It Comes From.* New York: Free Press.

Pipes, R. (1992). The Great October Revolution as a clandestine coup d'état, *Times Literary Supplement,* 6 November, 3–4.

Poliakov, L. (1974). *The History of Antisemitism (4 Vols.).* London: Routledge and Kegan Paul.

———. (1987). The topic of the Jewish conspiracy in Russia (1905–1920), and international consequences. In C.F. Graumann and S. Moscovici (Eds.), *Changing Conceptions of Conspiracy.* New York: Springer-Verlag, 105–113.

Popp, R.K. (2006). History in discursive limbo: Ritual and conspiracy narratives on the History Channel. *Popular Communication* 4 (4): 253–272.

Popper, K.R. (1966). *The Open Society and Its Enemies, Vol.2: The High Tide of Prophecy, Hegel, Marx and the aftermath.* London: Routledge and Kegan Paul.

———. (1972). *Conjectures and Refutations: The Growth of Scientific Knowledge (4th Ed.).* London: Routledge and Kegan Paul.

Posner, G. (1993). *Case Closed: Lee Harvey Oswald and the Assassination of JFK.* New York: Random House.

Potter, J. and Wetherell, M. (1987). *Discourse and Social Psychology: Beyond Attitudes and Behaviour.* London: Sage.

Powell, M. (2006). The Disbelievers: 9/11 conspiracy theorists are building their case against the government from Ground Zero. *Washington Post,* September 8, [online] http://www.washingtonpost.com/wp-dyn/content/article/2006/09/07/AR2006090701669.html (accessed 1 December 2010).

Pulzer, P. (2003). The new antisemitism, or when is a taboo not a taboo? In P. Iganski and B. Kosmin (Eds.), *A New Antisemitism?* London: Profile, 79–101.

Rai, M. (1995). *Chomsky's Politics.* New York: Verso.

Ramsay, R. (2000). *Conspiracy Theories*. Harpenden, Herts.: Oldcastle Books.
———. (2008). *Politics and Paranoia*. Hove: Picnic.
Roberts, J.M. (1974). *The Mythology of the Secret Societies*. St Albans: Paladin.
Robertson, P. (1991). *The New World Order*. Dallas, TX: Word.
Robins, R.S. and Post, J.M. (1997). *Political Paranoia: The Psychopolitics of Hatred*. New Haven, CT: Yale University Press.
Robison, J. (1797). *Proofs of a Conspiracy Against all the Religions and Governments of Europe, Carried on in the Secret Meetings of Free Masons, Illuminati and Reading Societies*. London: William Creech.
Rödlach, A. (2006). *Witches, Westerners and HIV: AIDS and Cultures of Blame in Africa*. Walnut Creek: Left Coast Press.
Roisman, J. (2006). *The Rhetoric of Conspiracy in Ancient Athens*. Los Angeles: University of California Press.
Ronson, J. (2000). *Them: Adventures with Extremists*. London: Picador.
Rosenfeld, A. (2004). *Anti-Zionism in Great Britain and Beyond: A Respectable Antisemitism?* New York: American Jewish Committee.
Rosnow, R.L. (1980). Psychology of rumour reconsidered. *Psychological Bulletin* 87(3): 578–591.
Rosnow, R.L. and Fine, G.A. (1974). *Rumor and Gossip: The Social Psychology of Hearsay*. New York: Elsevier.
Ruotsila, M. (2004). Mrs Webster's religion: Conspiracist extremism on the Christian far right. *Patterns of Prejudice* 38 (2): 109–126.
Ryan, K.R. (2009). Demolition access to the World Trade Center towers: Part one – Tenants. 911Truth.org. http://www.911truth.org/article. php?story=20090713033854249.
Sagan, E. (1991). *The Honey and the Hemlock: Democracy and Paranoia in Ancient Athens and Modern America*. Princeton, NJ: Princeton University Press.
Sales, N.J. (2006). Click here for conspiracy. *Vanity Fair*, August issue, [online] http://www.vanityfair.com/ontheweb/features/2006/08/loosechange200608 (accessed 1 December 2010).
Schlafly, P. (1964). *A Choice, Not an Echo*. Alton, IL: Pere Marquette Press.
Shaw, C. (2005). The Gatekeepers of the So-Called Left, www.911 Truth.org [online] http://www.911truth.org/article.php?story=2005050522171876919 (accessed 1 December 2010).
Shibutani, T. (1966). *Improvised News: A Sociological Study of Rumor*. Indianapolis: Bobbs-Merrill.
Silverstein, P.A. (2000). Regimes of (Un)truth: Conspiracy theory and the Transnationalisation of the Algerian Civil War, *Middle East Report, No.214* [online] http://www.merip.org/mer/mer214/214_silverstein.html (accessed 1 December 2010).
Simmons, W.P. and Parsons, S. (2005). Beliefs in conspiracy theories among African Americans: A comparison of elites and masses. *Social Science Quarterly* 86 (3): 582–598.
Smith, D.E. (1978). K is mentally ill: The anatomy of a factual account. *Sociology* 12, 23–53.
Smith, D.N. (1996). The social construction of enemies: Jews and the representation of Evil. *Sociological Theory* 14 (3): 203–240.
Smith, T. and Novella, S. (2007). HIV denial in the Internet era. *PLoS Medicine* 4 (8) [online] http://www.plosmedicine.org/article/

info%3Adoi%2F10.1371%2Fjournal.pmed.0040256 (accessed 1 December 2010).

Southwell, D. and Twist, S. (2007). *Conspiracy Files*. London: Carlton Books.

Spark, A. (2002). Conjuring order: The new world order and conspiracy theories of globalisation. In J. Parish and M. Parker (Eds.), *The Age of Anxiety: Conspiracy Theory and the Human Sciences*. Oxford: Blackwell, 46–62.

Spier, H. (1988). Restructuring Soviet anti-Zionist propaganda. *Soviet Jewish Affairs* 18 (3): 46–55.

Stern, K.S. (2006). *Antisemitism Today: How It Is the Same, How It Is Different and How to Fight It*. New York: American Jewish Committee.

Still, W.T. (1990). *New World Order: The Ancient Plan of Secret Societies*. Lafayette, LA: Huntington House.

Strauss, J.S. (1969). Hallucinations and delusions as points on continua function: Rating scale evidence. *Archives of General Psychiatry* 21 (5): 581–586.

Sunstein, C.R. and Vermeule, A. (2009). Conspiracy theories: Causes and cures. *Journal of Political Philosophy* 17 (2): 202–227.

Sutton, A. (1974). *Wall Street and the Bolshevik Revolution*. New Rochelle, NY: Arlington House.

Swami V. and Coles, R. (2010). The truth is out there. *Psychologist* 23 (7): 560–563.

Swami, V., Chamorro-Premuzic, T. and Furnham, A. (2010). Unanswered questions: A preliminary investigation of personality and individual difference predictors of 9/11 conspiracist beliefs. *Applied Cognitive Psychology* 24 (6): 749–761.

Swann, J. and Coward, B. (2004). *Conspiracies and Conspiracy Theory in Early Modern Europe*. Aldershot: Ashgate.

Taguieff, P-A. (2004). *Rising from the Muck: The New Anti-Semitism in Europe*. Chicago, IL: Ivan R. Dee.

Taibbi, M. (2009). *The Great Derangement*. New York: Speigel and Grau.

Tajfel, H. (1981). *Human Groups and Social Categories: Studies in Social Psychology*. Cambridge: Cambridge University Press.

———. (1984). Intergroup relations, social myths and social justice in social psychology. In Tajfel (Ed.), *The Social Dimension*. Cambridge: Cambridge University Press, 695–716.

Thomas, S.B. and Quinn, S.C. (1991). The Tuskegee syphilis study, 1932 to 1972: Implications for HIV education and AIDS risk education programs in the Black Community. *American Journal of Public Health* 81 (11): 1498–1505.

———. (1993). The burdens of race and history on Black Americans' attitudes toward needle exchange policy to prevent HIV disease. *Journal of Public Health Policy* 14 (3): 320–347.

Thompson, D. (2008). *Counterknowledge: How We Surrendered to Conspiracy Theories, Quack Medicine, Bogus Science and Fake History*. London: Atlantic Books.

Thurlow, R. (1978). The powers of darkness: Conspiracy belief and political strategy. *Patterns of Prejudice* 12 (6): 1–12 and 23.

Trachtenberg, J. (1983). *The Devil and the Jews: The Medieval Conception of the Jew and Its Relation to Modern Antisemitism*. Philadelphia: Jewish Publication Society.

Tran, M. (2007). Castro says US lied about 9/11 attacks, *Guardian Online*, Wednesday 12 September, [online] http://www.guardian.co.uk/world/2007/sep/12/cuba.september11 (accessed 1 December 2010).

Turner, P.A. (1993). *I Heard It through the Grapevine: Rumor in African-American Culture*. Berkeley: University of California Press.

Van Os, J., Hansen, M., Bijl, R. and Ravelli, A. (2000). Strauss (1969) revisited: A psychosis continuum in the normal population? *Schizophrenia Research* 45 (1): 11–20.

Vankin, J. and Whalen, J. (2010). *World's Greatest Conspiracies, The History's Biggest Mysteries, Cover-Ups and Cabals*. Secaucus, New Jersey: Citadel Press.

Vogt, J. (1975). Old images in Soviet anti-Zionist cartoons. *Soviet Jewish Affairs* 5 (1): 20–38.

von Bieberstein, J.R. (1977). The story of Jewish-Masonic conspiracy: 1776–1945. *Patterns of Prejudice* 11 (6): 1–8 and 21.

Von Bülow, A. (2003). *Die CIA und der 11. September* [The CIA and September 11]. Munich: Piper Verlag.

Wagner-Egger, P., and Bangerter, A. (2007). La vérité est ailleurs : corrélats de l'adhésion aux théories du complot. *Revue Internationale de Psychologie Sociale* 20 (4): 31–61.

Webster, N.H. (1921). *World Revolution: The Plot against Civilization*. London: Constable and Company.

———. (1924). *Secret Societies and Subversive Movements*. London: Boswell Printing.

Wegner, G. (2002). *Anti-Semitism and Schooling Under the Third Reich*. London: Routledge.

Weisberg, H. (1965). *Whitewash: The Report on the Warren Report*. Hyattstown, MD: Harold Weisberg.

Willman, S. (2002). Spinning paranoia: The ideology of conspiracy and contingency in postmodern culture. In P. Knight (Ed.), *Conspiracy Nation: The Politics of Paranoia in Postwar America*. New York: New York University Press.

Wistrich, R. (1979). *The Left against Zion: Communism, Israel and the Middle East*. London: Valentine, Mitchell.

———. (1991). *Antisemitism: The Longest Hatred*. New York: Pantheon Books.

Wood, C. and Finlay, W.M.L. (2008). British National Party representations of Muslims in the month after the London bombings: Homogeneity, threat, and the conspiracy tradition. *British Journal of Social Psychology* 47, 707–726.

Wood, G. (2007). Riders on the storm. *Atlantic Magazine*, October issue, [online] http://www.theatlantic.com/magazine/print/2007/10/riders-on-the-storm/6177/ (accessed 1 December 2010).

Wood, G.S. (1982). Conspiracy and the paranoid style: Causality and deceit in the eighteenth century. *The William and Mary Quarterly* 39 (3): 402–441.

WorldPublicOpinion.org (2008). International poll: No consensus on who was behind 9/11, Press release issued on September 10, [online] http://www.worldpublicopinion.org/pipa/pdf/sep08/WPO_911_Sep08_quaire.pdf (accessed 1 December 2010).

Wulff, E. (1987). Paranoic conspiratory delusion. In C.F. Graumann and S. Moscovici (Eds.), *Changing Conceptions of Conspiracy*. New York: Springer-Verlag, 171–189.

Young, T.J. (1990). Cult violence and the identity movement. *Cultic Studies Journal* 7 (2): 150–159.

Zarefsky, D. (1984). Conspiracy arguments in the Lincoln-Douglas debates. *Journal of the American Forensic Association* 21, 63–75.

Zonis, M. and Joseph, C. (1994). Conspiracy thinking in the Middle East. *Political Psychology* 15 (3): 443–459.

———. (1996). Response to Letter from Dr. Robert M. Dorn. *Political Psychology* 17 (2): 357–359.

Zukier, H. (1987). The conspiratorial imperative: Medieval Jewry in Western Europe. In C.F. Graumann and S. Moscovici (Eds.), *Changing Conceptions of Conspiracy*. New York: Springer-Verlag, 87–103.

Index

CPSIA information can be obtained
at www.ICGtesting.com
Printed in the USA
LVOW04s0907051215

465458LV00014B/458/P